SPIRITUALITY AND SPIRITUAL COUNSELING

In the twenty-first century

Raymond PHANOR, M.Ed (in Mental Health)

Copyright © 2013 by Raymond Phanor, M.Ed

Spirituality And Spiritual Counseling
In The 21st Century
For A Profound Understanding Of Human Spirituality And The Techniques
For Assisting People With Life-Related Issues
by Raymond Phanor, M.Ed

Printed in the United States of America

ISBN 9781625091529

All rights reserved solely by the author. The author guarantees all contents are original and do not infringe upon the legal rights of any other person or work. No part of this book may be reproduced in any form without the permission of the author. The views expressed in this book are not necessarily those of the publisher.

Unless otherwise indicated, Bible quotations are taken from the New International Version. Copyright © 1973, 1978, 1984, 2011 by Biblica, Inc. Used by permission.

"Let the wise listen and add to their learning, and let the discerning get guidance" (Proverbs 1: 5. NIV)

www.xulonpress.com

Contents

Acknowledgments .... *vii*

Forward .... *ix*

Introduction .... *xi*

1. Spirituality and Spiritual Counseling 13

2. The Aims and Purposes of Spiritual Counseling 16

3. The Various Forms of Spiritual Counseling 26

4. The Features and Practice of Spiritual Group Counseling 39

5. The Techniques and Foci of the Spiritual counselor 50

6. The Main Foci of Spiritual Counseling 63

7. Exploring People's Obstacles to Change and their Desire for Change –
   The Techniques for Assisting People with Life-related Issues (TAPLI) 70

8. Assessing Uncomfortable and Disturbing Feelings to Spiritual Counseling 99

9. Human Sexuality and Spiritual Counseling 133

10. Prevarication and Spiritual Counseling to the Prevaricators 143

11. The Ethics for Being a Spiritual Counselor 151

- *Epilogue 165*
- *Checklist for Spiritual Self-Assessment 167*

Acknowledgment

    I can't help thinking of scholars, family members, friends and coworkers who, generously contributed to the fineness and success of this project on human spirituality. First and foremost is Cristina Ajemian whose intensive work of proofreading was greatly appreciated. Cristina Ajemian (former instructor of ERSL at Massassoit Community College - MCC) assisted the manuscript in its early stages in the areas of conception and clarification of concepts to human spirituality. My heartfelt consideration goes to the staff and faculty members of MCC. I am thankful for the helpful support of proofreading and comments on controversial issues by Charles Serneve, former librarian at Caritas Carney Hospital, MA. Michael Shanahan, one of my coworkers also contributed to this tremendous assignment.

    Special words of gratefulness to my wife, Linda, my daughter Raydana Chistie, and my extended family members for their loving support (my brothers and sisters, Nola, Emise, Joseph, Pierre Phanor and their respective children. I am grateful for my friends: Garvens Bonhomme, Gina Mars, Albert Pierre Canel and their family for their occasional assistance. Primarily, I wish to thank God who blessed me with the presence, caring, input, prayer and support of the many wonderful people that helped to make this book possible.

Foreword

In this book, author Raymond Phanor, presents a reference guide for spiritual counselors. Central to successful spiritual counseling is the understanding that because of their consciences, human beings are a higher order of God's creation.

When a spiritual counselor helps people fulfill their needs in ways that are consistent with their intrinsic values, he or she acts on the basis of their "True Conscience." Under certain favorable circumstances, individuals can naturally discern right from wrong and, falsehood from truth, and make most appropriate decisions. The more one learns, and the more one knows, the stronger is the development of one's "Educated Conscience". In this book, the author explores several settings and instances that contribute to the formation of the "Educated Conscience." These show how the quality of spiritually informed religious based counseling varies and how this can contribute to the counselees' quest for ordering their lives, or lead to massive and irreversible confusion.

This focus on spiritual counseling requires awareness in spiritual counselors of their need to incorporate in their counseling session spiritual values and goals. An awareness of the counselee's spiritual need, and the moral obligation to fulfill those needs without harming themselves and others in the process, counselors need to act truthfully and behave righteously. Counseling should be connected to the love and redemption that God revealed through Jesus Christ.

The author calls upon spiritual counselors to recognize the fact that any spiritual counseling given to those they counsel can either truthful or misleading. As spiritual counselors are doing the educating that leads to the transformation of hearts and minds, they should help the counselees to understand and adopt corresponding rules for their spiritual and physical welfare. As they counsel and educate, they should also think of the human "need for redemption." This need for redemption, according to the author, is evidenced in "disordered reflection" and emotions and feelings resulting in spiritual disturbances (e.g. resentment, jealousy, guilt, dejection, suicide, and homicide). This need is also intertwined with fear of death, which is the major concern of humanity. The author maintains that for human beings to live life at its best and its fullest, they must seek redemption in the divine power for transformation.

The author holds that fallen human beings cannot live invariably by moral judgment (as dictated by their TC).

Spiritual counseling removes the idea of "self-efficacy." This often serves as an obstacle to spiritual breakthrough and improvement. He appeals to spiritual counselors to give up unrealistic "pictures of perfection" in counseling and allow God to be their guiding light and inspiration in doing the work of counseling. Spiritual counselors rely on the "ultimate spiritual counselor;" who empowers counselors who depend on Him to counsel in accordance with His will.

This book is a must reading resource for all counselors engaged in making a difference in peoples' lives.

By Dr. Ernan Norman, M.Div., D.Min. – Pastor, Author, and Associates Professor of Theology and Religion.

Introduction

Human beings face vital difficulties in acquiring a clear-cut definition of their spiritual nature and purpose. This deficit seems to persist due to a lack of awareness of the spiritual needs and the motives correlated to the satisfaction of those needs. Fundamentally, the major dilemma is about self-awareness. Some individuals are skeptical about their origin, doubtful about the purpose of their existence, and uncertain about their destiny. Therefore, an understanding of 'self' remains a big mystery.

Today, topics on scientific matters are more suitable to debates than those that are spiritually orientated. There exists a large variety of campaigns against spirituality itself. In order to demean the humanistic value of spirituality, critics tend to relate it to a restricted domain of religiosity. Spirituality, however, is not necessarily a religious notion. It is not appropriate to assume that a person cannot be spiritual without being religious. This assumption is false, since we are, by nature, spiritual beings, whether we are religious or not. In contrast, one may be religiously devoted without being spiritually renewed.

Scientists know that spiritual science is not infallible. Leon Eisenberg (2001), in his personal memoir, "50 years of Child and Adolescent Psychiatry" wrote,

> The history of science is the guarantee of its freedom. The mistakes of our predecessors remind us that we may be mistaken; their wisdom prevents us from assuming that wisdom was born with us; and by studying the processes of their thought, we may hope to have a better understanding, and hence a better organization, of our own" (L. Eisenberg. 2001. Journal of the American Academy of Child and Adolescent Psychiatry. Web site).

Humans have the ability to reason and interpret life in a spiritual way. Animals, on the other hands, lack this higher mental ability to reason and to explain; thus, they remain the passive victims of the oppressive forces of life. Man's aspiration for an eternal life results from a spiritual need that the animals do not have. Human motives and needs are spiritual and can clearly be distinguished. The concept of spirituality itself infers that human beings have the faculty of reasoning. Human beings are capable of conceiving marvelous ways to satisfy physical and emotional needs either with or without moral standards. People know what it is to choose to live with trust (e.g., live with will and with confidence in what they believe), live safe, and live fair. These are the four foci in our essay of spiritual counseling. Human life is conditioned by two spiritual mechanisms: the *True Conscience* (TC) and the *Educated Conscience* (EC), which help determine our values, beliefs and lifestyles.

When our motives are confounded, we are confused as to how we should fulfill our needs. When our motives of living are discordant, we are perplexed. While all men agree that peace is good, there may be no center of awareness concerning the way and means for achieving peace. This is also true when it comes to love. While love is valuable to all, sometimes, people are confused about the way and means to make love a happy and fulfilling experience.

Spirituality and spiritualism are two distinct concepts. Spirituality is conceptualized as a function of a human conscience. Spiritualism concerns itself with an inexplicable assump- tion that the dead might be able to communicate with the living. As such, spiritualism involves reincarnation, which is the passage of the human soul at death to another body. This is a belief that is irrelevant to the nature of the human beings. Spirituality negates the belief in reincarnation. Spirituality places the emphasis on human needs, which are condi- tioned by functional fears. These fears are imperceptible and have the potential to inspire either self-improvement or spiritual degradation as a result of spiritual disturbances.

The philosophy of relativism that suggests that ethical truths are different among individuals and the groups holding them does not help boost human spirituality. For human beings to reach the desired level of spiritual revival, they need a unique and irre- versible alternative to the truth. The spiritual results vary according to how individuals utilize their internal resources. From a spiritual perspective, our conscience is the ultimate guide to the truth. The existence of standards of judgment, which provide the rationale of being "ok," can shadow the pathway to the desired truth. The nature and characteristics of the truth are clearly established by the Bible, which is an explicit set of values in the pursuit of a truthful and better life.

I will explore how we can help people to recognize that we all have a spiritual nature. I hope to develop an understanding of the 'self' in our spiritual being and demonstrate the ways and means used to satisfy human needs which affect our spirituality. I will also explore the ethics and responsibilities which relate to the work of spiritual counselors.

Chapter One

SPIRITUALITY AND SPIRITUAL COUNSELING

Spirituality is the key to understanding individuals' beliefs and behaviors. Although spirituality is often denied in understanding human thoughts, feelings and behaviors, individuals may undergo inner disturbances relative to failure to live with trust, live with will, live fair, and live in security. Spirituality and spiritual counseling emphasize a foundation of willpower, fairness, and security.

Trust is the basis of all interpersonal relationships, relationship to people and relationship to God. On the premise that people surrender their spirits to whatever is considered to be "truly gratifying" and that which serves as the basis for assessing whether peoples' commitment, or passion, derives from a choice to trust or a command to trust. A command to trust, which constitutes manipulation, may be self-damaging. From a spiritual perspective, people think, speak, and behave as a result of fear-driven inspiration. These fears when they are efficiently managed prevent people from internal disturbances and enhance an *upward spiritual experience*. The knowledge of what is good and what is evil may infuse a desire for change. At any particular moment, people may become concerned with what is needed to improve themselves and their perspective of self-improvement can be consistent with their best expectations in life.

Peoples' failure to manage their spiritual disturbances can lead to a *downward spiritual experience*. Human beings have a particular vision of life and freely look for internal comfort. That vision can challenge other people's beliefs or trust. Their habits can render life more difficult, while dealing with the inner self. These individuals might be infused with the spirit and with feelings that could lead them to believe, there is no hope for personal improvement with the risk of spiritual pitfall.

From the spiritual perspective, people think, speak and behave as a consequence of their fear driven-inspiration. These fears, when they are managed in an efficient manner, can increase the prospect of an uplifting spiritual experience and prevent people from suffering internal disturbances. In contrast, these fears can be the source of internal disturbances in human beings.

A desire for change is significant, and it should be examined. A person can start by considering what should happen to make the desired change a reality. Spiritual uplifting is associated with a drastic shift in the individual's vision of life. People understand the causes of their underlying ambivalence and their resistance to accept fulfillment of their need for redemption. In helping individuals to gain this self-understanding, spiritual coun- selors should know each individual's spiritual needs. They should also know each per- son's limitations for solving life-related problems and issues. Spiritual counselors' have the responsibility to help the counselees understand and take responsibility for their own problems. Counselor should help decrease the individual's desire to find solutions without divine help.

The True Conscience (TC) acts to encourage each of us to do the right thing. It reveals mistakes and errors that we make and shows us how to correct them in the future. The TC spiritually screens our thoughts and feelings, and counsels us to make informed decisions.

Individuals may seek spiritual counseling due to their concerns about their conduct in life and their thoughts that are not always in line with one another. An individual may come to the realization that he is unable to solve his personal problems. He might feel powerless and helpless in conjunction with fears of vulnerability. A person might be confused and discover himself becoming panicked, while reflecting on the reality of life. One might present other motives for seeking spiritual counseling that could be related to broken relationships, separation, grieving over the loss of a beloved one, a terminal illness, and other life-related issues.

The role of a spiritual counselor is to attend to the counselees' present problems and provide a solid understanding of the change desired through wise guidance. The spiritual counselor expresses compassion when it is appropriate and re-directs the counselees to the One who can help deal with all problems and provide solutions. Here are some hints for intelligent spiritual guidance:

1. Working with the counselees develop a positive and realistic plan in order to meet their spiritual needs: internal struggles, and their problems pertaining to their relationships with God and others;
2. Working through the two spiritual steps slowly: 1) make them aware of their misdeed, sin, or uncomfortable feelings, 2) get them to manifest a willingness to abandon the wrong answers;

3. Help them to remember that their troubles did not take God by surprise. He is still in control. Assuring them that God has a loving purpose for them;
4. Help them to trust God to work out God's perfect will. "We must give up our ambitions and allow Christ to dictate our goals," Dr. James Dobson advised (2007. p.15).
5. Encourage them to affirm their faith in God and express their confidence in Him through prayer and praise even before He acts – "the closer we walk with God, the clearer we see His guidance" (Our Daily Bread. May, 2008).

Charles F. Stanley (2003) wrote, "As long as we think we are tough enough, wise enough, educated enough, or strong enough to make our decisions 'on our own', then we will never seek the guidance that the Lord offers through the Holy Spirit" (p.19). In reality, those who deny God's existence tend to live their lives in accordance with their wishes and passions. The human need for redemption coincides with a change of lifestyle consistent with God's plan of redemption. In order to live life in accordance with God's plan, people must: 1) Accept God's way to redemption, 2) Acknowledge God's expectations and be willing to live accordingly, 3) Assure oneself that the changes expected are realistic and attainable through God's manifestation of grace and mercy. This form of counseling, which aims at facilitating a life-changing experience, requires a collaborative process. The counselor helps the counselee to know the meaning of life and "live a life with a sense of responsi- bility," (Ephesians 5: 15) as told by the Apostle.

Methods and techniques let individuals realize through insights the complexity of a life without God. Through the spiritual teaching of the Bible, a counselor can help his counselees find the way to love, justice and hope. Within a Christ-centered approach, the counselees learn to be responsible for themselves (Phil 2: 12) and learn that there is no redemption (or salvation) in no one other than Jesus Christ (Acts 4: 12, Rev. 7: 10). Crowder (2008) said, "Like a compass, the Bible always points in the right directions." A case in point is that a counselor's clarity of mind and commitment should inspire and moti- vate the counselees to make changes in their vision of life and their lifestyle. It is not good for a spiritual counselor to speak in favor of change and then find himself embroiled in a life full of controversy. Spiritual counseling consists of assisting the counselees through the process of interpreting their "must-change self-appeal" by their True Conscience.

David McCasland (2008) argued "When the unthinkable happens, it may seem impossible to believe that anything can overcome the emotional scars" (Readers Digest. April). Spiritual counseling urges people to prefer right over wrong. It holds the greatest function in human awareness of each individual is through gained acquiring motives for loving one-self, caring for self, forgiving one's debtors, and reconciling with one's Creator – a human experience that is consistent with undergoing a rebirth of spirit.

Chapter Two

THE AIMS AND PURPOSES OF SPIRITUAL COUNSELING

Spiritual Counseling is always challenging but not insulting. The core focus of spiritual counseling is to help improve the counselee's self-knowledge and confidence in the change experience. The process of empowerment, in spiritual counseling, coincides with the ability to better understand one's self through the acknowledgment of one's spiritual needs for action-taking and for self-improvement. There are strong indicators that people have an increased desire for knowledge of self. One of the relevant concerns that pertain to spiritually counseling an individual or a group revolves around the kind of reflection that is going on in the person's mind - the seat of all human interpretation. These individuals, when revisiting difficult circumstances in their lives, may go through a *time of wondering* which can enhance learning and counseling. At this point, the aim of spiritual counseling is to facilitate awareness of the need for redemption.

Spiritual counseling helps individuals become attuned to their True Conscience. In a time of honest interaction, a counselor may ask the counselee, "What did you do when you were feeling guilty about. . .?" (Such questions fall within the context of counseling.) The spiritual counselors can help their counselees clarify their own feelings and reactions in new ways. There could be a concern raised regarding guilty feelings that counselors can help the counselees articulate more clearly by asking, "I am not sure if you remember, when you spoke about the time you felt a sense of guilt about. . . .would you like to elaborate some more on this?"

The following is an example of how a biblical character was able to effectively communicate with someone in power, who suffered fear of God's reprisal.

To get the message through David, Nathan used wisdom and courage. Nathan told David the story of a rich man, who had exceedingly many flocks and herds. But the poor man had nothing, except one little ewe lamb, which he had bought and nourished; it grew up with him and with his children. It ate his own food and drank from his own cup, and it laid in his bosom. It was like a daughter to him. And a traveler came to the rich man, who refused to take from his own flock and from his own herd to prepare one for the wayfaring man who had come to him; but he took the poor man's lamb and prepared it for the man who had come to him.

David was receptive to the message in this story as told by Nathan, and it gave him insights into his wrongdoing. David naturally assumed the Nathan's story was true. David wondered, "How that is someone who possessed many sheep killed the only one of his neighbor's?" Nathan's counseling skills helped David to recognize his wrong behavior in which he had killed one of his officers so he could cover up an affair he had with the man's wife, Beersheba.

The technique used by Nathan was aimed at disquieting David's True Conscience to a point where he made David feel remorse for his wrongful act. Other ways of spiritual coun- seling should include helping the counselees reflect on the virtues of compassion, kindness, humility, patience, forbearance and love.

Spiritually speaking, one cannot be clear minded and confused at the same time. We talk about spiritual disturbance, when an individual has no clarity of mind and center of awareness of what he or she means by a life-changing experience. Someone who says, for instance, "If I don't change my lifestyle, I will die," and yet makes mistakes leading to more confusion, worry and panic, will have difficulty managing his or her conscience. This individual's confusion is more likely to cause involvement in situations and activities that engender worry and panic. Such inability to reason may evolve into a chronic spiritual disturbance (CSD) characterized by *mindlessness*.

Contextualizing Spiritual Change - *evidence of facts and evidence of opinion in spirituality*

Human beings are the only species that have the ability to reflect on their experience and understand the concept of failure and success, the concept of progress and regress. Individuals go through a variety of experiences that impact their life towards either a spiritual improvement or a degredation of their lives. We have thoughts and feelings that are habitual. Such thoughts and feelings may result in a reflection-based interpretation regarding the risk involved, or they can be simply automatic. This pattern of thinking elicits the purpose and meaning that we ascribed to our beliefs and lifestyle – the basis of our philosophy or vision of life. On December 4, 2004, Time Magazine published statistics that emphasized every-day risks from falling out of bed due to a heart attack. Also, this article provided a few examples of the individual's ability and strategies to manage potential risks. In this article, Guy Billout stressed, "Sensible calculation of real-world risks is a multidimensional math problem that sometimes seems entirely beyond us."

Sexual abstinence has two components - *a strict sexual abstinence* and *sodomitical abstinence*. A strict sexual abstinence, for example, must be a fact or it is not existent. It is a fact, whenever a person obviously stops any sexual activity. Abstinence results when some activity poses a grave risk to intrinsic concepts of what constitutes a safe life. When this occurs, the True Conscience is operative. Because strict sexual abstinence can negate propagation, such a commitment is not likely to foster an upward spiritual experience.

The more pain we suffer, the more we tend to abstain from what causes the pain. It is a normal human experience to seek relief from inner disturbances resulting from fear of some spiritual burden. An individual can become very disturbed while reflecting on his sexual abstinence or other sexual experiences that he had. In spirituality, the individual's decision to give up on certain sexual practices relates to the degree of distress resulted from such practices.

Sodomitical abstinence refers to the cessation of sexual activities pertaining to sodomy (any sexual intercourse regarded as abnormal, as between individuals of same sex, incest, or sex between a person and an animal).

The practice of abstinence can be temporary; as such, people can embrace this *utilis*, but fail to persevere in it. This is an indicative of disappointment with the *utilis*, meaning that the necessity of being abstinent is no longer effective. The time abstinence is practice constitutes in itself an evidence of fact.

I conducted a survey in two groups: 16 young Christians who regularly attended their church, and 16 students from Boston University. I surveyed them, while they were sitting at the lunch tables in the George Sherman cafeteria.

The participants of this study on sexual abstinence ranged from 13 to 23 years old. The data were collected by means of a structured questionnaire of 24 items that measured teenagers' attitudes toward sexual abstinence. The data showed that the group was heterogeneous in terms their religious affiliation, some of them claimed to be religious and others claimed not to be.

A correlation study determined the extent to which teenagers' devotion to their Christian religion increased the likelihood of their positive attitudes toward sexual abstinence. One of the first questions in this study was intended to determine whether the participants, who claimed to be "non-religious," had some interest or inclination to participate in church activities.

The study revealed that those who claimed to be "not religious" had some degree of religiosity as evidenced by their answers. To determine the highest rank of religiosity between the two groups, the study compared the frequencies of positive answers provided on the basis of three criteria: highly devoted religious, moderately religious and "not religious". The study showed that the frequencies of answers provided by the Christians were:

2 (highly devoted religious: 8 to 10 positive answers), 3 (moderately religious: 4-7 positive answers), 2 (not religious: 0-3 answers) and 9 unanswered questions. Paradoxically, the frequencies of the "non-religious" were: 5 (moderately religious: 4 to 7 answers provided), and 11 (not devoted religious: 0 to 4 answers provided), zero highly devoted found. Among Christian responders, the Mean for the degree of religiosity is 8.13 SD 2.47. For "non- religious" responders $M = 2.69$, SD 1.78.

The study demonstrated that the correlation between devotion to churches is stronger among young Christians than among those who claimed to be "not religious." In light of the results, the hypothesis that Christian youngsters are more likely to have positive opinions toward sexual abstinence than those who are "non-religious" was confirmed.

We concluded that Christian churches have greatly contributed to preventing young church members from contracting Sexually Transmitted Diseases (STDs). We have established that sexual abstinence has two aspects: awareness of health consequences and fear of getting STDs. The results showed that 82% of the Christian teenagers advocated sexual abstinence and not just out of their fear of getting STDs. Of those young responders who were in favor of sexual abstinence, their reaction was not essentially motivated by the "fear of being victimized from infectious diseases," but it was a deliberate choice of not having premarital sex.

In general, young church attendants (especially Christian churches) have been exposed to messages regarding the risk of premarital sexual intercourse including getting STDs. The results showed an equal percentage of young Christians, 69%, who answered the questionnaire and agreed, "Not all parents who pressure their teens into not having sex before marriage understand the reality." This study also predicts that 50% of young Christians will eventually make attempts to convince their boyfriend or girlfriend about sexual abstinence prior to a date, in comparison with 13% of nonreligious youngsters who might not do likewise.

Some limitations to this study were that it did not currently explore the effects of some important factors such as, moral ability of the teenagers; parental education; media influences on the teenagers' attitudes toward sexual abstinence. Primarily, the focus was on the level of awareness and compliance of the young responders, who attended Christian churches vis-à-vis sexual abstinence vs. those of the same age group, who did not have such learning experience.

Other considerations of evidence of fact vs. evidence of opinion coincide with individuals' belonging to a group, but are not compliant with group standards and principles. *Affiliation* has an undeniable meaning in spirituality. Some individuals, even after years of attendance in a Christian Church, decide not to get baptized, even though baptism is one of the Christian requirements. In reference to the Christian standards of discipleship, this is a case of evidence of opinion, not of fact. As stated by Jesus Christ to all authentic Christians, "He who believes and is baptized will be saved" (Mark16:16). Evidently, without exag- geration those who believe and are hesitant to get baptized are far from being Christians. Other aspects of Christianity are embedded in loving God by observing His living precepts. The Bible clearly states that love and obedience are intertwined. In other words, someone, who claims to love God needs to be asked how profoundly he or she believes that God's commands should be kept and taught. Christ strongly reminds all His followers "If you love me keep my commandments" (Jn. 14: 15).

Testimony, from the perspective of spiritual change, is an oral statement regarding personal knowledge or personal experience by which another person may be persuaded. Individuals give testimony for the purpose of communicating to others knowledge of some- thing, the other person does not know. It takes a much self-confidence to relate facts that concern personal beliefs and lifestyle. In an atmosphere of trust and mutual respect, one cannot help sharing amazing and truthful events with others which are highly persuasive. Some people had dreams and visions in which they received a message from the Divinity or some apparition.

A dream can have a distinct meaning to the dreamer and to those to whom the dream is told. To the dreamer, a dream could be the evidence of something real if he can see some correlation between the dream and a real-life experience. This dream-and-real-life correlation constitutes the strongest evidence that often drive people to share with convic- tion about their dream. The dreamer's degree of belief in the dream experience depends on how strongly he or she is motivated to share his or her dream with others. Like dream experience constitutes an evidence of fact for the person, who experiences it.

I had a talk with a young married Christian woman, who shared with me a dream in which she saw a tall person, with long hair, announced to her the date when a specific event would occur. She was eager to tell me that the event that was foretold in the dream hap- pened exactly as it had been predicted.

Despite the woman's conviction in sharing about the effect of the dream on her life, it was hard for me (the hearer of the dream) to recognize the existing correlation. The dreamer is more likely to take the correlation between a dream and a fact in life than the person to whom the dream is told.

For the purpose of conveying respect to the dreamer's belief, the spiritual counselor should stay silent, and listen carefully, while demonstrating empathy through eye con- tact and nodding. The counselor should be caring enough to be attentive to the story teller. At times, when the spiritual counselor wants the dreamer to look into the meaning of his dreams, the counselor can have the dreamer explain his or her thoughts regarding them.

The spiritual value of a dream comes from the individual's decisions that show they have trust in their dreams. A dream can determine a certain course of action in the life of the dreamer, "We are all pilgrims on the same journey, but some pilgrims have better roadmaps" (Nelson DeMille). A lady once told me about a dream she had about the cut- ting of a cake from which many people were expecting a piece. Following this dream, the woman moved into her mother-in-law's house, and felt compelled to share the "good news" (her cake) with her house mates. She had some concern that the people with whom she was living were not receptive to her spreading of the 'good news' - the message from the gospel. The woman's step-mother sudden hostility to her message of hope showed not everyone is willing to accept a dream and the message it carries.

After listening to her dream and how strongly she felt about the dream, I shared with the woman a few simple techniques. I told her how she could be efficient in her task of spiritually counseling others. I explained that people's share of the "Good News" with others can force people to face the reality of their needs; as such they may cause them to feel offended. I explained finding hope, overcoming a fatal diagnosis of a deadly disease, finding love, and living differently can all be signals for a spiritual change.

One woman, who was diagnosed with a rare illness at age 20 confided, "I truly enjoy taking extra time in the day to sit and talk to God by myself. It's a way for me to connect personally with God and let Him into my life." In addition, she declared, "I know he's there sitting next to me, willing to listen and talk about anything that is happening in my life. He's the one who has been carrying me through all the tough times in life. I couldn't have done it without him" (St. Anthony Messenger. April, 2008. p. 52).

Because a *miracle* can be hard to prove, it may pose a controversy of faith. Miracle was defined by Hume (1955) as "a violation of the laws of nature, and as a firm and unalterable experience has established these laws." A miracle, by nature, will generate many judgments, interpretations or considerations among people. Even, when witnessing a miracle, a miracle may be difficult for certain people to accept. A miracle may be seen by some people as a person's testimony founded on his or her past experience, as it was only an incident, a coincidence, or natural phenomenon.

Hume (1955) also said, "The proof against a miracle, from the very nature of the fact, is as entire as any argument from experience can possibly be imagined." Hume meant that some people may try to deceive or manipulate their audience; testimony of witnesses may be false or inaccurate. There may be other reasons to believe the miracle reported was a fake story when, for instance, witnesses contradict each other or have a personal motive in what they have been reporting, or appear unsure or distracted from what they believe occurred.

The spiritual counselor's responsibility is not to weigh one miracle against another or determine whether a miracle is real or not. The counselor and counselee should share respect and the counselor should provide the counselee undivided attention and does not need to know the accuracy or falsehood of a shared miracle. The very same principle of respect for every person's core belief which brings us (Spiritual counselors) and the counselee to a certain degree of camaraderie is pertinent in giving them our undivided attention and regard. The idea is not to wonder whether or not the miracle (as it was reported) is credible or not. However, being attentive and respectful is a requirement for an effective spiritual counselor. The counselor may get a sense of the teller's belief system by examining whether or not the miracle is an intervention of God. One may ask the following, "To what extent do you think this miracle was an intervention by God into your life?"

Repentance is a spiritual experience that is to be taken as evidence of fact. Repentance entails an upward spiritual experience. Teasdale (2004) wrote, "Change takes an open mind and heart; it requires courage and vision, as well as imagination and hope in the future (p. 113). The process of repenting sexual misdeeds, for instance, may be a long-lasting struggle that may lead to the belief that overcoming the bad sexual habits is impossible. For this to happen, the person should experience a renewal of mind. Laurel King in her book "Living in the Light" affirms, "Many people still suffer from the mistaken idea that spiritual energy and sexual energy are opposite, instead of recognizing that they are the same force," she said. In addition she said, "People split themselves; they try to deny their sexuality in order to be more spiritual, create a tremendous conflict within themselves, and end up blocking the very energy they are seeking" (p. 121).

Sexuality is such an integral part of our spiritual life that we would be disturbed without it. A biblically oriented sexual lifestyle does not aim to make individuals "more spiritual." The goal is to accomplish a sexually disciplined lifestyle, which has two aspects: monogamy and a heterosexually marital relationship. The purpose of repentance is to help individuals avoid spiritual disturbances regarding their failure to conform to the healthy guidance of their True Conscience.

In the chapter, "Sexuality and Passion," Laurel King talked about "sexual energy [that] has the power to create and transform." In this matter, she emphasized, "There is nothing safe, stable, or entrusting about it." This brings us to the understanding that L. King does not envision any escape from sexual misconduct. From a perspective of upward spirituality, those who practice polygamy may need to break their pattern of marrying with more than one partner and decide to commit to only one person of the opposite sex.

In a television interview, a young woman talked about her journey in prostitution and how she was "redeemed by Jesus." She stated, "If I can't tell the girls that there is a way out who's going to." This constitutes evidence of fact that the former prostitute experienced a change in her worldview. Her testimony regarding her redemption and her determination to tell other girls about "a way out" demonstrates that she is committed to make a moral value commitment and live her life differently.

Repentance as it is experienced entails determination to translate obstacles into victories - a switch from an immoral value commitment to a moral value commitment. Individuals refer back to their past experiences to give testimony about changes that they experienced. Repentance brings spiritual insight and gives rise to regrets over past behaviors. It gives rise to guilty feelings, and in most cases, ends in confession to God. The biblical repentance concept of becoming a "child of the light" results in a newfound discomfort with the unfruitful effects of darkness.

H. Spaulding (1989) when stressing the meaning of love said, "Sexual freedom seemed to many the opportunity to express true love. Alienation and estrangement led some to reach out for the closest person, and what often resulted was a strictly physical experience." He added, "The image of a man and woman waking up after a sexual encounter without knowing the other's name is tragic. This mentality indicates confusion about the meaning of love" (Spaulding. pp.50).

Sexuality is comprised in the ten commandments of God that give evidence of the healthy direction in life (Ex: 20:1-20). Therefore, human sexuality is not the only spiritual life experience that may give rise to challenges to seek redemption. When one of these laws is trespassed, the trespasser is likely to feel guilty feelings.

The concept of 'spiritual ambivalence' defines an individual, who is halfway between denial and repentance. This is a category of individuals, who are living with a rationale for evil. They may,, at times, feel disturbed by doing what is wrong, but under certain circumstances, they, with pride and arrogance, justify their mistakes or sins. They have an inability to commit to the reality of a need for change. As they are exposed to unhealthy ways of dealing with life, they may not know how to manage uncomfortable feelings. They may not clearly understand the origins of their confusing thoughts and behavior that they need to change. There are those, who talk about God, but who they are not entirely ready for divine guidance. They may not be ready to give up the illusion that they can control all circumstances or manage their life alone. As a result, they become overwhelmed by the hard work, they have been doing.

Spiritually speaking, individuals who are confused and ambivalent are in a stage of *inexplicabilis*. These individuals are not fully aware of with what they are dealing with, and they cannot clearly spell out their goals and purposes in life. In this spiritually, there is no value commitment, and the distinction between what is true and what is false remains undetermined. They have neither evidence of fact, nor evidence of opinion. They may say, "My whole life was changed" or "I cannot tell what happened, and why my life would change for ever?" These people have no clarity of what they can get out of a life-changing experience.

The Fundamentals of an Upward and Downward Spiritual Experience

The True Conscience of humans, as we explained, provides the resources for an enjoyable life without regrets or unvarying disappointment. The basic aspect of an *upward spiritual experience* is that it produces, as stated in the Bible, the fruit of the spirit that comprises, "love, peace, joy, self-control, compassion" (Galatians 5:21). Knowing that different life experiences may have a constraining influence, an individual's upward spiritual experience to be relevant needs to be framed on the basis of three aspects: (1) A change in vision of life, (2) a renewal of spirit, and (3) behavior that is consistent with the spiritual condition of improvement, i.e., a life relevant to redemption.

The highest level of spiritual improvement that a person individual may reach is the *sanus*. Following a reflection-based interpretation of his past behaviors, an individual's con- trition for sins may lead to a change in vision of life and of lifestyle. Spiritually speaking, *exertus* (or trial) is considered common to all stages of spiritual revival. The biblical expla- nation is that we "fall short of the glory of God" (Rom. 8:18). Under like circumstances, individuals who have natural motives to do well may have a decline in their spiritual life. An example of *exertus* occurs when someone, who is firmly committed to the principles of living with trust, living with will, and living fair, feels offended and becomes out of control. This tried person may say: "I knew what I was doing was wrong, but I could not help myself."

Given that the intrinsic values taught by our True Conscience may be compromised, we may feel compelled to do evil. To remain in the *sanus*, we need to continually turn to God for guidance and counsel. These dynamics in human spirituality are consistent with the understanding that individuals may be prone to do evil without weighing the implica- tions of their actions. *Profligatus* is the most degrading or declining spiritual level that an individual may attain. This spiritual stage in which a person is given shamelessly to vice or immorality is the end result of a chronic spiritual disturbance (CSD) that a person can undergo.

The main difference in the spiritual outcomes between *sanus* and *profigatus* is this a person in the *sanus* has God at the center of his life; however, the person, who lives in a state of *profligatus* does not place God at the center of his life. This person plans and acts on his own. He views himself as self-sufficient.

Having considered the two extremes of human spirituality in light of upward and down- ward experiences, let us examine how someone who was offended can, either have a spiri- tual revival, or suffer a spiritual degradation. In order to get over a grudge, a person has to:

Level A: go through the process of forgiving;
Level B: inform the offender that he or she has been forgiven;
Level C: re-establish casual relationship with that person through a mediator, and
Level D: Integrate the idea that the conflict is indeed solved.

As a consequence, an offended person, who had a grudge, reaches the sanus stage. This is evidenced by the reflection of those feelings and peace is restored within him.

From the perspective of a spiritually downward experience, the resentment over some personal grudge can build and eventually it could result in violence against the per- petrator of the offender. If the violence results in murder, the person who retaliated might attempt to justify his action in a shameless manner.

Dr. R. Puff (2005) was involved in a very challenging spiritual experience, while teaching people "how to express their anger and still be kind" (Anger Work. 2000. p. 1). Dr. Puff's challenge people to be kind while expressing their anger may not be effective for someone, who is only gradually experiencing an upward spiritual experience. I understand Dr. R. Puff's motive is to help people shift from anger, which is an uncomfortable feeling to a comfortable one. The rationale of being angry carries with it a *taedium feeling* (i.e. feeling of bitterness) that often takes time to go away. Someone, who has "good reasons" to be angry with another, may not be able to easily get over his anger. One of the greatest concerns with "teaching people how to be kind in all situations, even when they are angry" is that it may turn to be some kind of manipulation. As such, participants in this program may feel misunderstood and quit.

With this approach, spiritual counselors, who are attempting to mend counselees' anger, may not have sufficient time to assess the rationale behind the counselees' feelings; counselors may find it harder to help their counselees overcome their disturbance. Spiritual counselors in order to help people heal and get over their pain, need to remember the beliefs and feelings of their counselees must be considered when advising them. When spiritual counselors cause counselees to believe their concerns are being ignored or ridiculed, they might cause the counselees to develop further negative feelings and even become belligerent. If spiritual counselors want to accomplish a permanent good, they must keep in mind a counselor's spiritual background may be different from the people they counsel.

A relevant question is why angry people take time for spiritual improvement. This question was answered by David McCasland (2008) who said, "When the unthinkable hap- pens, it may seem impossible to believe that anything can overcome the emotional scars." This question has also been in a different way by the people, themselves, who have felt serious anger with the statement, "I am not God!" or "God alone is capable of forgiving all reprehensible deeds."

Chapter Three

THE VARIOUS FORMS OF SPIRITUAL COUNSELING

Counseling through writing

*I*t is well known that writing is a powerful means of communication. The motives of writing are various and involve the enthusiasm of sharing opinions, ideas, and counsel with others. One may not be given an occasion to speak in public, or have a delightful opportunity to have a conversation with the socially high-ranked persons, but to these individuals one can relate a message of importance by writing a note, a letter, a card, an email, and text message in a very convincing way.

A letter can be a special occasion or the most favorable means to invite someone to have a reflection on some common issues. In other words, a letter can promptly be persuasive to help people seek meaning and direction in life. For the success of the spiritual counseling through writing, the primary focus of the writer should be the sharing the good news of the Gospel.

Writing whose aim is to convince people regarding the fruit of the spirit (joy, love, peace, and hope) should not be dominated by personal experiences and achievements. This spiritually-related correspondence can be done by the awareness of someone who is facing difficult times, on the verge of a marital vow, moving away, or giving birth to a new born.

In light of human limitations to problem solving, Sweller and Levine (1982), researchers of cognitive psychology, called our attention to the fact that, "It is important to note that people can solve a problem but learn very little about its structure, with the result that they show only modest improvement when the problem is repeated"(Cognitive Process p. 263).

Fundamentally, a purposeful solution to a spiritual problem is relevant to an in-depth understanding of the spiritual challenges of humanity. In fact, for any forms of spiritual counseling, the primary source of inspiration is the Bible. There exists an effective flow to disclose personal knowledge of salvation and the internal security experienced through reading the Bible. The knowledge that a Christian writer acquired through personal experience in church and Bible reading may have powerful results in the message delivered either vocally or in writing.

Spiritual counselors are also talented writer. It is important to keep in mind that the spiritual counselors are not problem solvers, but through writing they can facilitate insights into change Buckingham and Clinton defined talent as "any recurring pattern of thought, feeling or behavior that can be positively applied." Given that some people can productively apply writing to teach something about the structure of a particular problem, these people are talented writers.

Although "Scientific problem solvers are well trained to recognize unanswerable problems or answering questions about a formula" (Cognitive processes p. 263), the Christian counselors must feel confident in God's supremacy for solving any problems. By doing this, these counselors draw a specific conclusion without supporting the evidence - the evidence of God's merciful power manifested itself through Jesus Christ's ultimate sacrifice.

In the face of contradictory evidence, the wisest way to proceed is to respond by alluding to some Bible characters who, by faith, overcame severe trials, and quote their words of success and triumph. This is a formal way to tell your correspondent: "For those who believe in Jesus Christ or in God every thing is possible," or "All things concur to those who believe in Him." This procedure of life review of believers in God can help the readers discover meaning and accomplishments through others' spiritual journey.

By definition, an "expert is a person who is extremely skilled or knowledgeable in some field" (Cognitive Processes p. 267). As a counselor who communicates through writing, one should avoid imposing on others values as an "expert." When counseling about death and the unique solution to death, the counselor concentrates on an irreversibly spiritual need for all human beings, for which he or she encourages the counselee's responsibility and self-confidence – a position that challenges scientific ways of problem solving.

A letter can serve as a clarification of options and facilitation of choices. It comes out that the success of this spiritual activity depends on the source of inspiration. The spiritual counseling prioritizes inspiration by God of the Bible.

After hearing several announcements made by a pastor of a mega church to formulate questions regarding "Grace and the Law," I wrote a letter to clarify what I think might have been useful to the Christian fellows. Here is the content of my letter:

Dear Pastor,

I cannot help writing to you about an important theological aspect of Christianity. I am persuaded that your audience and I will find an accurate and satisfying answer concerning the two challenging concepts for all believers in God, that are Grace and the law of God.

Some people assume that their belief in Jesus Christ, the Savior and the Lord is sufficient to their salvation by denying and ignoring the law of God. According to the Bible an authentic Christian whatever his religion or his culture has no duty to reject the laws or the commandments of God since these laws or commandments are written in their heart (Jer. 31:33). The main objective of writing to you today is to confirm what Jesus Christ said about following him "he who follows Me will not walk in darkness," he said (Jn. 8:12). In a spiritual context, darkness is similar to confusion. Are Christians confused about what God specifically expects from them? If they are confused it is because too many religions teach what is incoherent about the law of God. Our God, my God, is a very conservative God concerning His precepts, His law, and His commandments. Jesus Christ the Son of God shows complete submission and respect for the commandments of His Father. He said clearly that "Think not that I have in come to abolish the law and the prophets; I have come not to abolish them but to fulfill them. For truly, I say to you till heaven and earth pass away, not *an iota*, not a dot, will pass from the law until all is accomplished" (Matt. 5:17). My question to all theologians, preachers, deacons, and believers is this: Is Jesus Christ disobeying the law of His Father? The answer is not at all, since He has willed that those who claim to be His friends, brothers and sisters observe the commandments of his Father as quoted in Matthew 12 verse 48. These days Christians are *confused about loving God* or loving Jesus Christ.

The solution to this dilemma of faith is also stated in the Bible: "He who loves me keeps my commandments" (Jn. 14:15). Loving God is proximate to the situation of man who wants to show his wife how he loves her. The intelligent man has to be aware of what kind of appreciation that his wife would like best. If the man realizes that his wife loves flowers, he will bring her a bunch of flowers just to please her. If it is something else such as a poem, cruise or walking in the garden, he would try his best to meet such an expectation in a reasonable period of time. This is the reason that it is never too late to do what the Bible displays about the kinds of expectations that God has for every one of us who believes in Him through His Son Jesus Christ.

Dear pastor, - I have been listening to you and several other pastors since my commitment to Christ. I realize that one of the Ten Commandments remains a puzzle to be put in its proper position to get the exact picture of God (who is a God of love). This piece of puzzle is the fourth commandment. Do you think that it is permissible for a particular person or famous character to cross out one of the ten or to preach against it? The Bible thesis that commonly serves to support the introduction to the everlasting statement of the law of God, the Ten Commandments, is the following: When God recalled for His beloved people their slavery in Egypt, it is like making an allusion to our slavery of being sinners or Pageants. Some Christian critics say that the law or the Ten Commandments were given to the Israelites only. If we consider our status as Christians, or as being servants of God, we shall also show obedience to God and to His law. In addition, Moses was the witness of His law given on Mount Sinai which counseled the Israelites to teach strangers who visit them or dwelt among them (Deut.6:9).

What is the actual meaning of being saved by Grace through the sacrifice of Jesus Christ, the Messiah? Every Christian knows that salvation is related to the bloodshed of Jesus in the same manner as the apostle Paul taught it in Ephesians 2:8. Therefore, he said: "you are not under the law but under Grace (Rom. 6:14). The apostle Paul also said in Romans 6 verse 1 "Are we to continue in sin that grace may abound?" At this point, the new genera- tion of believers in God might be perplexed how best to understand and acknowledge that God, the Creator to whom they commit and serve has precise and unchangeable expecta- tions. What God wants us to do in a clear purpose? The answer is the same for all believers; He wants us to observe His commandments by surrounding our mental energy of belief and faith in Jesus Christ. To better understand this, this is what I personally call the *efficacy of the Grace*. In this precise context, the Apostle Paul says: "I can do all things in him who strengthens me" (Phil. 4:13).

Dear beloved brother, I do not wish to propagate an element of confusion within your devotion of preaching the Gospel of God. I am providing you and your sincere audience an opportunity to "test the truth" as it is advised by the Bible. You may have an objection to my counsel or completely reject it. My prayer to you all Christians is to meet consciously and deliberately the sacred expectation of God. Even though they are summarized' they are still the same in a concise way. David, one of the beloved servants of God was wise when he said; "Lead me in the path of thy commandments" (Ps. 119:35). As a result of his will he concluded: "The precepts of the Lord are right, rejoicing the heart, the commandments of the Lord are pure, enlightening the eyes" (Ps. 19:8).

I want to close my letter by encouraging you in the name of Jesus Christ our Savior and Lord to set yourself in agreement with the laws of the Father that are also the laws of the Son. I am sure that you are going to follow the example of David in favor of whom God said; "I have found in David a man according to my heart."

Please believe in my sincerity of teaching the truth and nothing but the truth. As it is written, "By Him we may be sure that we know the truth, if we keep His commandments. He who says, "I know Him" but disobeys His commandments is a liar, and the truth is not in him, but whoever keeps his word, in him truly the love of God is perfected. By this we are sure that we are in Him: he who says he abides in Him ought to walk in the same way in which He walked. My last question to you is that, did Jesus Christ observe the Sabbath as the authentic Jews have?

God bless all!

Letters from significant others can unexpectedly impact readers in a profound and posi- tive way. A man, for example, may write a letter or a card to a lady that he dated to reassure her how he has felt about their dating experience. In situations where fiancés are living at a distance they may be involved in a love correspondence that would allow them to warm up the romance and fight chances of doubting the integrity of the partners in the relationship. One day, I wrote to my wife a letter in an attempt to convince her about my committed love for her. Here is what I wrote: I came to realize that you're still holding some doubts about my sincere affection to you. Today, I am in a great hurry to write to you, one more time, to express my heart-felt love to you alone, which is as a burning bush that will never extinguish. I remembered that my sexual experience, in the past, could be compared as a butterfly sucking from multiple flowers. In August 3, 2003 (the date of my wedding with her), from the lesson I learned from God, I became a dedicated young married man . . . .

In October 2003, I received a letter from Pastor Joel Osteen that was to me very helpful in a moment of serious financial turmoil. In a moment that I felt discriminated and rejected by the school system that I attended. "Nothing is beyond your Reach," Joel wrote:

> Your heavenly Father wants to supply your needs, fulfill your hopes, and give you the desires of your heart. His favor is surrounding you. He will open doors for you that no man can shut. But before you can receive all the good things He has for you, you need to develop a *vision of victory* for your life.
>
> I want you to remember something extremely important – God is with you, God is for you, and God is in you. His goodness and mercy are following you. No matter where life takes you, He has promised to go before you and make crooked paths straight. There is no way you can lose as long as you follow Him.
>
> And once you start seeing your future through the eyes of faith – once you develop that vision of victory – you will discover that nothing is beyond your reach.
>
> Let me explain what I mean. Begin to see yourself the way God sees you. If you can see yourself happy, you will be. If you can prosper in business, you will. If you see your relationships fulfilling, they will be better. Every area of your life will be better. Start believing for God's best today, and you will begin to see His victory come to pass in your life.
>
> **You were born to win:** When you've got a vision of victory for your life, you can't be intimidated by anything! Not terror. Not loneliness. Not financial problems, cancer, or even death. Yes, these are giants, and they strike fear in the hearts of many people. But the giants you face don't have to frighten you.

Begin today to focus on God instead of your problems. He will empower you to face the "giants" of your life and say, "You are defeated." He will help you and you all the wonderful new things He is just waiting to give you.

Declare your victory: Let me encourage you to rise up today and see yourself as the overcoming champion He made you to be. You will be victorious – start today by taking the first step on your way to a new beginning.

I want to help you begin a life of victory. You are very important to us, and we pray for you every day. We continually ask God to strengthen you with His mighty power. We're always looking for ways to help you like the champion God created you to be. . . .

Bible Study

Bible study constitutes a prevailing avenue to a successful spiritual counseling. Instead of focusing on individual values and cultural differences, there is a need to explore principles and values through the Bible, if acquired, will result in wisdom and understanding. There is a spiritual correlation between wisdom, understanding, knowledge, and spiritual success. This correlation is explained as, (1) "Happy is then man who gets understanding" (Prov. 2:11), (2) The mind of him who has understanding seeks knowledge (Prov. 15:14), (3) "A people without understanding shall come to ruin" (Hos. 4:14). In the New International Version "wisdom" is equivalent to "discerning."

Two hours spent in studying the Bible indicate a great deal of interest in exploring the core values of living with trust, living with will, living fair, and living safe. The learners, at a particular moment of Bible study, can benefit from their counselor's kindness, patient, respect and consistency.

In a case where individuals do not want to share their problems with others, the need to spend a quality time exploring the obstacles is relevant. One can explore what makes these persons uncomfortable being a part of the discussion and what needs to change in order for them to commit and actively participate.

The purpose of any Bible study is to help the counselees ascertain the presence of Jesus Christ in each session. The first step is to present Jesus as the "victory." At the very beginning of each session, it is recommended that the spiritual counselor and the counselee(s) spend a special moment in prayer. The attendants implore divine assistance, address the need to know Christ, and come into agreement regarding the topic to cover in the session.

Acceptance of Jesus Christ should never be imposed. A reason of being part of this belief system should be presented as an open teaching option. This knowledge of Christ once mastered can be followed by other more advanced topics such as, God's holiness, His justice, His graceful plan of redemption, and the prophecies. These studies are exciting because they, not only, add more information to people's archives, but precisely, they are worth storing. At the time of learning about these topics it is hard to say when and why one might need them, but nobody knows when they might become useful. With all this practice, the learner may find himself (or herself) wanting to know everything about the Bible and feel uncomfortable knowing paradoxical topics.

Let us now imagine that a person is sincerely interested in becoming a Christian, starts with a Bible study and has to leave, after a few sessions, for a very distant area. This supports the idea of allowing all Bible students first to get familiar with knowing the redeeming work of Jesus Christ and His ever-lasting guidance who said, "I am with you everyday, until the end of this world." Once the person starts knowing and integrating who Jesus Christ is, he or she would get the "flame" to continue his spiritual journey under God's direction wherever he or she may be. The spiritual counselor, in that instance, has the responsibility to follow up with the counseling process by providing this counselor with learning materials concerning Jesus Christ and other related Bible topics that can be forwarded by regular mail or via emails. By teaching the person how to fish, the spiritual counselor is teaching him the skills of solving problems.

I learned in psychology counseling that one of the proper ways to answer the client who asks a psychotherapist or a counselor (using the rogerian therapeutic model) a spe- cific problem is to say, "I wish, I would give you the solutions." Paradoxically, a pro- fessor of psychology counseling said, "Clients get frustrated when, they do not get the answer." "Everybody's coming to us to feel relieved," he added. In spiritual counseling, however, spiritual counselors are bound to accompany their counselees through clarifica- tion of thinking, speaking and writing of people who are seeking a sense of meaning and direc- tion in life.

The Bible is exciting because of its infinite variety and complexity. The Bible is revealing the strengths and weaknesses of ancient servants of God. Given that God is the business of inspiring people on how to figure out problems and the solutions to these prob- lems, Bible students who are paging through his or her Bible may get the precise answer(s) to their questions and concerns, which is an amazing spiritual experience to these readers. By reading about the gigantic issues that biblical characters went through, a Bible reader can think about things they did to overcome their life-threatening issues (e.g., their hum- bling attitude, persevering prayer, fasting, and faithful speaking), and follow suit.

The Bible is the "instruction book" that gives us a clear-cut understanding of the course of a spiritual counseling. There exist in the Bible instructions on how to deal with our sinful nature and our sinful deeds. Jesus Christ only instructed on how human beings can withstand temptation, which is a very important learning experience for the Bible readers who are seeking direction for their lives. In the history of divine rewards and punish- ment, Christ's teaching of *instilling hope* and of *anticipation of reward* is the center of the

Christian belief and faith (Mat. 19: 28:30). The Bible enlightens conflicting spirits toward clarity and hopefulness.

The Bible has been is the most inspiring book that people use to learn about God and about servants of God. Here is an example:

What I can say of "our own God"? Words fail to express the depth of joy and delight that is contained within these three monosyllables, "our own God." He is our own by the eternal covenant in which He gave Himself to us, with all His attributes, with all that He is and has, to be our portion forever and ever. "The Lord is my portion, said my soul" (Lam. 3:24).

Following a series of Bible reading, one may say, "He is "my own God, mine to trust, mine to love, mine to run to in every dark and troublesome night, mine to commune with on every bright and sunny day, mine to be my guide in life. He is my help in death and our glory in mortality." He is "my God" by providing me His wisdom to guide my path, His power to sustain my steps, His love to comfort my life, His every attribute to enrich me with more than royal wealth. The person who can truthfully, out of a pure heart, looks up to the throne of the infinite Jehovah and calls Him.

The following presents some questions followed by their answer in a biblical approach of a Christ-centered spiritual counseling:

- *How dependent are we upon Christ for Salvation?*
"Without me ye can do nothing" (John 15:5).
- *What three essentials for a Savior are found in Christ?*
Deity: "But unto the Son He said, Thy throne, O God, is for ever and ever" Hebrew 1:8).
Humanity: "When the fullness of the time was come, God sent forth his Son, made of a woman, made under the law" (Galatians 4: 4).
Sinlessness: "Who did no sin, neither was guile found in his mouth" (1Peter 2:22).
How did Christ show from the Scriptures that the promised Savior of the world must be both human and divine?
"While the Pharisees were gathered together, Jesus asked them, saying What think ye of Christ? Whose son is he? They say unto him, the son of David. He said unto them. How then doth David in spirit call him Lord, saying, The Lord said unto my Lord, Sit thou on my right hand, till I make thine enemies thy footstool? If David then call him Lord, how is he his son?" (Matthew 22: 41-45).
What two facts testify to the union of divinity and humanity in Christ?
- Concerning his Son Jesus Christ our Lord, which was made of the seed of David according to the flesh; and declared to be the son of God with power, according to the spirit of holiness, by the resurrection from the dead" (Romans 1: 3, 4).
- *How complete is the Salvation obtained in Christ?*

"Wherefore he is able also to save them to the uttermost that comes unto God by him, seeing he ever lived to make intercession for them" (Hebrews 7:25).
- *What should we say for such a Savior?*
"Thanks be unto God for his unspeakable gifts" (2 Corinthians 9: 15).
- Concerning "New Birth" or "Conversion":
- *Why did Jesus emphasize the necessity of New Birth?*
Unless you turn from your sins and become as little children, you will never get into the Kingdom of Heaven" (Matthew 18:3).
- *In what other statement did He teach the same truth?*
"With all earnestness I possess I tell you this: Unless you are born again, you can never get into the Kingdom of God" (John 3: 3).
- *What takes place when one is converted to Christ?*
"When someone becomes a Christian he becomes a brand new person inside. He is not the same any more. A new life has begun!" (2 Corinthians 5: 17).
- *From what is a converted sinner saved?*
"Let him know, that he which converted the sinner from the error of his way, shall save a soul from death, and shall hide a multiple of sins" (James 5: 20, see Acts 26:14-18).

Preaching

Preaching is the most common form of spiritual counseling. It occurs in churches, on radio stations, on TV and in the open-air crusades. . . The question is what is the role of preaching in the business of spiritual improvement? In his article "Social-psychological Causes of Faith," Bruce Hunsberger said, "Religious people typically report that they have greater support in their lives than do people with no religious affiliation" (*The Science of Religion*. p.34). Another psychologist Ken Pargament affirmed, "Religion aids people in coping with life's problems. Greater social support means more potential resources to help one deal with stress, illness, death of loved ones, and so on" (Ibid. p.35).

In addition to personal confidence in their ways of coping with negative life events, religious people seem to be more sharply connected with their True Conscience than non-religious people. As a matter of fact, remarkable changes may occur in their lives following their experience of listening to a sermon that calls them to reflect on what is right to do and the dangers to avoid. In order to measure positive effects of an upward spiritual experience, Altemeyer developed a questionnaire that aimed to assess individuals' "Happiness, Joy, and Comfort" that he administered to over 500 parents of university students in 1997. The answers reflected the extent to which "traditional religious beliefs brought them happiness, joy, and comfort in the following way: (1) they tell me the purpose of life, (2) they help me deal with personal pain and suffering, (3) they take away the fear of dying."

These parameters (happiness, joy and comfort) triggered by religious experience were contrasted to logic and science in the same context of bringing people happiness, joy and comfort. The results are as follows: "The parents indicated that religion brought them substantially and significantly more happiness, joy and comfort than did logic and science" (idem). This empirical outcome helps to better conceptualize the difference of undergoing religious activities and positive outcomes from that religious experience.

In general, people often are misled by the concept of being religious, and having an actual spiritual life. To clarify this, I am making allusion to my personal experiences in several Catholic and Protestant churches to substantiate that all individuals are spiritual persons, but not all are religious, and those who are nonreligious do experience an upward spiritual lifestyle. Let me emphasize that the concept of "being born again" preached in the Christian churches is an indicator that this religion has promoted an upward spiritual experience because it brings to awareness all-inclusive aspects of lifestyle changes. When it comes to matters about changes in life- style this implies a Moral Value Commitment (MVC) that has no involvement in whatever is unsafe, self-destructive, and injurious to others. This in what comprises the job of a preacher who is also a spiritual counselor. Preachers often stress the spiritual breakthrough that happens when persons surrender to Christ's means of redemption. Such messages are likely to facilitate changes in the listeners' meaning of life.

Visiting in a Moment of Turmoil - *the ministry of caring and praying for people's healing*

Another feature of spiritual counseling is to devote self to minister for those who are in need through prayer and support. This ministry of caring and praying is done in a group of two or more - which feature is evidenced by Christ's instruction in Mark chapter 6 verse 7. When talking about those who are physically, emotionally and mentally healed, Hagin, author of *"You are an Heir"* affirmed: "Sometimes God manifests Himself in special ways for people to be healed, but at other times He does not." This is a very powerful statement that corroborates the following: "My wife and I ministered personally to people when doc- tors have shaken their heads and said, 'We've done all we can do.' They will be dead in a matter of hours'" (Hagin. *The World of Faith*. Dec. 1994. p. 6). Hagin recognizes that his faith cannot force the will of God to fulfill his wishes (Idem. p. 6).

It takes a lot of confidence, trust, assurance or faith to intercede for individuals who have a terminal illness. Interceding means "to plead on behalf of another person." This other person may be a believer or a non-believer in God. Faith encores the reality that God is powerful and merciful enough to forgive any sins and to solve any problems. This developing conviction is the spiritual process by which the sick may have realistic expectation regarding God's healing intervention, the broken hearted person will mend, and the unsolved problem of evil may be hopefully faced. This realistic expectation is grounded on faith, an experience, and a way of life. The greatest assurance is that the ministry of praying for people's insurance is embedded in the individual's trusting experience with God.

Hagin reported what a patient said to him: "I want you to pray for me. I have high blood pressure and heart trouble. My doctor is concerned about me, and he doesn't think I'm going to make it, I want you to pray that I'll have the faith to be healed." From this statement, there are two important elements to consider. First, the speaker has a reason for not relying on her doctor's lack of trust – the *ratio decidendi*. Second, the speaker who is a believer in God did not feign faith. Her trust in God demonstrated confidence in the healing process through prayer intercession. Another consideration to make is that this woman "wants to have faith to be healed," which is biblically grounded. Although she was awfully ill, she was aware of the biblical instruction according to which there could happen no healing without faith. Jesus Christ, in many occasions, emphasized the healing power of personal faith when he said, "Your faith has healed you" or "Your faith has saved..." (Mt. 8:10, Lk. 7: 50, Mt. 21: 21). Substantially, the ministry of praying for others' physical and spiritual welfare is a faithful ministry in Christ.

The insidious pressures of modern life can wear prayer ministry down to a point that ministers rush to the conclusion. This article brings the opportunity to understand and show compassion to the individuals who confess about their lack of faith. A spiritual counselor ought to avoid commenting on people's words of faith. The nature of these comments may be repugnant to sensitive people. They may be misinterpreted and endanger a desired working relationship - the individual who is feeling "misjudged" will be ill-disposed to benefit from the ministry. The spiritual counselors should be cautious not to overcome their counselees by a feeling of repugnance to a point of display of rejection of prayer.

It is not judgmental to ask a visited person if he or she is a believer. The point of the matter is that *faith confession* of any sort should be respected. The following story shows how personal ministry of caring for others can bring blessings to the one who cares: Sister Maude told me a story about her church member who insisted that she accompany her to a medical appointment. Sister Maude who had seen her doctor for eight years had not been diagnosed for any disease. She often said, "Everything is all right." It was only when she went to the hospital with her daughter and the church member that she was not feeling well and was kept for an emergency surgery. She had the operation and since then her life condition had improved. The lesson behind this story is that merciful works can turn into personal blessings. Sister Maude's benevolence brought blessing to her through a medical intervention that was successful.

In their prayer, those who are involved in caring ministry should ask that their iniquities be forgiven. This is not a time to get involved in religious debate of any sort. One should avoid constant criticism that can be provoking and derail from the objective. At all times, one should avoid being an intruder. In an attempt to win the sympathy of the person served, it is recommended that Bible reading should not be inflicting guilt or remorse. This suggests that the choice of literature to give out should be uplifting rather being a curse.

The following is valuable in understanding that pastors may at times need other church members' spiritual support:

A pastor, just like anyone else in his congregation, can feel weak and inadequate at times.
I remember one day when I was particularly tired and weary and felt I had to talk to the Lord about it. I trudged across the parking lot from my office to our worship center and went in to pray.
It was late afternoon, a time when no one else was in the building. It was dark, quiet, and cool in the big auditorium. Perfect praying conditions. I knelt down between the pews, buried my face in my hands, and began to pray out loud, as I like to do sometimes.
"Lord," I said, "I don't want to feel this way. Really – I feel bad about feeling this way. But – well, I just feel like I'm done. Don't think I'm pastoring all that well these days. But Lord… it would be nice, really nice if …I mean, I'd just kind of like to know if you're still concerned at all about how I'm doing. It'd be nice to hear from You could, You know, just give me a little bit of a reason to believe that You really care – that You're really involved in my life and ministry…
So I went on with my sad little recitation, complaining a bit maybe, remember that David got away with it in his psalms.
I just about worked myself up into believing I was pretty much alone, abandoned, and washed up when, suddenly, a few yards away from me, a head popped up from between the pews.
It's was a little startling. I had to squint into the semidarkness to make sure it really was a head. (But what else would it be?) In a moment I saw that the head attached to a body – a man's body – because he walked over to my pew and sat down beside me, where I'd been kneeling.
"Pastor," he said. "I'm terribly sorry to disturb you. Sorry to bother you while you're praying. But, well, I heard you, and I felt like the Lord wanted me to come over and offer to pray for you. I felt like the Lord moved me to come here today – right here – to pray for you. Funny thing is…I really don't know why. You're not the sort of person who seems to need anything. You're so positive all the time. Never seem to need encouragement. But I thought I'd better do what the Lord said and come ask if I could pray for you. I felt maybe you needed it today."
I nodded, and with that he placed his hand on my shoulder and began to pray that I would experience refreshment and strength in my life, and encouragement in the work of the ministry.

I had been surprised to see that head suddenly pop out of nowhere in that big, empty auditorium. I had been amazed to learn – just when I was feeling so weary and alone - someone had been praying for me, only a few yards away.

I guess I shouldn't have been surprised. God knows very well when I'm approaching the end of my strength. Truthfully, He knows it long before I do. And He knows just when to send along an angel or a brother or sister in Christ to fill my empty cup.
It's just what He did for Elijah, when that good prophet had finally reached the end of his tether. Someone popped in on Elijah, too, and taught him what to do at a frustrating dead end called fatigue (Ron Mehl, 1996. *Meeting God at a Dead End*. pp. 62, 63).

Chapter Four

THE FEATURES AND PRACTICE OF SPIRITUAL GROUP COUNSELING

The more precise goal of discussing spiritually related topics in a group is to establish a friendly rapport leading to exchange of the truths of life, e.g. everything in wisdom is grounded in the knowledge of good and evil. Individuals will find the truthful insights through others' shared experience, feedback and clarification in reference to the Bible. It is clear that a group pertaining to spiritual counseling have specific criteria and features.

A spiritually oriented group leader needs to clarify a spiritually specific matter that fits the group's behavior. We all, youngsters and adults, have been undergoing a morality test on a daily basis. In addressing some vital issues that are mostly challenging such as, the ones that pertain to abortion, to marital status and ethics, we need to be aware that people become uncomfortable for the reason that those topics may inspire relevant past experiences.

The question that ties to any topic related to spirituality is often what is the true purpose or meaning of living. Authoritarian need versus simplicity and humbleness, the death penalty, and materialistic trends are all relevant to this question. These are topics that pose a challenge to reflection-based interpretation. Most likely, in a group debate some individuals may become extremely aggravated to a point where they may leave the room, and curse.

I suggest that a spirituality-based counseling session lasts 45 minutes with one hour the maxim length. Because counseling groups have different objectives and distinct purposes, a group interested in psychotherapy or psycho-education should not change into a spirituality-based group. A group that participates in psychotherapy may be of interest to a spirituality- related group.

What is a spirituality-based group and what is its objective? The Alcoholic Anonymous (AA)'s group philosophy is consistent with the idea that "individuals cannot cope with addiction on their own but need the help of something greater than themselves" (Judith A. Lewis. *Addictions - Concepts and Strategies for Treatments* p. 148). This approach to treating addictions is based on the principle that "Relying on the support group is probably as important as the reliance on the higher power (Idem). It is obvious that AA's plan to foster awareness in group participants of their need to comply with divine guidance through various slogans, meditations, and prayers does very little to achieve this goal. Through this means, AA has been educating attendants on humility in the face of the pow- erful disease of alcoholism toward renewal of the mind with the assistance of God.

While I was running spirituality-based groups, I was involved in chatting with participants about their viewpoints on the concept of "Higher Power." Their responses varied as to what and who they consider to be the Higher Power in their life. Of these participants, several told me that "The Higher Power can be anything: A tree, a lake, the sky, the moon, or something else." This information suggests that their concept of the Creator of the universe has no basis of uniqueness

A spirituality-based group is a discussion group for individuals who are willing to take the risk of experiencing a change in their vision of life. Change is always frightening, but a spiritually-based group creates a new environment with new challenges that bring insight for the change needed. The group empowers its participants to live worthily and not merely to get on in the world, but to develop a goal they can attain. Leading a spiritually-based group is not about teaching religion, but guiding individuals to a place where they begin to believe that their need for redemption cannot be met unless they surrender to the transforming power of Jesus Christ, the Redeemer. Again, the purpose of spiritual counseling is not to tell someone he or she is a "bad person." Its aim is to counsel individuals to seek physical excellence, which we call good health and moral completeness - moral value commitment (MVC). Instead of letting people feel that they are "so bad that there is nothing that they can do to change the course of their lives, rather prepare them in what they *must do* in order to meet their need for redemption when it becomes apparent.

Group members tend to be altruistic toward people who share personal problems and assist in making specific value judgments through reflection-based interpretation of their own mistakes. This involves a strong sense of mutual obligation toward group participants who become close throughout shared alternatives for problem solving. In the attendants' best interest, a spirituality-based group helps explore and solve a current issue or persistently unresolved problems.

Participants in a spiritually-based group must promote qualitative meaning to one another. As we pointed, the role of the group leader is to deal with the content of what has been discussed to inspire the attendants about their need for redemption. The leader of a spirituality-based group may introduce a session by asking: "How many of you possess a Bible at home?" and proceeds with: "Today, together, we are going to take a great risk. We are going look humbly at the idea of 'must be born again' (the Bible). The leader presents information on the topic drawn from the Bible as clearly and compassionately as he or she can – it is a task with a clear goal with the expectation that everyone in the room would participate in the interesting and spiritually-challenging debate.

Given that a group leader should not dump bad news on the attendants, he or she should artfully process concerns, feelings, and needs of the group participants in a way that is not distressing. Between the leader and the participants there should be close bonds of learning. The spiritual counselor needs to maintain a rapport of persuasive helper by putting emphasis on "what works" and "what makes life better" in light of biblical instructions. This suggests that a moment of reflection on what is healthy and productive in life is not necessarily creative – it can be clarified by use of the Bible. Some participants may not be willing to comply with what the Bible teaches in terms of values. When a spiritual group leader encourages his or her attendants to practice the discipline as required by the biblically suggested way of living, the leader may face an internally self-defending reaction on the part of the counselees. This internally self-defending reaction may generate an outburst. Suppose that a leader says "Let us look at what the Bible says on this matter in. . . ..," a participant may not partly agree or fully disagree with the cited biblical reference. As the group leader strives to build close bonds of independence, he or she must be consistent on the matter of living with trust, living with will, living fair, and living safe.

From a humanistic standpoint, a spiritual group leader ought to convey respect for individual freedom by encouraging the attendants not to cut themselves from the counseling resource that is the Bible counsels. There are ways by which a counselor and the counselees (in a group) can articulate a mutual awareness of the Bible as a book of reference. One of the ways is to acknowledge that the speaker may totally disagree with what a statement in the Bible. Suppose that a group participant argues "I have the right in not forgiving," a group leader may process the speaker's right by saying, "It seems to me and many of us that you do not share the biblical instructions on 'forgiving one's debtors' and that it is upsetting when others are talking about the spiritual outcomes of "forgiving. Is that true?" If a group participant argues, "I have the right in not forgiving," the group leader may add, "I under- stand that you have had some serious concerns about what the Bible instructs on the matter of "forgiving one's debtors. It is true that not all people agree on all biblical instructions and that some of you may not be in a mood of solidarity. At this phase, the group leader may make a call for solidarity by saying: 'Unless our group achieves solidarity, we will be unable to accomplish our goal."

During this period of search for solidarity, the group leader ought to convey attention and respect for the participants' right of disaccord by reflecting back what they said as well as their feelings. The intervention can be stated as such, "You openly said that 'you disagree with the biblical instruction on forgiving and when hearing other people discuss this topic you get upset. On a score of 1 to 10 (1: being in total disagreement and not willing to talk about forgiving and 10: finding the topic helpful and wanting to continue with the topic) what is the number that describes your point on the discussion? A participant who is between "5 to 10" suggests that he or she wants to stay in the group. Otherwise, he or she will continue acting in exactly the same manner i.e., having a contradictory stand.

It is obvious that individuals may be feeling uncomfortable discussing matters that tend to be challenging to their spirit. At all times, spiritual counselors are involved in a working relationship, especially with participants who are reluctant to the diversity of individuals' values. Through this working relationship, the group leader smoothes the entire process of spiritual counseling by clarifying that religion is not the foundation of a spiritually based counseling.

During the first group, clarification that pertains to the difference between religiosity and spirituality could be helpful. Freedom of speech on issues that are challenging is the primary criterion to a spiritually based group. Once the group participants are well-informed of the nature of the topic in discussion and the goal to be achieved, chances of antagonism and dissension will decrease relatively quickly. By doing so, participants whose philosophy of living is unconcerned with religion are less likely to feel stigmatized or judged by other group members with various religious convictions. The question as to why people feel targeted by others' comments on a particular topic has a spiritual basis. Often in uncomfortable conversations, one or several participants may abruptly react to others' viewpoint on a matter to a point of rushing away from the room.

An instance of protest that is often tied with a statement such as, "Who are you to summon my conscience for a change?" Such abrupt reaction on the part of one group participant may stem from guilt and be expressed as follows, "Why can't you just believe what you want to believe, and let me believe? As long as we both really believe in something, what's the difference?" Such reaction may cause other members' frustration and reactions as well. Under like circumstance in which close bonds of interdependence has not yet been established, transfer of confusion and mutual frustration in a group are to be expected.

Let us pass on to the matter of a leader who sends inconsistent messages to a group. All the aspects of spiritual counseling must be geared to this goal of being a reliable model. The importance of goal setting in spiritual counseling is grounded in the biblical instruction according to which "A blind man cannot lead another blind man." (Mat. 15:14). Some speakers may attempt to derogate a spiritual group leader from his/her influence or reputation by directly attacking his questionable habit. A spiritual leader ought not to launch into excuses of bad habit, rather he or she is to practice what he or she asserts to be true. Even when a leader is hurt by derogatory remarks on the part of the group participants, this leader should remain confident in his or her basic conviction or moral commitment – an adequate self-confidence that is highly persuasive. Given the damages that smoking cigarettes causes to an individual's health, it is therefore a poor idea to choose a non-repentant smoker to talk to a group about health-related issues of any sort. This restriction to spiritual counseling is a prevailing principle to always remember that the lifestyle of a spiritual counselor should not be misleading. The values shared by this group, are values that are divinely inspired and biblically established. From a biblical perspective, a spiritual counselor is portrayed as "the Light" shining in the darkness and "the Salt" transforming a tasteless world.

Another striking analogy concerning the power of modeling in spirituality conveys that "Different kinds of fruit trees can quickly be identified by examining their fruit. A variety that produces delicious fruit never produces an inedible kind. And a tree producing an inedible kind can't produce what is good" (Matt. 7:17, 18). As such, a leader's lifestyle must be inspiring to the rest of the group or of the church.

As a group progresses, a participant may become extremely aggravated and derange the group cohesiveness. The journalists participated in the conference press by the US President George W. Bush challenged him for reasoning over the risk of making war to Iraq as opposed to pursuing peace through negotiation. This is a classic example of the dynamics that may take place due to controversial worldviews of group participants. These journalists endeavored to inspire the US President a moment of contemplating a life of fairness and safety. The speaker (the US president) and the attendants (the journalists) were speaking through different level of conscience. The former spoke through his Educated Conscience, and the latter functioned by the influence of their True Conscience.

There is a need for a homogeneous group. Homogeneous groups that gather people of congruent philosophies would be less conflicting than those with a dissimilar vision of life. In a sense individuals who claim to be atheists are unlikely to be thankful to God and more likely to feel annoyed when believers are happily expressing their gratitude to God. Knowing that the homosexuals strongly suggest that heterosexuals are 'homophobic," and that the heterosexuals perceive the homosexuals as "morally promiscuous," a group with these two sets of incompatible lifestyles can be conflicting in a way that is irreversible. Andrew Sullivan unveiled a clear reason why the homosexuals would feel uncomfortable being among the heterosexuals as such, "It's possible; I think that whatever society teaches or doesn't teach about homosexuality, this fact will always be the case. No homosexual child, surrounded overwhelmingly by heterosexuals, will feel at home in his sexual emotional world, even in the most tolerant of cultures" (What is homosexuality. Massasoit Community College – course pack for English Composition I. p. 95).

When commenting on Sullivan's perspective of homosexuality, Dolan Jill argued:

> Sullivan's determination to see gay and lesbian and trans people as self-powered makes him foolishly blind to the practices of hatred that makes us very vulnerable indeed, of the vagaries of public opinion and to the practices of malice that many of us are unluckily enough to face, sometimes on a regular basis" (Jill. 2010. The Feminist Spectator.).

This statement supports the fact that a decision to incorporate the homosexuals and heterosexuals will lead to an inter-group conflict. Such a heterogeneous group nests heating confrontation over an irresolvable issue that even the most knowledgeable and skillful group leader(s) will fail to manage. We maintain that a homogeneous group is more likely to foster solidarity between its participants who will eventually experience a polarization in their vision of life, and progressively improve in their desire for living with trust, living with will, living fair, and living safe.

Subsequently, when group members share common concerns, the likelihood of cohabitation would increase. A way to conceptualize a heterogeneous group refers to the idea that a group can include "forgiven sinners" and "unforgiving sinners." Because of their experienced spiritual breakthrough, the forgiven sinners are more receptive and ready to learn about different lifestyle choices, and are less likely to assert that they are right and that other people are wrong. The unforgiving sinners, however, can boastfully defend their lifestyle choices, which attitude can engender confrontation.

We have highlighted some factors that can deter cooperation between group members and turn into an irresolvable conflict. A group leader should bear in mind that, when discussing issues such as a, *being born again*, the audience may react in an unpredictable and irascible manner. William Carr Peel et. al. explained the grounds for confrontation in a spiritually-based individual counseling or group when they said: "*Born again* is [another] a perfect good biblical term that sadly had begun to raise red flags when we use it in conversation with some non-Christians" (p. 100). The authors of "Going Public you Faith" added, "If you tell people they need to be born again, they may think you're trying to get them to join the 'religious right' rather than inviting them to experience new life in Jesus." This remark and others made by the authors are essential when dealing with attendants' resistance to change their worldview. As they counseled, spiritual counselors should be ready to "face offensive behavior inoffensively" (p. 128).

There will come a time when a spiritual leader will express openly the truth about what has brought him (or her) true happiness in life. Martin Seligman (2004), a social psychologist, believes that happiness is a "useful core" of positive emotion - "the energizing force that drives us toward the sweeter things in life, like friendship and romance, and probably keeps us healthier and living longer" (*Whole Living*. p. 100). In addition to explaining the benefits of friendly and romantic relationships that are necessary for fulfilling our existential need for connection, a spiritually-based leader ought to capitalize upon how his or her need for redemption has been met. I agree with Seligman when he said, "Happiness means so many different things to different people." From this perspective, Seligman prescribed "The third form of happiness, which is meaning." The idea is to "know what your highest strengths are and deploying those in the service of something you believe is larger than you are" (*Eudaemonia*, the Good Life: A Talk with Martin Seligman, 3.23.04)

Through the leader's testimonials, the group attendants will gain a sense of the ben- efits of being in a relationship with Christ who made the changes in their lives. By cred- iting the gracefully transforming work of Jesus in their life, the testifiers show how truly they were engaged in the process of being spiritually renewed by God's intervention. The counselees who are listening to the leader's testimonials and are struggling with the concept of *being born again* would have a reflection-based interpretation that God's plan of redemption can bring meaning and purpose to themselves. When talking about "leaders' ability to overlook outward sinful behavior," Peel and al. pointed out the Apostle Paul who "entered a city more decadent than ours" and "did not preach to the nonbelievers about moral issues." This suggests that more than anything else the Apostle Paul's focus was on the benefit of being in a relationship with Christ. When describing the spiritual effects of this relationship, Peel and al. considered it as "a relationship that can change people to the very core of their being" (p. 129).

Commonly, when people sin, they feel guilty and go on alleviating the spiritual effects of their guilt by seeking pleasure and happiness in ways that may turn to be spiritually detrimental. A *realistic acceptance of one's sinful nature* occurs when sinners come to a point to acknowledge that they are spiritually incapable to prevail over their tendency to sin with their own will or self-persuasion and are resolute to turn to the Redeemer. From a perspective of being a persuasive helper, a truly repentant homosexual may clearly com- municate how, in the past, he or she railed against his or her wrongdoing without making any progress until he or she surrendered to Jesus. A powerful testimonial of such aims at promoting qualitative meaning in others' resistance to accept the reality according to which "we all are sinners," and therefore, we have a need for redemption.

For success of a spirituality-based group the number of participants should not exceed twelve. Such a recommendation is based upon the fact that Jesus Christ chose twelve dis- ciples. From a group psychotherapy standpoint, management and communication among group members is related to the size of the group. In this way, the level of irritability can be better controlled when there are limited possible interactions among members. The group size of choice is more likely to be affective in producing adhesiveness with regard to Wicker's (1969) statement, "Smaller groups are likely to be more attractive than large ones" (*Group Therapy and Experience*. p. 87). This suggests that in a group of this size (twelve or less), the leader will successfully establish the level of involvement, self-commitment, and distractibility of the participants, and will also better control intercommunication among group members.

Let us now put anger management in a context of a spiritually-based group. In a Spiritual Anger Management Group (SAMG) members should be a good fit and are expected to par- ticipate freely in the debate. Individuals who want to be part of a SAMG must disclose about what inclines them towards irritability. An indication of desire for change is when participants perceive anger as noxious and detrimental to themselves and interpersonal relationships.

Prior to participating in a SAMG a structured interview must take place (with at least a ten-item questionnaire). This pre-screening aims at determining the necessity for the solicitors to be a part of the group. This will help the SAMG facilitator not only to select the potential members, but also to know the prospective group participants in terms of the severity of their anger. Three out of the ten questions should address the chief condition of SAMG eligibility: the frequency (How often he or she feels angry and react out of anger?), the gender (whether the participant is a male or a female), and the situation in which anger occurs (i.e., at home, work or in public). This suggests that the SAMG is contextual and gender related. The benefit of this model is that the selected participants are likely to be on the same page. Though people are intimidated by talking with strangers, participants would feel a sense of belonging to a group of people who understand and accept them. Due to commonality of interests, members of the SAMG will engage in the process of cohesive- ness. Members would identify with the others by reflecting that others had the same "bad" thoughts and feelings that they had. Such commonality among participants will enhance cohesiveness and facilitate openness. They would be able to reveal things about themselves that they felt embarrassed. At times, the group facilitator can stress the sense of not "being alone" in their attempt to personal life issues.

At the first contact, a person selected to be a part of the group is provided with information on how the group operates, its scheduling, the duration of each session, and the matter of confidentiality. A spiritual group counselor who leads a SAMG assists the attendants in exploring the reasons for their interest in attending this group in a meaningful and constructive manner. Given that anger is an emotional state that can vary in intensity, the *working focus* generally consists of enhancing communication among members and preventing the expression of anger with violence. Group participants will benefit from a biblical overview of anger and the biblically oriented therapy for it - materials handed out should be biblically oriented. Jesus Christ is at the center of freeing believers from worry, hatred, and resentment from which anger derives.

Through three consecutive sessions, the SAMG participants will be involved in a skill building experience by giving the participants an opportunity to evaluate their anger. Here are the guidelines for the three sessions:

In session I: The group leader gives participants the ability to recognize and acknowledge the beliefs that caused them to be angry. This recognition and acknowledgement of causes of anger may bring about the necessary motivation to change their patterns of beliefs and thoughts. The group leader continues the process by encouraging the prospective members to acknowledge their angry behavior and express the desire to reflect on the evil that they did to themselves and others and to embark on a more favorable lifestyle.

In session II: The group leader enhances the counselees' awareness of the changes in the counselees' perception and improvement while interacting with others. Participants who had observed other people verbalizing their anger may gain insights into their own problems and learn ways of coping with anger, and successful management of outbursts. The role of the group facilitator is to encourage the integrating of new communication styles through the process of trust and hope.

In session III: At the end of a group discussion, participants volunteer to role-play relative to real-life situations. Role-playing can be relevant to the participants' issues and concerns by mimicking, for example, a tense household, a hostile job setting, or something else. The group facilitator asks the volunteers to pick a role written on a folded piece of paper. Regarding a tense household, the roles assigned could be the following:

- A single parent that is authoritarian and has various complaints about his or her children's behavior
- A difficult child who does not want to comply with his parent's directions
- A guest invited to the diner who feels embarrassed and reacts because of his or her feeling of embarrassment.
- Another teenager insisting on going out with her friends, which friends keep on calling her on the phone, etc.

The group leader who is observing is also taking notes with regard to: the situations, the behaviors adopted, and the decisions to change – the SBD. After the role-play, the group leader may proceed by asking the role-players a few questions that are consistent with the problem, the thought related to anger, the responsibility, and the likelihood of hurting the targeted person:

What is the problem?
Have you ever thought of expressing your anger to him or her, or at the person? How could you sort out who is responsible for your angry feeling?
How could you express your anger without hurting the other person? (question open to discussion).

In addition to role-playing, the group leader pairs the participants. This method of paring is likely to bring the drive understanding that is essential for self-examination, and help with many problems, which were not easy to solve over several years. One alternative is to choose six actual anger role-players paired with the other six members of the group. Each player should have a "coach" with whom he or she can practice the techniques of anger management for fifteen to twenty minutes.

The coaches facilitate a reflection-based interpretation by the anger role-players. These six coaches assist the paired participants in exploring the various aspects of their reactions (or behavior). That is, how they can improve their behavior by smoothing one's tone of voice, by taking a deep breath before talking and/or positive self-talking, and processing their want in a modest manner. At the end of this paring session, each coach takes five minutes to lay out to the group their personal observation, and the difficulty encountered in the process of redirecting the anger role-players. The emphasis is on the basic goal of developing a working relationship with each anger role-player. A working relationship, if successful, modifies whatever obstructs the human relationships. It enhances ability at negotiation and produces a time of peace. This endeavor for a working relationship may create qualitative meaning in the anger-role player's life and in that of the coaches. Both parties are in the process of learning how to solve problems without having a destructive response. In regards to their observation, the coaches' intervention should include comments and suggestions that can help the role player find out exactly what was wrong with their attitudes, actions and reactions. Here are some examples of questions that coaches might ask:

What did they notice?
What conflicts did they see, when?
What, according to them, did the central person feel?
What attitude might have helped reduce the conflict?
What could have been done to succeed in building a working relationship?

Yalom said, "Therapy is an emotional and corrective experience...We must experience something strongly; but we must also, through our faculty of reason, understand the implications of that emotional experience." The SAMG gives to its participants an opportunity to learn about themselves and the feeling of trust when reflecting on the loss that predisposes to anger. This group experience happens in a context of discovering the unknown part of one's self and enables its participants to relate to others in a more favorable fashion. *Learned sympathy* takes place through observation of other group members whose struggles with issues may be much more severe than one's own. This consideration refers to what Yalom said, "Over time, the client's deeply held beliefs will change - and these changes will be reinforced if the client's new interpersonal behaviors shifts can reflect a profound change and need to be acknowledged and reinforced by the therapist and group members." (p. 30).

The group leader is to be an effective facilitator. The SAMG is to be a "freely interactive group" in that the leader encourages the participants to be open to comments and advice from other members, which are as important as the leader's comments and advice

(Yalom p. 570). The group leader may clarify the interactions and reactions about what group members said or did in the group without providing direct advice.

Because of the legal issues that may be involved, a special group, for individuals who are dependent on alcohol and drugs, perpetrators of domestic violence, and criminal offenders are to be part of a group that we lay claim to a spiritual group for special-need people (SGSNP). A SAMG is a closed group, meaning that new participants are not allowed to join after the group starts. Individuals who want to participate after the group starts should wait for the formation of the upcoming SAMG. In our spiritual construct, anger and petulance are used interchangeably.

Chapter Five

THE TECHNIQUES TO SPIRITUAL COUNSELING

*I*n order to succeed in helping individuals identify their spiritual needs and find relevant alternatives to their problems it is important to develop skills and implement appropriate techniques in the course of counseling.

Spiritual Counseling requires some preparation. In certain cases, it takes place in public places such as at a birthday party, at a barbecue, on a train, in a wedding celebration, etc. Spiritual counseling in a private and relaxing place involves some measures such as turning off cell phones and TVs, avoiding physical barriers by not sitting behind a desk, and having open arms not clenched fists. When visiting the spiritual counselor, he or she may gently ask the person visiting to turn off his cell phone, radio or TV.

Introducing self is the initial step in meeting with an individual for counseling purposes. It is not recommended to identify self as a Christian and how long you have been a Christian. Such disclosure could be made only if the counselee or the group is curious to know about it. Spiritual counselors have to show themselves considerate by stating the person's name, being delighted in having the person listening to them and showing interest in discussing topics of such a great concern.

Clarification is one of the greatest needs in spiritual counseling. Clarifying occurs with three distinct purposes: (1) acquiring the appropriate skills for effective conversation (2) Assenting that the need for redemption is common (3) Considering that the need for redemption is common.

Clarifying entails use of powerful and appropriate skills. The main purpose of spiritually counseling someone is to be natural helpers, not enablers. All professional helpers in their business of counseling individuals need to acquire appropriate techniques and skills by facilitating self-disclosure. A spiritual counselor is an active listener. He or she listens for experiences, ideas, and perceptions that imply cumulative, adequate and inadequate self-confidence. He or she carefully listens to the counselee's desire for change and explore with him or her ways change can occur. Other advantages pertaining to active listening include reflecting the counselees' feelings and insights, evaluating their progress in their efforts to fulfill their spiritual needs, and giving feedback.

In spiritually counseling someone, there is a very definite difference in the techniques whether it is a short or a long-lasting conversation. Since all day long most of our conversations are short, let's first take into account short ones by observing some of the following principles: 1) Being genuinely interested in the other person and in his life history; 2) Smile; 3) Showing the person that you remember his or her name is of great importance; 4) Encouraging the person to talk about himself or herself; 3) Talking in terms of the coun- selee's interests.

Conversation is an exchange of feelings, thoughts, and attitudes. The art of conversation suggests the ability to tell the truth with no presumption that "other people are wrong." When meeting someone in traveling, time constraint is obvious. The moment the counselor forgets "exchange," the counselor is in danger of offending. In spiritually counseling someone, conversation has a purpose. It is neither for pleasure, nor a leisure pastime. Therein lies the necessity for learning techniques of spiritual counseling that often starts by free conversation. This technique consists in *starting with something that constitutes mutual interest*. That is to say, the conversation may be about jobs, the latest news on global warming, natural disasters, or anything else. Do not introduce politics, religion, or race. If these subjects are brought up refuse to be intolerant. Critics consider them the most provocative topics of our time.

Thus, spiritual counselors give their counselees the opportunity to talk about their own business and eventually be questioned about their personal activities as well. By allowing the individuals to give input on possible solutions to certain ongoing or past issues on the planet gives them *a sense of respect for their ability to judge and make choices*. Initially, when someone is asked what aspect of his or her work he or she enjoys the most, this person feels satisfaction when he or she met a challenge and overcame it. The spiritual counselor by hearing the counselee making a good point can proceed with: "That seems to bring you strength and satisfaction? The point that needs clarification is that what this person actually meant by "challenge." This inquiry probes a little deeper in the search of understanding the veracity of this person's feeling of satisfaction – "you either feel it or you don't". This approach suggests that the counselor is helping somebody to pay close attention to the description of something (i.e., a *utilis*) that seems to bring him satisfac- tion. This exercise of identifying sources of satisfaction is important to future moments of pinpointing values and lifestyles and reexamining those values and lifestyles. Spontaneous responses regarding what is enjoyable in life will all help detect the speaker's spiritual strengths ad weaknesses.

Minimal encouragement, as its name indicates, is a way to make the counselee feel he or she has been listened to, accepted, and understood. Spiritual counselors foster openness in a counselee by using "minimal encouragement." Saying "Ha -hah!" is the most common minimal encouragement through the counseling sessions. Nodding occasionally is a simple movement that signifies acceptance and can sometimes convey a minimal encouragement. In a case where somebody is firmly disclosing his feelings of guilt, a spiritual counselor may ask, "How did you arrive at the understanding that was a guilty feeling?" This approach offers the speaker the chance to clarify what feeling guilty means to him or her, it can also facilitate more disclosure.

One of the most common ways to urge someone to elaborate on a subject matter is by asking open-ended questions. After listening, the counselor can begin with the speaker's own phrase and add, "You said that you are a smoker, what is like for you?" Another way that can stimulate more talk is by saying, "Tell me more about that." When used appropriately, and in convenient time, this type of questioning ease the conversation compared to closed- ending questions that can be boring and intrusive.

To someone who subtly or clearly states, "I don't even want to change right now," the counselor can sort out the belief that he can change, the counselor can go by saying, "I am not asking for any change, is it ok to talk about what works and is enjoyable in life?" The counselor can add, "You can also talk about how 'smoking' affect your life." This procedure in which the counselor deliberately tunes into the counselee's preferred modality of problem solving, before presenting the alternative that is the most productive, is called "bridging."

A spiritual counselor is somebody who knows how to communicate on the basis of the individuals' needs. This counselor should acknowledge that the need for redemption is common to all. In helping people with their spiritual-related issues, the spiritual counselor facilitates self-awareness by conveying recognition to people's efforts of problem solving. The key indicator of development of self-awareness is in the will to get counseling. Biblically speaking, the individuals who are seeking counsel are the ones who are wise. The individual's interest in having someone to talk about a personal issue is associated with the fear of recurrence of previous mistakes. This typical fear, as spiritually experienced, enhances the individuals' desire for self-examining and self-improvement in conjunction with their need for redemption. Along the road, spiritual counselors provide constructive feedback on the counselees' expressed desire for change –the focus is on strengths rather on weaknesses.

On every phase of counseling, one ought to restrain from rushing to the point. Although the goal is to clarify redemption through surrender to Jesus Christ, before engaging in such a conversation, one should take time to listen to the person talking about herself and her belief system. The success of clarifying the need for redemption requires a profound understanding of the speaker's cultural belonging. Spiritual counselors should be aware of the cultural differences of their counselee (counselees if in group) in regards to three facets of spirituality: (1) those who are skeptical about the existence of God, (2) those who relapsed from their commitment to God, and (3) those who have no interest in the domain of spiritual life. After listening to the person's talk of spiritual journey, the counselor does not need to use any theological words. Clarification may start by stressing the importance of being guided by the spiritual Mentor. "I am wondering if it is a good time to talk about someone who can read our mind and know our hearts." Added to this introduction, one may say, "This divine character knows when we are undecided and sincere about changing our directions in life." If the counselee goes on denying that truth, counseling can be deferred with respect.

Spiritually guiding someone helps to shield him or her from false concepts of God, of others, and of self - false concepts always lead to bad actions. Meaningful relationships with God and with others occur not by force, but only by reason and evidence. Hence the notion of *attending behavior* in stressing the solutions to all human spiritual problems already exists. As long as counselees sense that someone is open-minded and is there for them, they learn through modeling of prayer - a simple way of expressing the heart sincere desire to God. They also begin to develop awareness of their own spiritual needs, espe- cially their need for redemption. In the long run, they may decide to find peace with them- selves, with God and with others. Once their fear of being punished by God is gradually dissipating they will be in touch with their spiritual selves.

Before being committed to a new-birth experience, individuals need moments of clarification. The function of spiritually counseling someone is to accompany this person as he or she is "working out his own salvation with fear and trembling." In order to avoid interminable argumentation, the spiritual counselor ought to explain the value of spiritual redemption. As the counselee grows in grace and in the knowledge of Jesus Christ, the spiritual counselor will nurture him or her by positive modeling, personal experiences, and exhorting him/her more and more with compassion and patience. It is an ever-ending process. This process of change is known as *perseverance toward sanctification*. Thus, human beings will not realize God's plan of redemption in their lives, unless they sincerely acknowledge their need for redemption. This notion of perseverance, confirms that spirituality is an ongoing personal experience through the individuals' lifespan. Without a desire for repentance, self-improvement will not take place. Without purity, there is no power, and there is no salvation without power. The point is that as long as the believer keeps faith and perseveres in the transforming power of God, salvation is guaranteed. The Scripture states, "Everyone who trusts in Him is freed from all guilt and declared righteous" (Acts 13: 39.

LB). It is only by the human surrendering action to the divine plan of redemption that a spiritual growth happens.

Sharing experience

As counselor, we need to experience a true connection with our counselees. Sharing one's personal experience is one of the practical ways to show empathic connection. This initiative conveys conviction and fortitude. This shared experience may raise an immediate enthusiasm in the hearer that will eventually empower the counselee to face similar circumstance (dangerous or painful) with courage. There is no need to be creative. The speaker omits any comment about his/her role in the development of the event. This is not a time to overvalue one's experience and to make up one. Following a sincere self-disclosure by the counselor, a counselee is likely to have a reflection-based interpretation with the likelihood of opening up to the best interest of counseling.

Self-disclosing is a powerful technique; when used it can persuade people about a significantly life-changing experience. In our business of helping people with serious issues, sharing a relevant life story can catalyze the counselor-counselee rapport. Testimony about divine intervention corroborates the reality of human need for redemption that God only can fulfill. A life transforming experience is often accompanied with enthusiasm in sharing. Louise L. Hay (1987) stated, "When something works well for us, we often want to share it with others" (*You can Heal your Life*.)

Redemption is an acquired value. When a counselor is putting emphasis on God's graceful intervention, he or she may go on introducing a personal experience such as, "There is a freshness, a cleaning, a good feeling of starting over…" (Charles Stanley. *The Reasons of My Belief*). The preceding can be followed by: "I remember a time when. . . ." The following life stories highlight changes that occurred in the tellers' lives because of God's intervention:

> Proud and arrogant is the simplest way to say what I was. I was convinced of my own superiority. I believed not that I was necessarily smarter than everyone else was but that most everyone found it easier not to apply any cognitive skill to what they said or did. I realized that at an early age. I felt that my skills and abilities were responsible for my quick rise in the company I work for. Needless to say, I was forever hesitant to share any credit with anyone, much less God, at any time. It was this attitude that made me responsible for that which followed. My life came crashing down. I thought because I went to church and occasionally read the Bible that I was a Christian. After all, I was raised in a good Christian home with Christian parents with firm godly values. I always had followed half-heartedly. I

have had the problems before and I had come to rely on myself. Yes, of course sometimes I resorted to prayer but I always somehow felt I was just spinning my wheels. The reason behind this is that although I prayed it was different. I had lost everything that mattered to me, including my family. Brokenhearted and crying, I made an honest assessment. Now my prayer is different. I am very grateful to my Lord for even being concerned with an insignificant piece of dust, which I am. Best of all, that a wretched creature like myself could be considered God's child is a true miracle. Now I have learned to put God first and trust that His will for me is what is best. Amen.

Shared experience could take different forms. Here is another history told by Cliff about his spiritual redemption from his alcohol addiction:

My demon was alcohol. I was raised in a family that drank.

Whenever life got tough, I turned to my crutch, alcohol. Now, with my life in trouble, I reached for the bottle again. I should have been comforting Ann after her suicide attempt, but instead I was drunk out on the front porch. Days later, standing in the kitchen, Ann asked me what I was going to do when she went to prison. Would I file for divorce? I honestly didn't know. We had two daughters, ages 8 and 16, and I wanted to do what was best for them.

Ann and I had been church goers, or you might call us "pew sitters" for years, but we didn't have a personal relationship with God. I remember the tug-o-war in my heart between religion and alcohol. I felt separated from God and everyone else when I drank, but I did not stop. During this difficult time, one of my co-workers relentlessly invited us to her church. We finally gave in, Ann and I found ourselves at. . . . . (a Christian church). I had never seen anything like this church in my life. The people were so happy and loving. A few Sunday mornings later, during praise and worship time, I looked up and cried out, "Jesus, I can't go without you." I felt the Spirit of God, and I dropped to my knees. I began to weep openly. I wept for 45 minutes straight that Sunday morning, right through the pastor's sermon. I gave my heart to Christ that day. I finally felt free from the heavy sin I had carried for years.

After Jesus came into my life, I was ready to give Ann an answer to her earlier question. She had stood by me through all the years of alcoholism. I would stand by her life while she served time in prison. I told Ann that I would be there for her when she returned. She broke down and wept for joy. God was beginning to bind us together, preparing us for the storms to come. . . .

Months later, my oldest daughter rebelled and left home, saying she couldn't live under the rules of the house. When my daughter walked out, I felt like a failure. Broken-hearted, I sat in a chair and wept. I threw a pity party for myself that night, and decided to open the bar. I went to the liquor store after one and a half years of sobriety. As I consumed the bourbon through my tears, I knew the Lord was speaking to me. I realized He was with me. And I began to see that God was in control. I poured out the last little bit of bourbon. Even my fall back into my addiction could not separate me from His love. From that day on, I have not touched one drop of alcohol (Turning Point Magazine and Devotional. March/April 2001. p. 12-14).

The following is an experience that I shared with my classmates in the year 2005 via emails:

Hello everybody,

It is always of great courage when someone remembers and shares about his past. I appreciate that Sean shows such a courageous character to tell us about his experience when he was a child with Phenylketonuria (PKU) (e.g., a rare condition in which a baby is born without the ability to properly break down an amino acid called phenylalanine). This enterprise comes to confirm that we all need to be grateful to the merciful God, our Creator. One of the reasons is that He created us all for a purpose, which is to worship Him and be reverent to Him. Other reasons are to firmly attest that our existence is by His grace and mercy. Jesus Christ's sacrifice on the cross suggested that God's outstanding way of communicating with human beings (His creatures) His unconditional love. There are people who believe and surrender to this alternative of making peace with God; others are still skeptical and reluctant to accept it (often taken for not a religious fallacy. The truth is we all need a way to communicate spiritually and this way is through Jesus Christ only. As He said: "I am the Way, the Truth and the Life" "No one can come to the Father but by me." This statement is very important to all who are desirous to develop an effective relationship with God.

O.K. folks, please don't think I am preaching religion. I am also one who had a very powerful experience with God who saved me from three consecutive years of chronic diarrhea. I had prayed insistently, when one day I was taking a nap and I saw two hands giving me an injection. I was delighted and woke up and went straight to my older brother's house to tell him about the great miracle that God had performed in my life. Truly, I was not diagnosed for any disease, but I was severely depressed with a delusion of a fatal disease.

I hope this attempt to convince you about the fact that God has been in the business of saving those who have despaired and are in spiritual and physical need is to be taken as real and serious.

Have a nice night,

See you on Friday.
Raymond Phanor

This preceding experience is one that I already shared with family members, friends and in church services on several occasions.

Fraternizing

Fraternizing with someone means "to associate or mingle as brothers or on fraternal terms" (*Merriam Webster's Collegiate Dictionary*). People do not only need someone to talk about valuable subjects, they also long for earnest companionship. Fraternizing with someone always has significant spiritual impact on both the counselor and the counselee or a group of individuals at large. Individuals who are involved in persuading others about good-life spirituality have to have an understanding between them and the person who has been receiving the counseling. They need to have a good grasp of the needs of the individual in order to envision what particular assistance they may offer to the person, either material or emotional. It requires collaborating with the person in all aspects of his life.

It is good to understand that the conversational technique one uses depends on how well one knows the other person or persons involved. As we observed earlier, before get- ting to the point that God has a plan for humanity, a spiritual counselor who meets someone for the first or second time ought to begin conversation on topics of general interests. From a biblical perspective, the concept of discipleship is time wise. Having a *discipleship rapport* with somebody is equivalent to being friends of long standing with a shared belief system. This includes the remembering of names, and knowing the needs. This kind of relationship prepares spiritually the counselees to receive advice (taking suggestions and Bible references into consideration). Max Lucado & co. stated, "The remembering of names is a discipline that will win you much admiration" (p.193).

Fraternizing comprises emphasizing the spiritual impact it can have on peoples who have been helped through showed consideration, caring and compassion. The later is an emotional ability to demonstrate awareness and understanding of the situation of the individual by acknowledging and processing understanding of his feelings and thoughts – analogically, it is getting into the shoes of one's interlocutor. When fraternizing with someone one has to show not only an understanding of the problems, but it requires conveying sensitivity at a practical level of assisting the person in need. In other words, fraternizing with people infers caring in an objectively explicit manner. It includes visiting the person, making phone calls at convenient times, spending time in prayer with the person, and formulating wishes in time of delight and of sorrow. One has to be mindful when sympathizing with people not to ask questions that pertain to private issues; it is wise to let those typical matters be first addressed by the individual prior to any proposal of support. It is biblically recommended that it is up to the needy person to start talking about a relevant issue, and the counselor may proceed by showing concern about the unfortunate event (Matt. 7:7,8). The counselor may implicitly say, "If there is any way that I can be helpful to you, do not hesitate to let me know," or he or she may ask, "Is there some way in which I can be useful?"

One aspect of a family is companionship. The parent-child relationship is essential in the spiritual development of all human beings. The fundamental role of a family is not to empower its members to achieve societal standards, but rather to prepare human beings not to lose the benefits of a relationship. On several occasions, the Bible stressed how important the family relationship really is. Jesus gave relational directives concerning one's *need for connection* and its fulfillment in a healthy manner, which are applicable to all relationships – God does not want us to be a loser in a relationship. In order to save human beings from the anguish of loneliness that all forms of broken relations may bring, God, the Creator of all human beings, instituted the family to nurture and teach each of us on loving in a mutual way. Family life is for sharing, and modeling, and teaching about love and wisdom. The ideal family teaches on "loving one another" (John 13:34, NIV). Second, the ideal family models "doing to others what" one "would have them done to you" Matt. 7:12, NIV). And, third the ideal family models "loving" [even] one's "enemies" (Matt. 5:44, NIV). One parental responsibility is to spend time talking with children about the importance of marriage. Parent-believers in God live out their marriage relationships in harmony with the divine plan. Such families are more likely to succeed in meeting their children's spiritual need in an efficient way. Because God enables couples to exhibit love and grace in their marriage, children would seek to pattern their future marital relationships according to their parents'.

Individuals who lapse in their church attendance have a variety of complaints. One of their major criticisms toward their community of faith is grounded on a lack of fellowship. They may somehow exaggerate, but their need for a sincere fellowship is to be taken seriously. Whenever I have a chance to talk with somebody who stops attending Christian churches, I often address the matter of fraternizing in a context of the reality of Christian responsibilities. In reality, the popularity of the Christian community is attributed to its capability of caring and loving. A Christian is liable to value, initiate and maintain fraternization in the respective worship community. This is supported by the prophet Isaiah's call from God to stand and become an agent of change in his community: "I heard the voice of the Lord saying: 'Whom shall I send? And who will go for us?' (Is. 6:8). From this perspective, Christians are mandated to such a great job of facilitating fraternization in their church. One of the questions that one needs to ask a relapsed member from a community of Christian values is that "Don't you think that your church would be much improved if you stick to it and make the changes that you see necessary?" On the whole, every Christian has to play his part in consolidating his community of faith by valuing, initiating, and maintaining an atmosphere of fraternity. Fraternizing is not an ideology but it is spiritual fruit. There is no way to complain about a community for its lack of friendliness or of warmth. What one needs to affirm is that: "You will find love here, because you're here to find and to bring love" (Stephen C. Paul & Gary Max Collins. *In Love*. p. 3). There indeed exists a spiritual link between the pain of giving and the hardiness of self. As we quote, "The pain of giving often makes us feel less pain doing so, and we become hardened" (*Corner Stone*. p. 41. Vol. 36, No.3. Third Quarter, 2005). Often, the lapsed often grieve about various kinds of treatment from members of their church; it is because they cannot attest to fraternizing and their lack of contribution. It is clear that giving ourselves makes us feel vulnerable, especially for those who are selfish.

Given that spiritual counseling is a truth-oriented therapy, confrontation is therefore unavoidable. A counselor-counselee rapport may become confrontational. It could be because the counselor presents self as being the "expert" and is in a rush to counsel and pass on values and all the "good lessons" to their counselees.

Unsuccessful counseling often results from the counselor's concerns and precipitation to set goals that go against their counselees' will. This may be due to the counselor's fear of contradiction. In a sense, a counselor may form conviction that brings him a level of impatience to a point of compromising the process of fraternizing. Archibald Alexander said: "Men are more accountable for their motives than for anything else, and primarily, morality consists in the motives, that are the affections." Because spiritual counseling is a truth-oriented therapy, chances are confrontation unexpectedly happen. Spiritual counselors need to be clear on how to manage resistance on the part of their counselees.

For most, the individuals' desire for change can be frightening. So, it is easier for somebody to say, "I am sick," than earnestly acknowledge his or her wrongness. Edwin R. Thiele (1979) defined redemption as a "growing remorse over what happened in one's life that may lead to a sincere moment of confession to God, which is consistent with a desire for repentance toward self-improvement." Someone may become unreasonable and irascible. Through confrontation technique, counselors facilitate their counselees' discoveries of their current need for redemption. To the best of the counselee's interest, a "sudden bad news" may be seen as throwing a counselee into a state of disappointment that deranges the possibility of fraternizing with the counselor who confronted. Therefore, when con- fronted, individuals are likely to close the door to both the divine, and the human coun- selors. Confrontation may stem from a reminder of a chosen course of decision.

Thus, a person who seems temperate may start worrying because of a word or statement made by the counselor that recalls a similar experience. In certain instances, he or she may claim to have certain feelings, which they actually do not have.

The whole idea of confrontation throughout spiritual counseling does not consist in giving the appearance of superiority. A revealing truth could challenge the interlocutor to a reflection-based interpretation of his/her shortcomings. In light of the Bible, the listener may come to the realization that the character has something in common with him or her. He or she may identify that he or she has offended God and other people repeatedly. He or she was so desperate that he/she attempted to end his life. All these aspects of life when addressed, have the power to challenge and cause inner disturbance on the part of the counselee. Adler's philosophical standpoint is that "individuals are neither good nor bad." As creative and choosing human beings, we have the ability to "choose to be good or bad." Confrontation, as practiced in spiritual counseling may require telling the counselee that the expected peace with himself will not be earned unless he or she surrenders to God. This is a unique way for spiritual growth.

We all have to remember that *all behaviors are purposeful.* The question as to which extent individuals can get irritated about the way they were approached by a question or an assumption is answered by Nathaniel Brendan (1994). Brendan called our attention to the fact that "We tend to be more conscious in some areas of our life than in others" (*The Six Pillars of Self-Esteem.* pp. 88).

In raising a moral issue on a particular behavior or a lifestyle, we must be careful of what we say and do; of what we did or did not say. Confrontation, from its broadest perspective, consists of persuading the offenders to stop offending the resented, and the resented to value forgiveness, and turn from hatred to love.

The work toward awareness is powerful and vital. It serves to bring the individuals to a level of responsibility for their choices and actions. The idea of confrontation as irritable is explained by an example given by N. Branden (1994) in these terms: "Suppose my supervisor is trying to explain why something I have done on the job was a mistake. She speaks benevolently and without recriminations, and yet I am irritable, impatient, and wish she would stop talking and go away. While she is talking, I am obliged to stay with the reality of having made an error. When she is gone I can banish the reality from my conscience – I admitted my mistake, isn't that enough? Which increases the likelihood that I will make the error, or one like it, again" (pp. 93). A 'conscious sinner' needs to be encouraged to seek God's grace, forgiveness and redemption. This draws us to the conclusion that, individuals who become irritated and threaten their counselors when confronted with a mistake are not spiritually receptive to learning from the mistake they made. A successful reflection when one is confronted has three components. One may wonder: 1)"Why do I do that?" 2) "Why did I say that?" 3) "Why am I like that?"

In a case where an individual exhibits a spiritual lethargy that may prevent him from believing in self-improving, confrontation is a way to inspire him that a changing of self is always possible. These spiritually lethargic people constitute the category of individuals who often utter "After all, who is perfect?" As in session, be quick to admit nobody is perfect. In the same token you may say that there exist individuals who are striving to live a better life through gaining a desired internal peace.

As we are counseling people they might be feeling confronted when, in reality, we do not mean it. Sometimes, spiritual counselors may feel driven to draw individuals from their spiritual lethargy in a way that may be unwelcoming. When facing indifference and resistance on the part of counseling, we need to bear in mind this wise counsel: "A gentle answer turns away wrath, but a harsh word stirs up anger" (Proverbs 15:1). Under all circumstances, a counselor needs to be more aware of their counseling style and needs to reflect on exploring the possibilities to resolve their personal issues. As we demonstrated, confrontation may be inevitable due to values differences or it can be purposeful.

This process of confrontation resulting in the counselees' resistance should be done skillfully, in a proper time, and in a very respectful manner. One way to evaluate if previous confrontation in effect was fruitful is to see whether the person that you confronted repels you, the confronter, or keeps seeking counseling from you. In several occasions, for example, I wisely and respectfully confronted my classmates on various controversial issues, during breaks or after class some of them enjoyed questioning me on various spiritual matters, which therefore reassured me that my way of confronting them was effective.

Giving Feedback

An example of positive feedback that may benefit counseling is by saying, "When we started meeting together, you were resistant. In the tree most recent meetings that we had, you have been cooperative and more open to discussion on a consistent basis. It is uplifting for both of us that we continue discussing real-life issues, praying, reading, and meditating biblical messages." Other examples can highlight improvement in the person's lifestyle and behavior: "In the beginning, you were more inclined to blame other people i.e., unwilling to take responsibility for your decisions and behaviors. Nowadays, you are more likely to feel remorse when expressing concern about your wrongdoing. This is good sign of spiritual improvement. That's awesome!"

An effective way to evaluate a counselee's desire for change and the progress made in his or her decision to change is through providing feedback. Milne (1999) said, "The benefit of working with others is that you give and receive feedback" (Counseling. p. 74). A spiritual counselor must master effective ways to give feedback and be attuned at the positive and negative counselee's attitude toward the given feedback. Here are some general principles in giving feedback:

- Spiritual counselors have to make a review of all that happened in the nearest previous session.
- Spiritual counselors are to check on what their counselee's personal feelings, their perception of the helping process, and what they plan to do after this.

Following the counselee's viewpoint, the spiritual counselors relate genuine thoughts and feelings about being present with the counselee in his spiritual journey.

As we are giving feedback, we then become sensitive to the humanistic counseling approach, which stresses the "person's capacity for personal growth, freedom to choose one's own destiny and positive qualities" (Santrock, 2000. p. 425). We underscore that one of the counselee's essential needs is to be empowered, meaning to feel having the capacity of fully functioning as a person. Positive feedback provided to someone may be for him an occasion to realize, "None has ever talked to me like you have."

Spiritual counselors should always encourage individuals to attain their very most positive self-concept and adequate self-confidence. When Jesus Christ performed miracles for on people and said, "your faith has saved you," these people were eager to talk about their "deepest secrets" that brought them their feelings of humiliation, guilt, and shame.

As a result of their received feedback, the counselees may feel highly valued and identify with their counselors whom they view as a 'real brother' or a 'real sister,' or some kind of 'divine angel.' Counselees who were defensive may, after acquiring positive and constructive feedback, experience show wisdom and understanding in their spiritual journey.

This technique that focuses on positive feedback is effective in helping the counselees solve the discrepancy between their real self and their ideal self. Such spiritual experience may bring them to the realization of big gap between their actual capacity of changing self and a the need to seek after the ultimate spiritual Counselor.

Here are a few techniques that would allow a counselor acknowledge thoughts and feelings of the person who has been counseled:

- Get engaged in an honest and active listening.
- Gently ask questions to get a sense of what the person thinks might be at the origin of the spoken problem.
- Use sentences such as "I heard that you said. . . ."
- Paraphrasing some points that are in agreement with of the change expected: "You said you want to be more. . ., but you don't know how this would be possible."

Chapter Six

THE MAIN FOCI OF SPIRITUAL COUNSELING

There are certain principles that need to serve as the foci of spiritual counseling. These principles are: trust, will, safety, and fairness. Although these concepts are not to be revealed during a spiritual counseling session, the spiritual counselors should keep them in mind as the framework for their intervention. Once the spiritual counselor has a grasp on the individual's concerns and desire to change while being counseled, he or she may focus on one of several of these concepts:

Living with Trust: From a spiritual perspective, living with trust is equivalent to having an adequate self-confidence. Not all human beings have an optimistic spirit in their spiri- tual journey. One's educational and cultural background influences one's ability to trust. A change in perspective is sometimes necessary in order for a person to live with trust. For the purpose of enhancing individuals' quality of life, it is important that the spiritual counselor maintains a straightforward focus, which is teaching how to live with trust throughout. As Yalom said, "faith in a treatment mode can itself be therapeutically effective."

The reluctance of accepting the truth about oneself may derail from the Greater TRUTH. The truth is that Jesus Christ is the "Way, the Truth and the Life." This trust in God's investment is evident in all human beings testifying to His supernatural love. Therefore, a spiritual counselor needs to put emphasis on the fact that God has offered a way for the spiritual redemption of all human beings. In his article "Learning to Trust," David C. Egner wrote, "If we are to please God, we must learn to trust Him." In addition, he added, "Just as a pilot must learn to trust his instruments, we must learn to trust God. Our feelings lie, our vision is shortsighted. What may seem to be a sudden wrong turn could from God's perspective be exactly the right course for us. As we stay close to Him and acknowledge

His direction, we will begin to depend solely on His guidance. That's learning to trust" (*Our Daily Bread*. June-August, 1986).

Trusting and having hope have common spiritual ground. From *Time of Healing*, we quote: "From each of life's misfortunes large or small comes a new beginning, an opportunity to renew your faith in the future" (Marie D. Jones et al. p. 16).

Living with Will: A great number of individuals believe and practice willpower, and many are professionally accredited to counsel about the results of their convictions. Some people develop such a great trust and will that they bring many others to believe and accept the proposal of certain alternatives to pertinent human problems. When they are driven to gain social approbation by exerting their force of power - their motives are not spiritually well-grounded.

The most effective way of living with will is to humble self before God. When it comes to growing up spiritually, a genuine motive to personal change is inspired by the True Conscience (TC), which may originate from the Holy Spirit. When, someone believes and says, "Thy will be done," he or she is a believer in God who yields to the Almighty, and acknowledges that God is in control and they are not. In the same toke, changes in one's philosophy of living and in one's disturbing habits should be attributed to divine intervention. The idea that "I can get what I want and when I want it" is not applicable to various domains of spiritual life.

For experiencing an upward spirituality, living with will has to be distinguished from being self-willed, being stubborn, being uncooperative, being refractory, being recalcitrant, being disobedient to God, being intransigent, being a difficult person, being wild, and being obstinate.

Living Fair: This is one of the greatest spiritual challenges. 'Being fair' means, being impartial, unprejudiced, just, courteous, and gracious. The ethic behind this lifestyle is to love justice and honesty. The golden principle consistent with this spiritual focus is: "Do unto others as you wish they would do unto you." In a context of exercising fairness, this principle can be translated as, "be fair to the same extent you wish others to be fair to you." It takes giant self-confidence to commit to living fairly. The pressure to pay back evil with evil is always present. It could be internal mental pressure or external pressure from society. The world has been giving us negative messages regarding these principles of living, especially when it comes to revenge.

Our human tendency is to take revenge when we are victimized. Beccaria's question is significant: "Is it not absurd that the laws which detest and punish homicide, in order to prevent murder, publicly commit murder themselves?" People lose self-control when they are offended. Living fair is not to be occasional. It stands for a desire to do and say right things to others even to one's oppressors! Jesus Christ counsels us to forgive others prior to any attempt to soliciting God's forgiveness in prayer. In addition, He advises us to reconcile our differences with those who hold a grudge against us, before bringing our offerings to church.

Jesus Christ demonstrates good lessons of being consistently fair. Remember, when a a group of men caught a woman in adultery and her accusers brought her to Jesus; Jesus' response to them was the words he wrote on the ground. In fairness to this woman can you imagine what he wrote on the ground? According to Scripture, the woman's accusers responded by throwing away the stones that they were about to use as a weapon against her - Jesus brought equality to the situation by showing everyone their sin.

Living Safe: Everyone has his own definition of being safe. As we grow up we develop a sense of being safe and tend to repeat the patterns of activities that bring internal assurance. The search for comfort is not strictly a physical need; it is mental and emotional. Our safety or fragility depends on how we are driven to satisfy our needs. Once, we have the confidence of being spiritually redeemed, we experience the internal safety that God promised. Therefore, destructive thoughts, behaviors, and activities are no longer an issue.

Living safe requires an attitude of vigilance under all circumstances. Under certain circumstances, one may feel threatened by constant appeals to conformity that is very distressing. The purpose of steadfastness is to live safe, because it reflects strength of mind. Strength of mind is characteristic of vigilance needed for distancing and strong self-affirming that is necessary for one's personal safety. In other words, one should be able to discern invaders of souls. One should wisely plan the resolution of a problem or the satis- faction of a need, or with the aid of well-intended individuals.

On the Internet, there are people who have been suggesting evil actions, and anxious people may go crazy by following their advice. Here is what I quote from the "Dating & Personals" site, in the article, "10 blind-date dos and don'ts": "Do say yes to all the blind dates people offer. My grandmother always told me 'you get invited, you go; you never know who you are going to meet.' ...Even if your blind date doesn't prove to be the one for you, you never now whom that person could introduce to you." The same author wrote: "Do go for drinks instead of dinner. Drinks are much less pressure. Dinner can feel daunting for a blind date because you have to make it through the entire meal before you can leave whereas drinks can be brought to a close at any point. And keep in mind that if you are hitting it off, drinks can always turn into dinner or the scheduling of a second date" (Samantha Daniels). There is no element of safety in "blind dating." These quotations are relevant enough to show the extent to which individuals may be drawn into wrongdoing. These activities of coaching other people through the media can be a form self-destructive enterprise, since they are done in the shadows. Youngsters especially, who have a facile conscience for not being able to say "No," may unreasonably fall into these traps.

A counselor who is involved in family counseling has to be cautious about the prevailing issues that compel to counseling. It is easy to fall into a trap of misguidance. Let us take as an example a third person who is about to cause a rupture in a marital relation- ship; the couple is then threatened; they are not living safe because of the dissident char- acter that is suggesting the break-up. Under such a situation, it is not the counselor's role to advise the couple to break off relations with the dissident. This is a situation of complex spiritual counseling, in which the counselors have to stay at a distance and pray for the fortunes of the family or pray for them upon request. The counselors have to pay attention and show empathy. Prayer and Bible study are also good avenues to help manage the discordance between the couple and the third person. Spiritual counselors have to be vigilant when advising or counseling in order not to take away the safety of the person with whom they are counseling.

Spiritual counseling is a Truth-oriented therapy

One of the primary skills that all spiritual counselors ought to bring to the table is the capacity to bring their counselees to a full acknowledgement of their spiritual needs. The primary need is the need for redemption. This particular need is evident when someone has a remorse, a desire for repentance, which inspires a upright living. Once this need is acknowledged on the part of the counselee, the spiritual counselor can then provide the needed guidance and support to encourage spiritual growth – no spiritual therapy can be truly effective without this experience.

Self-evaluation is the key to maintaining the truth of one's spiritual growth. For people to acknowledge their need for redemption, they need to ascertain that their self-insufficiency is inadequate to solving all problems. When an individual's actions conflict with their values and beliefs, it is a time to seek counseling. In spiritual counseling, guilty feelings are not only different from feelings of shame, they are agents of change – positive evaluation of guilty feelings often leads to positive changes. Helping counselees to acknowledge their guilty feelings means bringing them to admit that "I did something wrong." The spiritual significance of being in touch with one's guilty feelings is that they can motivate people to be honest with themselves. As such, true guilt is a powerful spiritual motivator to seek the truth.

The human need for redemption is consistent with the desire for being freed and mastering from one's fear of spiritual burden. One of the spiritual outcomes of this need is the acknowledgment of being a innate sinner. Individuals may have this need of redemption in conjunction with a feeling of humiliation. This feeling of humiliation may bring individuals to a higher level of self-awareness, of personal growth and hope. Therefore, spiritual counseling is centered around Jesus Christ who is the ultimate spiritual Counselor and the TRUTH. James McDonald, a spiritual counselor wrote, "Just as a person cannot come to Christ until he comes to the end of himself, so you cannot experience the power to change until you are done with your own efforts" (*I Really Need to Change. . . So Help me God*. p.160). The Holy Spirit generates a spiritual discernment between the truth and the lie. When an individual is incapable of recognizing a problem as a problem and argues: "There is nothing in my life that I need to change," the individual's spiritual condition is one of *stagnation*. It is advisable not to impose the truth on someone who refuses to hear. The idea that there is no good living standard outside of God's way is the truth, but this may be uncomfortable for the resister. The following is an example of how someone who acknowledges his misdeeds can express a desire for repentance through confession to God:

> Dear God, I've been living my life my own way. Now I want to live in Your way, I need You and I am now willing for You to take control of my life. I receive Your Son Jesus Christ, as my personal Savior and Lord. I believe He died for my sins and has risen from the dead. I surrender to Him as Lord. Come, Lord Jesus, and occupy the throne of my life. Make me the kind of person You want me to be (Buckingham. p. 55).

Since Burchingham trusts God for every detail in life, his message to the world is that "God is real and has a plan for me." His prayer tells everything about how to make the change that is needed in someone's life who wants to grow spiritually. There is evidence that he is not self-sufficient. He is relying on the Higher Power. With a new born-vision of life, Burchingham is more concerned for being biblically correct instead of being politically correct. The Apostle Paul, as he was speaking on behalf of the authentic Christians, affirmed:

> All of us used to be just as we are, our lives expressing the evil within us, doing every wicked thing that our passions or our evil thoughts might lead us into. We started out bad, being born with evil natures, and were under God's anger just like everyone else. But God is so rich in mercy; he loved us so much that even though we were spiritually dead and doomed by our sins, he gave us back our lives again when he raised Christ from the dead – only by his underserved favor have we ever been saved – and lifted us up from the grave into glory along with Christ, where we sit with him in the heavenly realms – all because of what Christ Jesus did. And now God can always point to us as examples of how very, very rich his kindness is, as shown in all he has done for us through Jesus Christ" (Eph. 3: 3-7).

Jesus Christ who is the ultimate spiritual Counselor strongly affirmed, "You will find the truth and the truth will set you free" (Jn. 8:32). The "Spirit of Truth" (Jn. 16: 13) does not allow people to err from Him. It is not exaggerated to say, prior to their personal expe- rience with Jesus Christ, people are unlikely to acquire the wisdom, understanding, and knowledge, which lives substantiate a spiritual bondage. In other words, spiritual coun- selors do not need to know how the problem becomes a problem in order to help their counselees figure out their problem. Through techniques of processing desire and wants of their interlocutors, spiritual counselors can come to the point of recognizing whether their counselees have or have not experienced the liberating power of salvation. So to speak, prior to this spiritual experience, individuals may live in happy ignorance.

The role of a spiritual counselor in orienting toward the TRUTH includes:

A - Accompanying their counselee through the process of examining self and encour- aging him or her to explore his or her need for redemption. The counselee must be spiritu- ally ready and receptive to a learning experience.
B - Helping the counselee move forward in his or her personal growth by dealing with guilty feelings in a healthy way.
C - Putting "God's plan for life" in perspective based upon clear biblical directives.
D - It is important to remember that change is promoted by insight as we act on what we believe. Someone might be motivated to change his life course based on certain truth, and other people might think that what this person promotes and lives by is totally worthless.

The most obvious difference between psychotherapy and spiritual counseling is that in psychotherapy people are believed to have the inner resources to solve their problems. As such, their counselors or psychologists have to help them figure out the problem and empower them to generate in their lives the changes that they desire. Spiritual counselors, however, help individuals find insights into their impossibilities until they take full respon- sibility to surrender their life to the ultimate spiritual Redeemer. This model of counseling aims to encourage awareness of one's spiritual incapability for self-improvement.

Often, individuals may know the causes of their current problem, but cannot do any- thing to change the pattern. The point is that the knowledge and the good will to change one's smoking habit are not sufficient to change the habit. James MacDonald strongly avowed the following: "There is absolutely nothing in [us] – not an once of strength… not a smidgen of anything…not a thimbleful. And until we recognize and embrace that truth, we will always fail the process of change" (*I Really Want to Change…So Help me God.* p. 161). Thus, the primary condition to experience spiritual change is to humble self. Humility is the first spiritual indicator to change. It is by this state of mind that indi- viduals may want to do things differently than the way they have done them before. They usually think, behave, and decide out of pride. The reflection-based interpretation is typi- cally: "I know that is the usual way of doing it, but I am not sure it is the best way." This kind of thinking often gives way to a degree of doubt such as, "I'm not sure there is one 'best way'." At this phase, the spiritual obstacle is the counselee's fear of being contradicted. For personal growth to occur, one needs to be grounded in truth, which is fundamental to the fear of contradiction, at this instant of life.

The question is: Is the spiritual counselor orienting the counselee to the TRUTH, or is the counselor promoting the TRUTH? Be careful! What we need to bear in mind is the principle that spiritual counselors are facilitators to change; they are not to be engaged in "producing" a desired change. The problem establishes another dangerous set of false alternatives. When preaching, the message delivered is not directed to one person, but in an ongoing counseling session, a counselor should avoid saying things like, "It's time you started controlling your own destiny," or "It's time to accept Jesus Christ as your personal Savior." Such radical invitation may sound provocative or offending. A desire for change has to come from within. Our core responsibility, as spiritual counselors who recognized and have experienced the TRUTH is not to force the truth on our counselees. Our role as spiritual counselors consists of presenting the TRUTH without alteration or adjustment. The motive behind being a consistent presenter of the TRUTH is to help others to think success in order to become successful. Spirituality, as explained earlier, is a matter of thought and action, it is also a matter of accountability. We are appointed to get people to think of something without manipulating them.

One thing to keep in mind is that the counselees may be mentally and emotionally capable to engage in examining the lifestyles of those who offer them counseling. Spiritual counselors are not perfect. They have the need for redemption and should not lose sight of the divine truth, which is their noble responsibility. Spiritual counselors should model the truth concerning trust, safety, will, and fairness. The greatest of all is to show love for those in need for redemption. The truth is "The eye of the Lord is in every place. Keeping watch on the evil and the good" (Prov. 15:3 NKJV).

Chapter Seven

EXPLORING PEOPLE'S OBSTACLES TO CHANGE AND THEIR DESIRE FOR CHANGE - The Techniques for Assisting People With Life-related Issues (TAPLI)

When exploring people's thoughts, ideas, and lifestyles that hinder a desire for change, there are two fundamental aspects that need to be brought into consideration: the types of conscience in light of EC variants, and their state of confusion.

In the attempt of grasping the reasons why some people resist change in their worldview and lifestyles is to look back at the constructs of value commitment. People's philosophy and lifestyle grounded in rational activities is consistent with their value commitment that fuels their resistance to change. When people are chronically confused, there is neither commitment to nor a desire for change, they are inconsistent in every aspect of their lives. Confusion is spiritually characterized by resistance to learning and to changing. Because of their confusion, these people tend to repeat a life scenario with no concern for re-evaluating possible alternatives to life improvement. These individuals are prone to comply with others' suggestions, proposals and demands. They may reflexively say "No" when their interests would be better served by saying, "Yes," and vice versa. Confusion is associated with rough feelings that cause individuals to be undetermined regarding a life changing experience. A spiritual state of incertus keeps the confused persons from understanding what is going on in their life, and their incapability to foresee the consequences of their misdeeds decreases the unlikelihood for change to occur.

The level of persuasion regarding one's personal gratifying activities is relevant to how people differ greatly in what they value. This evaluation or judgment is not a mere means to improving conduct, although it may result in such improvement. This survival interpretation (failed judgment) of one's wrongdoing shows itself quite clearly in three variants of an individual's Educated Conscience, which are a *facile conscience*, an *obscured conscience*, and a *self-induced clear conscience* that leads to single-mindedness and decrease the likelihood for the need for redemption to be fulfilled.

A clear recognition of what is good and what is false is useful for a spiritual breakthrough to happen. The Educated Conscience strengthens individuals' belief that their self- concept is accurate. We have in fact multiple cases where a person voluntarily did a wrong act and that he deliberately and resolutely choose to do it. Or, people can do wrong under the influence of others' suggestions. This could be a case where an individual begins to think about making a life-changing decision and that he or she cannot withstand people's ill-intended advice resulting in a change of the course of action due to a facile conscience – a conscience that facilitate a great deal of social compliance.

The idea that "We make decisions on the basis of criteria that arise from our values, and when our values change our decisions change" (David Jeremiah. March, 2003. pp.32) infers conduct must be judged according to whether reason for what one did is good or good enough to commit to it. An act done for a reason is something upon which one can reason, evaluate, and correct. Here are two possibilities to look at when considering counselees' obstacles to change:

(a) A person who does not choose to avoid the wrong, but rather has chosen to do so with normal firmness.
(b) A person who chooses to refrain from doing the wrong, under certain circumstances, fails to be consistent with his choice and because of internal pressure of conformity does not acknowledge his or her wrongness – this increases the chance that this person's need for redemption would not be fulfilled.

In the state of happy ignorance, people tend to be offensive when they have an invitation to change. When individuals are on the verge of losing their ability to discern the truth from falsehood, their future life is critical. Nathaniel Branden (1995) in his chapter, "Internal Sources of Self-Esteem" considered the following statement as one of the basic principles of a healthy self-esteem, which we think is consistent with what individuals who do not desire to change might utter, "My life does not belong to others and I am not here on earth to live up to someone else's expectations" (*Six Pillars of Self Esteem*. p. 121).

One should first observe that God has given to man the capacity to know himself and to seek what is good for his wellness. Sometimes in life, reality is valued by the quality of a person's connection with others, their openness to the truth, and a careful evaluation of the truth. In the process of persuading self about the truth of a better living, people with a *cumulative self-confidence* seem having to face a great obstacle concerning the way they defend their rights of free choices and their actual needs. Research supports that "the less people focus on themselves, the happier they are (e.g. Nolen-Hoeksema & David 1999).

At certain times, people are more open to spiritual truth than at other times. People can be mistaken and lose the ability of having reflection-based interpretation of what in life can bring them happiness.

With an *obscured conscience*, individuals are perplexed about their spiritual and moral values, and they may not realize how much damage they are causing to their lives. *Profligacy* is the greatest spiritual pitfall that individuals may undergo. This will surely cause them to be unable to have a successful reflection about either living with trust, with will, living fair, or living safe. This misguided spirituality leads to bragging about "invulnerability" by ignoring the reality. Obscured conscience, which is in line with profligacy pre- vents people from reflecting on a new way to approach a matter. Their vain speech and indecency reveal that they are shameless of their immorality. Even after witnessing other people's distress and death in relation to their misbehaviors, their rewarding feelings is what prevent them from having successful reflection in regards to the fatal consequences of their own misconduct.

This conscience variant (obscured conscience) prevents individuals from refraining themself from wrongdoing, and it impedes the ability to identify and acknowledge the triggers or causes of their deeds. As such, a person with a typical conscience is not held responsible for their erratic behaviors. What of a spiritually disturbed person who knows he is killing someone and has chosen to do so, but whom, because of his obscured conscience, does not know that he is doing anything wrong? From a spiritual standpoint, an individual, who knows what he has been doing is wrong and continues to do wrong, has an obscured conscience that fosters his cumulative confidence in doing what he infers to be wrong. Individuals who have an obscured conscience may continue (due to confusion, worry, or relevant panic) denying the reality of their spiritual fragility and continue living a reckless life. Given that these individuals are hostile to virtue, they despise those who have a moral sense of purpose.

The third conscience variant that constitutes obstacles to human spiritual breakthrough is a *self-induced clear conscience*. These are people with a strong desire for "feeling okay!" as they engaged in convincing others about their righteousness. Therefore, they tend to hide their shortcomings. With this type of educated conscience, individuals may be in denial, and they are unable to acknowledge their responsibility in having their current situation or condition of living. Given their inability of having a reflection-based interpretation of their mistaken behavior, constant justification of their wrongdoing constitutes a normal frame of mind. Often, these individuals arrogate spiritual power of discerning good from evil, right from wrong, true from false by holding the assumption that "No one knows better than I do." When comparing themselves with others, they tend to exaggerate by assuming to be "better than them."

Self-eulogia is consistent with the biblical description of the church of Laodicea. It refers to a false self-perception accompanied with an extreme excitement that "Everything is perfect, which precludes them from the reality of their living. The biblical recommendation is stated, "For you say, I am rich, I have prospered, and I need nothing; not knowing that you are wretched, pitiable, poor, blind, and naked" (Rev. 3:17).

Self-justification hampers peoples' reasoning ability. They can rely on certain factors to support their weaknesses and conceal their increasing wrongdoing. They may argue, "I could not behave or decide otherwise than I did." Self-induced clear conscience deprives individuals from their natural will to take responsibility for their errors and fulfill their need for redemption. Charles Stanley (2006) in a Sunday message said, "The denial of the truth does not change the truth." People with a facile conscience, an obscured conscience, and a self-induced clear conscience are prone to a spiritual degradation. The question is how can a spiritual counselor discover in their counselee the presence of a desire for change?

Tips for Identifying a Counselee's Stages of Spiritual Improvement

Agnosia or Time of Ignorance

It has been established that human beliefs are aimed at behaviors and solutions of problems in ways that we perceive to be good. *Agnosia* or state of ignorance has dramatic implications for how we live our spirituality, in relation to our knowledge of self, and of the negative consequences of our actions. Individuals in this spiritual stage are deceived in believing that "whatever makes me feel good is actually good." This stage of ignorance is tied to disordered-reflection patterns and to the ways in which individuals express and satisfy their needs. Individuals may feel good when they accomplish "something important" and find it very satisfying to persuade someone to do likewise without being able to explain the benefits of doing what they did – this is the spiritual state of *inexplicabilis*. These individuals are likely to commit to the *utilis* with the least chance of having a second thought. In the process of seeking satisfaction, individuals of this spiritual stage often have survival interpretation such as, "life is fun," which interpretation serves as a boost in the pursuit of happiness (i.e., a straightforward feeling). This time of ignorance promotes a spiritual life that is void of true substance. Their acts have been free and do not wish to refrain from behaving contrary to their passion – they are committed to their misdeed. Peal (2005) wrote, "Conditions are created by thoughts far more powerfully than conditions create thoughts" (p. 166). For individuals to grasp a deeper understanding of self, they should have a spiritual experience that consists in *wondering*.

Existemi-A Time of Wondering

Following a *time of agnosia* (i.e., time of ignorance), the individual may have a *time of wondering*. It is a time when people reflect on self and on personal issues. In this precise moment, one may have a second thought "What if…" The course of action following a moment of wondering varies. *Wondering* is a cognitive activity. How strongly a person is determined to seek help and willing to tell about their core issues, indicates a time of wondering. The Latin expression, *Qui tacet consentit*, translated "He who remains silent consents" carries the idea that individuals who honestly share with others their personal problems are in the spiritual process of seeking counsel. Passive wondering is painful and ineffective. Some individuals acknowledge the danger of noncompliance with their Conscience, and yet function below their level of awareness.

From a spiritual perspective, no change occurs without being tied to a burden. Whether wondering leads to good or poor results is important. For a person to grasp a clear and pre- cise understanding of self and of his needs he should anticipate the benefit of the desired change (i.e., who has *remedial feeling*). This individual should be ready to carry the burden associated with a life-changing experience. The thought "What if…" may raise a second thought related to the challenges to change. For example, one may wonder "What if I give up on my fame?" "What if I give up on my wealth?" or "What if I desist on all my pleasurable activities?" etc. The "What if…" wondering that is equivalent to "What would happen to me if…" indicates the wonderer's fear of contradiction. Wondering has two forms that we identify as: *Ex more wondering* (according to custom) and *extra ordinem wondering* (beyond the usual order).

When wondering is ex more individuals have no desire for change, but prefer things to exist in accordance with custom. Self-indulgence entails a type of rigidity in the meaning ascribed to life. This decreases people's tentative explanation for their uncertainty of the way they are fulfilling their needs – a reward-eliciting lifestyle decreases the probability of having a successful reflection over one's lack or deficit. This increasing tolerance of ambiguity prevents wondering from being spiritually productive. When wondering is *extra ordinem*, individuals, at this time, raise concerns on important issues such as, the purpose of life on earth, the existence of God, the rationale of death and dying, and the like. Individuals before this moment never had a superior power of recognizing the truth about their need for redemption. When learning or reading about God's plan for redemption, someone may reflect and/or utter, "I wonder if God would accept me." In other instances, wondering about how to fulfill one's need for redemption may challenge the wonderer to seek knowledge of God and His plan of redemption. Fear of God's reprisal that brings discomfort within is likely to lead the wonderer to the steps he or she takes toward self-improvement in light of God's words. When the desire is strong a person will repent and learn God's plan for life. With a desire for repentance, one may wonder whether one should isolate oneself from the rest of society to enjoy life to the outmost Confusion, worry, and panic are the three disordered reflection that interfere with wondering causing it to be unsuccessful.

Carole whom I had counseled for six months in a residential program is a vivid example of someone who has been treated for nicotine dependence and had a grudge against her sister. Her sister visited her in the group-home facility. Carole often told me about her sister who is in possession of all her father's assets due to his death. One day, after her sister's visit at the group home, she led her out, closed the door and said, "I hate you." Like Carole, many people found it difficult to gain confidence - self-confidence, because their love- need for connection is not fulfilled. It is not unusual that individuals who are dependant on substance have underlying spiritual disturbances. A comprehensive treatment goal for Carole should include resentment. Even Carole experienced a decrease in cigarette consumption(...), chances are she would relapse. She has the right to hide or talk about her grudge and decide according to her own will. Carole's actual problem can help interpret every aspect of what she expects in life.

On several occasions, Carole who smoked one to two packs of cigarettes a day shared with me her concerns about her mother who was a smoker and dying with cancer. I let her into "opportunity for wondering" by allowing her to think of what could be the end result of her smoking pattern. One day, she came to tell me that "When you look at a person and see what cigarettes do to that person, it's sad; it's hard to see how sick they get." Then, she made me a brief description of her mother in bed." After listening to mother's medical condition, my intervention consisted in: "I understand, Carole, how painful it is for you to learn that your mother is dying from breast cancer and your uncle, recently, had surgery in the throat as a result of their smoking habits." How do you think you can avoid the con- sequences of your smoking?" Another day, right after she explained her mother's condi- tion, she, sporadically moved away by saying: "I've got to run; I have to puff a cigarette."

"Sarcastically, she added: "I know it is not good for me, but I can't live without having a cigarette early in the morning, which will make me feel happy for the rest of the day" – this statement indicates cessation of her wondering. This exemplifies how Carole's instant feelings from smoking were more important and essential to her survival.

Carole's survival interpretation of how "having a puff" is "indispensible" coincides with a lowered level of desire for change. As such, her fear of vulnerability is not helping her to withstand her tendency to self-destructive behavior i.e., smoking. Thus, cigarette was for her the *utilis* that made her feel adequate and "forgetful" about her sister's betrayal that she mentioned several time in counseling sessions. Carole was, indeed, confused about what could be the consequences of her smoking habit and her love for a "puff."

The question pertaining to whether one could have acted otherwise alludes to a time of wondering. Following this crucial time of self-assessing, if the person becomes concerned and holds accountability for his wrongful act, there is evidence of a desire for change or a *desire for repentance*.

*Nocham Thelem*a - A Desire for Repentance

From a spiritual standpoint, there is a difference between a "desire for change" and a *desire for repentance*. A "desire for change" is a vague wish for betterment. Such desire derives from judging a behavior to be other than what it should be. A common dilemma of wishful thinking of self-improvement is when people end up setting for themselves goals that are unreachable. The major difficulty associated with a desire for change is in its subjectivity that entails the notion of change. If a person is acting under recklessness, pride or resentment, then his decision to refrain from doing wrong will be ineffective, simply because such spiritual conditions stem from a disordered reflection that hampers a choice of refraining from doing wrong. However, if a person chooses to live life differently (i.e., a brand-new lifestyle), he must have successful reflection over all his wrongful acts and acknowledge his need for redemption. It may be a matter of practical impossibility to have a successful reflection regarding the spiritual resources that aim at assisting in one's desire for change.

When we consider that a person could have acted otherwise, if he had chosen to do so, we may ask, "Couldn't he or she have spoken and acted differently!" One such neces- sary condition consists of the knowledge and belief upon which repenting from a wrongful act coincides with a "change of mind (from the Greek: *Meta* that means" and noia "mind," literally it means "a change of mind"). A desire for repentance refers to the acknowledgement of one's mistake of judgment and a strong wish to maintain a level of conduct that brings restoration and peace inside – a spiritual condition that renders effective a choice to refrain from wrong doing by surrendering to God's plan of redemption. The type of reflection that is involved in contemplating an in-depth change is determinative to one's spiritual development and future. Ellen G. White wrote, "As we meditate upon the perfections of the Saviour, we shall desire to be holly transformed and renewed in the image of His purity" (*Steps to Christ*. p. 61). A desire for repentance to be spiritually successful has to be of first-grade importance.

The thought pattern, "I can because I think I can" is not suitable to repentance. In order for repentance to be genuine, the remorseful person, not only should be held accountable for having failed to do the right thing; there should be a necessary condition of a specific choice to spiritual growth. As the following quote suggests, "A fundamental change of mind not only turns us from the sinful past, but transforms our life plan, values, ethics and actions as we begin to see the world through God's eyes rather than ours" (Charles Colson. 2002. *Loving God*. pp.109). When someone desires to repent, the primary confession is directed to God. Typically, someone who is willing to repent makes no attempt at self-jus- tification, neither at lessening his guilt, but contemplates the most favorable spiritual exit for a renewal of mind through confession by saying "God be merciful to me a sinner" – the initial step to an upward spiritual experience. Repentance that does not hurt does not heal. Although repentance hurts, it carries the most powerful beneficial spiritual outcome, which is fulfillment of one's need for redemption. Someone who promptly admits his wrongness and expresses the desire for change with no mention of God's intervention does not have a true desire for repentance. For this individual it could be painful to think of "God" as the unique way to meet his need for redemption. Charles Colson explored important reasons for which repentance is ignored or misunderstood and affirmed, "Often we are simply unwilling or unable to accept the reality of personal sin and thereby our need for repentance" (p.111).

In the process of assessing a counselee's desire for repentance, the spiritual counselor should take into account the condition that renders the choice to avoid wrongdoing either effective or ineffective. A desire for repentance is the seedbed for seeking self-improvement in light of God's plan of redemption. By acknowledging the need to live life differently and by bringing this acknowledgment to God, the choice to refrain from wrong-doing becomes effective. An *indurate guilt* may compromise the possibility to fulfill one's need for redemption.

I had counseled a woman who was convicted after having sex with a 12-year old male neighbor. This woman who was overwhelmed by her wrongful act complained about her having been rejected by family members and by friends to whom she had disclosed her shortcomings. As I was actively listening to her, I got a sense that she tended to tell anyone she encountered about what she had been through. Her indurate guilt was evident in her statement: "Wherever I go (i.e., grocery store, gas station, or else), I get a sense that people are judging me." This woman who was self referred to therapy had a desire for repentance, but she did not know how to proceed. Her statement "I am worthless" suggested she had an inadequate self-confidence due to her indurate guilt. Throughout the counseling sessions, I conveyed respect to her and expressed appreciation for her honesty.

Another way to explore a desire for repentance in people is to grasp how they manage their pain and loss. Following a loss or pain, the thinker should create new ways of living; otherwise he or she would be dejected. A typical reaction to the pain that results from guilt because of a wrongful act is when people say, "There is nothing in life I have to be ashamed of." Other people, however, may start having a reflection-based interpretation of the nature of their guilt with the likelihood to develop a new meaning of life. In both spiritual responses, the fear involved is the fear of vulnerability. Fear of vulnerability when it is mismanaged can increase the individual's resistance by overcoming losses and fail- ures involved in this fear. When it is successfully managed, it enhances reflection over the "most appropriate alternative" to compensate the loss otherwise. Once individuals come to acknowledge that their insight about justice, loyalty, prosperity, and peace does not guarantee a solid spiritual breakthrough, they may seek after spiritual guidance by turning to the TRUTH. Rick Warren, a Christian Post Guest Columnist, asked the following question to which he answered, "Who are the most receptive people? I believe there are two broad categories: people in transition and people under tension." That's because God uses both change and pain to get people's attention and make them receptive to the Gospel." When speaking about tension that may trigger a desire for change, Warren said, "When people are fearful or anxious, they often look for something greater than themselves to ease the pain and fill the void they feel" (The Christian Post. How to recognize spiritual receptivity in your community? Apr. 6, 2006). Warren provided evidence-data to support this assumption:

> During the 1970s a man named Reeve Robert Brenner surveyed one thousand survivors of the Holocaust, inquiring especially about their religious faith. How had the experience of the Holocaust affected their beliefs about God? Somewhat astonishingly, almost half claimed that the Holocaust had no influence whatever on their beliefs about God. But the other half told a different story. Of the total number of surveyed of God, eleven percent said they had rejected all belief in the existence of God as a direct result of their experience. After the war, they never regained faith. Analyzing their detailed responses, Brenner noted that their professed atheism seemed less a matter of theological belief and more an emotional reaction, an expression of deep hurt and anger against God for abandoning them.
>
> Brenner also discovered that a smaller number, about five percent of his overall sample, actually changed from atheists into believers because of the Holocaust. After living through such abominations, they simply had nowhere to go (Philip Yancey, 2001. *Where is God When it Hurts?* p. 152).

Sanus-A Life Relevant of Redemption (LRR)

Many individuals who are referred by an agency for having medical attention do not experience a holistic approach of therapy. Some of the psychiatric patients are simply misdiagnosed because their "mental illness" was not addressed from a spiritual perspective. Because of internal disturbances that cause irrational thoughts and uncomfortable feelings in a patient (whose resentments are spiritually grounded), anti-psychotics or anti-depressants cannot help this particular patient function well in society, i.e., with their mates, co workers, and else. This consideration is central, not only in establishing a line of differences and contrasts between the medical and spiritual models, but gives enlightenment on the notion of causality related to these models.

Spiritual problems need to be addressed spiritually. Harol C. Sox, MD and Joseph M. Hubert (2002) in *What is a Good Decision?* Said, "Patients tend to overestimate the benefits of many medical interventions" (www.acponline.org/journals/ecp/julaug99/essays. htm). From television, we learned that "A government survey established that 70% of individuals that have been using anti-depressants are now having unresolved symptoms." Insofar, medications cannot help individuals who suffer from ill-sexual tendencies (IST).

From a spiritual standpoint, human intellectual abilities are a gift of God, not only to have dominion over the entire creation, but also to manage self rationally. The idea that True Conscience is innate and makes humans very superior to animals in terms of learning about self, discerning right from wrong, and true from false. In remembering decisions related to past experiences and the consequences of those decisions, the spiritual applicability of this human science confers to the ability that people have to ascribe meaning to their past experiences, which enhances their discerning ability. When someone's discerning ability is weakened, this person tends to deviate from his or her True Conscience coaching. Because True Conscience has a profound spiritual significance in inspiring people to make the healthiest decisions, people may need to be spiritually cured in order for them to be physically healthy.

Any counselors who ignore the spiritual aspect of lifestyle choices can reinforce confusion involved in people's aspiration to find the truth. For example, the likelihood for someone to repent from a sexually-ill orientation (SIO) decreases if such sexually related decisions are not viewed and processed as personal sins.

As we recall, people who are perplexed lose their ability to solve even the simplest problem. Even when they presume "there is nothing they are worried about and covering up," they do not have the peace of mind. It is an evidence of fact when people simply dissociate themselves from other people (of different life view) to avoid being bothered by their call for change. In certain cases, there happen repetitive public activities (i.e., lobbying and demonstrations) with the intent of dissuading the public of their lifestyle choices. These activities are neither relevant of a desire for change, nor of actual redemption.

Previously, we pinpointed the human need for redemption that is spiritual and how it can be fulfilled. We emphasized that the key to fulfillment of this need is to picture the reality of one's very spiritual limitations, and to surrender to God's established plan for redemption. As the following quote suggests, "The problem solver has to construct an optimal representation or understanding of the nature of a problem or issue (Biehler and Snowman. 1990. p. 448). In the same token, Charles Stanley (2008) said, "Individuals cannot be fulfilled until they experience the Lord's transforming and unconditional love" (*In Touch*. Feb. p. 43). Jesus Christ, the ultimate spiritual Counselor and the Redeemer urged His people to "bear fruits worthy of repentance" (Mat. 3:8).

The individuals' desire to live in accordance with the "kingdom of God" may develop into a radical change in their vision of life as evidenced in their decisions and lifestyle choices. Someone who was living a very bad life (i.e., covert or unveiled profanity derived from an inadequate self-confidence, negative perception of self, of God and of people, underlying or overt tendency of harming self and/or others) may come to experi- ence a life marked by morality and self-control. It was reported that "Velma Barfield (the first woman to be executed in the U.S. in 23 years) was under the heavy influence of pre- scription drugs when she poisoned four people. While in prison on death row, she accepted Christ. For the first time in her life, Velma saw herself as a person of worth. Although many factors contributed to her tortured life, she took full responsibility for her actions." The report also said, "In her Bible she wrote: 'Sin is being called all kinds of fancy names nowadays, but it's time we come to grips with ourselves and call sin what it really is – SIN.' "(Dennis J. de Haan. "Good Medicine." Our Daily Bread. August 12, 1986).

Redemption is not tributary to any religion, but rather to the knowledge of Jesus Christ who is alive and at work in changing believers' lives. Religions are powerless human efforts to fulfill their need for worship that is fundamental to spirituality. Redemption shows that Jesus Christ is evidenced-based in that all religion founders die and are not resurrected. Jesus Christ only was resurrected and was attested to by more than 500 eye witnesses. Therefore, Jesus Christ is the ultimate spiritual Counselor and the Redeemer/ Savior. Velma (in the previous story) had a reflection-based interpretation of her shortcom- ings that rendered her humble enough to choose Christ as her ultimate spiritual Counselor and Redeemer. Karmen also gave a meaningful testimony that demonstrates how her spiri- tual surrender to God brought her to an outstanding communication with God: "I felt as though the Creator of the universe spoke into my heart: *It's time to stop killing yourself and fight for life*." One needs to be cautious in taking Karmen's communication with God as an "auditory hallucination," but rather a call for repentance echoed in her True Conscience. Karmen also added that she had a sensation that "sank down from her head into her heart as she responded to that still small voice." In response, she said, "I'm willing to live for You. Take this pain and change me" (Focus on the Family. Dec. 2007. p. 16).

On the whole, a redeemed person has a high degree of understanding and determina- tion for living with trust, living with will, living safe, and living fair. The reality of love, happiness, death, and life after death is well established. As an evidence of the fact of their repentance and redemption after listening to someone's presenting problem, this spiritually renewed person may articulate, "If you are having difficulty solving such problems, pos- sibly it is because your knowledge of the Redeemer is incomplete." With no pretension of being "superior" or condemning others, these individuals have increased self-confidence that allows them to answer any personal questions related to their belief and faith in God. At times, the repentant person may feel spiritually weak, especially in moments of retro- spect, but they find strength in optimal methods of problem solving that include: prayer, meditation, Bible reading, and counsel from other redeemed people.

Redemption, which is a powerful spiritual experience, brings a lot of optimism and joy in the individual's life. People who embark on a life-changing experience live by *the reward of change*. Given their commitment to the Gospel, the redeemed persons are com- pelled to abide and live by the biblically-based moral standard. Redemption is, in effect, seen through a childlike vision of life that makes the spiritually redeemed to be at peace with self, with God, and other people. They look toward a positive future that is characterized by a life filled with hope, a life of service, a life compelling to integrity and a peaceful mindset.

In any problem-solving process, the redeemed individuals know exactly what their consciences want from them as they avoid disappointment, shame, or disgrace. This makes it obvious that individuals who are redeemed are more likely to seek after the ultimate spiritual Counselor than those who are not. They are less likely to deny responsibility for their behavior, and their likelihood to fix the blame on someone or something decreases.

The four tips for identifying the counselee's stages of change in a pyramid:

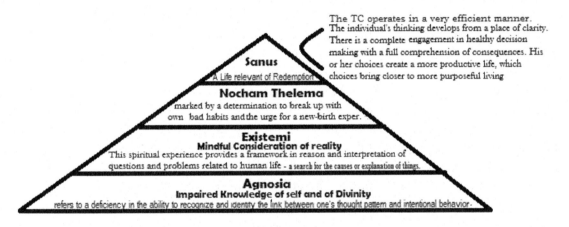

Figure 1
The Pyramid of an Upward Spiritual Experience

Christianity stands for the spiritually therapeutic model that pinpoint the need for redemption and for eternity, and a precise way to fulfill this need. The human search for "What makes life better" is consistent with the *desire for repentance* that all individuals have at times. Hal Lindsey (1997) speaking to this matter said, "Isn't it exciting to know that every decision we make in our lives has eternal repercussions?" In addition, he said, "Everything we do in this life - every act of obedience, every act of faith, and every trial endured is significant and can earn us eternal rewards. Nothing is without meaning" (Apocalypse Code. p. 290).

The Value of Modeling in the Individuals' Motivation for Change

Compared with various means and techniques of counseling, modeling has foundations and characteristics that consciously or unconsciously contribute to the formation of one's perspective of life. Richard A. Khalish affirmed: "Whatever the basis, much of our behavior is based on what we see others do." This illustrates the nature and purposes of modeling an individual's beliefs and lifestyle. John Fisher (1982) continues by saying that "A model is like a map. It represents selected features of its territory." So to speak, a model creates a meaning for the observer and the model chooser.

Let us now turn our attention to the spiritual significance of the choice of a model. In light of the effects of positive and negative modeling, an individual's ability to discern good from evil helps in making the choice of a *virtuous model*. This illustrates how the template of a model results from a reflection on the individual's lifestyle. Fiske encouraged individuals to be mindful in their "choice of a model" that he conceptualized as the "choice of a map" in that "we have to know when to turn to it and what insights we require from it." One must be cautious in using the concept of "perfect model" when we know that "nobody is perfect."

Children do not make choice of a model, but are subject to the emulation effects. If the adult's behavior is positive, the emulation is positive. If the adult's behavior is negative, the emulation is negative. A child may, publicly, declare his approval or disapproval of his father's belief system or of his mother's by saying, for instance, "I am doing it the same way as my dad/mom would do." In other instances, a child may state: "I hate his or her old-fashioned way of doing things." Childhood and adolescent memory of deceased parents or grandparents' modeling is relevant to the power of emulation.

Given the importance of choosing a model, the pertinent question that we need to look at is why individuals who are at the point of adopting a model may still change their mind. The notion of being persuaded by a model involves trust in this model. The ambivalence in the choice of a model or the rejection of a long-lasting model requires a successful reflection. This decision making process can make one vulnerable because it always upsets the equilibrium of relationships.

Two friends who enjoy smoking together have created a bond. If one friend decides to give up the smoking habit, due to successful reflection of the consequences of what could possibly happen to his life/her health, the bond between these friends can be threatened. Cessation of smoking based on negative consequences of nicotine on the smoker is due to the person's fear of vulnerability (which includes fear of being a failure, fear of death…). The friend who continues with the smoking habit will suffer from the loss of a smoking partner and will have moments of wondering, "Should I stop smoking too?" "Is my health really in jeopardy."

This moment of wondering will only be effective, if this person ceases to smoke. The friend who stopped smoking trusted the model of healthy living by others who were able to stop the habit. Yet, this friend has to deal with the loss of connection enjoyed during the time he shared smoking with his partner. From a spiritual standpoint, imitation of a model that is undertaken enthusiastically is risky and may enhance disordered reflection toward spiritual disturbance evident in unthinkable choices. The friend who was wondering may compensate his loss by continued indulgence in unhealthy habits.

Jesus Christ emphasized the outcomes of having two or several models - "No servant can serve two masters (Mt. 6:24), He said. This infers that a trustworthy model may become perverted and fails in his role of positive modeling. On the basis of his/her failure, this person may achieve little success in trying to help those who accept his/her guidance or leadership. At the sight of a decline in moral standard of a model, the deceived person goes into dissimulation of his choice. This person starts concealing his true feelings of appreciation with a decline in his trust in the spiritual mentor or counselor.

Many individuals disclose about their deception and disappointment in their parents' failure of being virtuous models. In light of progressive decline of emulation, a shared parental value of living may undergo a switch of preference. An indicator of a decline of emulation is when the emulator deals with his/her day-to-day priorities without begging for parental advice. Most miscalculated decisions that individuals make are often attributed to their family upbringing and experiences, so do the psychoanalysts. As we pointed out, a person may disregard his parent's lifestyle to adopt someone else's lifestyle that may cause him or her serious disturbances.

Parental Teaching of Moral Values is Powerful Modeling

No other place in the world has so much to do with the making of the human beings and the shaping of their destiny than their home. Home is the place where infants, children, adolescent, men, and women receive their strongest incentives and influences. Parental influence on children and adolescents is one of the most important factors to be considered if one wants to know the reasons why people speak and behave the way they do. The out- standing role of parents is to provide support for a child to grow in good character.

The solemn responsibility of all parents is to teach their children good manners and life-lasting values- thorough teaching about living trust, living with will, living safe and living fair. The idea of training young people to resist messages that draw them to passivity and stereotypical behavior is embedded in those four concepts. The question is: Do all parents succeed in teaching these concepts?"

To be an effective spiritual model, a parent needs to provide children and adolescent with the opportunity to examine their own belief by showing that they care about and trust them. The greatest spiritual challenge of all adults is to be consistent in the course of mod- eling. Parents need to teach young children how to silence their Educated Conscience and be receptive to their True Conscience. Often, parents fail to be consistent in teaching rectitude and are disappointed by the reaction of their children. From a spiritual perspective, the idea of being a consistent model has to do with how in tune one is with one's True Conscience.

Let us look at some examples of how parents teach their children incoherent life-styles: a parent who sends a child to church, but does not attend church, a parent who tells a child to answer the telephone and if the caller is requesting the parent, the parent tells the child to say, "I am not home;" a parent who has multiple sexual partners and teaches an adolescent to be committed to one sexual partner. These examples show the deviance from the goal of teaching moral uprightness. If parents expect positive outcomes of their modeling, awareness of the quality of verbal and non-verbal messages need to be examined.

Parents need to be watchful when expressing their frustrations, because this can lead to unsuccessful modeling. When adults are hurt and angry, they may not be able to refrain from impulsive talk (.e.g., swearing, cursing, yelling and threatening). There is nothing wrong with expressing frustration, but it should not damage someone's well-being. Therefore, in order for parents to be potential spiritual counselors, they should do their best to curtail their reactions in tense situations. It is recommended that postponement of correction is necessary to give time for parent to gather thought and feeling, so that they can respond appropriately. From the Bible "let all the bitterness, wrath, anger, clamor and evil speaking be put away from you. . . . And be kind to one another, tenderhearted, forgiving one another, even as God in Christ forgive you (Ephesians 4: 31-32 NKJV). Although uncomfortable feelings always have residual effects, it is to the benefit of the child that parents need to be consistent in their ways of conveying love.

Christian education tends to be idealistic in raising the spiritual level of a child. Parents may help children define their core values and true self by using the Bible. Parental faith in the Bible is an impressive way to inculcate in the youth the precepts of living trust, living with will, living fair, and living safe. Parents, as well as, children who attend Christian churches may be acquiring the support, the information, and the skills they need to make healthy-living choices. Focusing on biblical values, as a preference, can help both the parents improve their modeling and the children to incorporate these parental values. One of the fundamental values taught by the Bible is: "Train up a child in the way he should go. . . ." Prov. 22:6). This principle may increase parental awareness of their mod- eling as this principle becomes more consciously significant.

In looking ahead, a parent will determine the effectiveness of modeling so that the child will be influenced to be a productive adult. The conscience of this productive adult will prove to be the result of positive modeling. Christian churches give families strong role models through the Bible and the lives of morally committed church members. One of the fundamental goals of my survey on sexual abstinence among teenagers of 13-16 years old was to assess the risks of sexually transmitted diseases (STDs) and the likelihood of becoming pregnant. The results of the survey conducted in 2000 revealed that 50% of the respondents (religious and nonreligious teenagers) did not have great confidence in their parents' knowledge about the topic of sexuality. Several studies carry out the idea that girls who become sexually active at young ages are at high risk for teen pregnancy and other studies concluded that "Postponing sexual intercourse is an important goal for any program that seeks to reduce teen pregnancy" (*Developing Pregnancy Prevention Programs for Girls and Young Women.* p. 35).

Preaching in church about sexual abstinence before marriage and the good examples of faithfully married couples may influence young attendants in their sexual choices. Along the road, church attendants would develop the idea of sexual purity. Young children who are sexually active and attend Christian churches may easily draw the conclusion that "not everyone is doing it" and are likely to succumb to parental influence, simply because the two teachings reinforce one another. From "Tailoring Pregnancy Prevention Programs to Stages of Adolescent Development" "Sexually active youth, abstinent youth, and teen parents all have powerful messages to send to other young people" (p. 35).

One day, I heard a young preacher disclosing his struggles with watching football on the Sabbath - a day that is supposed to be kept holy (Gen. 20: 6-8). As he taught his children to refrain from all secular activities and concentrate on the sacred ones, he was very concerned and found it appropriate to set a good parental model by resisting the temptation. It is clear that this young preacher went through an internal conflict, before demonstrating trust and will in what he taught his children. This elicits that integrated biblical values can play a significant role in individuals' decisions, as well as, modeling.

Children remember what their family honors. When they think of doing something or planning something, they recall what the parents or adults in the house said to them: "Don't do anything that would make us ashamed." Obedient children adjust their lives in order to meet their parents' expectations and desires to gain parental acceptance. They get feedback from adults and change their words and actions accordingly. Such awareness on these values and parental expectations is vital in the formation of a vision of life (living will). As a person grows, they use their judgment regarding which values to adopt and which ones to deny. Sometimes, the influence of poor parental modeling gets children in trouble. The term "peer pressure" refers to the influence of one teen on the other teens. Individuals are extremely vulnerable to criticism from their parents and desperately feel the need for their acceptance. They end up doing things that they are not emotionally capable of handling by emulating what their parents would say or do under similar circumstances. Children who tend to keep their parents' values and reject their peers' are said to be spiritually well-oriented. Adolescents can easily be ambivalent about their parent's good values and bad morals; they are equally able to identify their friends' miscalculation. Some people are suffering to the point of death because of the models they pick. Role models should be carefully chosen.

A Lens on a Teacher's Failure of being a Spiritually Healthy Model

Individuals who are confused about their responsibility in modeling may fail to be good models. I watched an interview on "Day Date" television show with the title: "Daughter had sex with teacher." On the show, the teacher disclosed that he had a sexual relationship with his student. Here is a transcript of this interview:

Teacher: I could not have kept my job. I could not be effective, but I made that decision. In fact, I made the decision of having my teacher license cancelled voluntarily, so I won't teach anywhere else. I have no intentions that I will ever teach again; I will pick another career.

Interviewer: I want to know if parents are wondering if their children are safe in school. They are young women with developed bodies and are naïve about being so close to teachers. She is young, even if she were 25 it would be a danger.

Teacher: It's not a danger. It's a very difficult situation for students and teachers alike. The age of consent is very difficult to handle. I was not a danger to Becky. I had no intentions of ever hurting her. I cared very deeply for Becky; I cared for her well being, Ha! I made a mistake, and it is something that I can't take back and now I am asking for criti- cism. All I can say is the same thing that Jesus Christ said when He was crucified: "Forgive them all for they don't know what they do." I made a mistake, I fully admit that and I take responsibility for that.

Interviewer: Have you apologized to Becky?

Teacher: In the local Newspaper, I made a statement that I apologize to the Melzer family and to Becky if I may have hurt her self-esteem. I had no intention of ever doing that, I cared for her and I believed that she cared for me. And I was in a situation where we were able to reflect and I felt it was necessary for me to save my family, and not to continue the relationship with Becky.

Interviewer: Robert, thank you for being with us today. These are responses from interview with mother:

Mother (Marie Mouser): An apology would never be enough as far as I am concerned.

Becky: It did not make me feel any better; I wish it had.

Mother: I hope it doesn't happen to your children; there is nothing that you can do as a parent. Anger? I am angry as a mother. Someone you trusted, someone you depended on, someone that was viewed as a responsible adult.

Father: I don't understand how I trusted that man with my daughter. He violated that trust. He took away something from her and from me.

From this interview, there is evidence of a breach of trust on the part of the teacher who ceased to be a moral figure in the life of this female student. He failed in one area of the spiritual standards (living trust), he also failed in the other principles of life, which are: living with trust, living with will, living fair, and living safe. It was unfair for him not to behave as a moral figure and his behavior did not reflect morality. This teacher fell short in his will to be a model for his students; he became unsafe to the students and exposed them to his failure. As we notice, he was confused in his explanation about what brought him to that point in his life. Loss of clarity and lack of center of awareness are the two major elements that substantiate this teacher's obscured conscience and inadequate self-confidence. He indeed acknowledged having made a mistake that he thought he was unable to "take back." This interview confirms that in a case of manipulation both individuals, the manipulator and the person who was subjected to manipulation, are duly confused.

Modeling through the Choice and Ways of satisfying one's Need for Worship

The way individuals meet their need for worship may be a major cause of fellowship or of dissidence in a group or in a nation at large. Some people may be harsh when casting out judgments upon those who claim to be believers in God. Through ages, discordance between the believers and the unbelievers has been an issue of great importance. A brilliant philosopher from Harvard University made a critical comment concerning the believers' motives for righteousness: "If we have to be faithful to the God discovered by human understanding, we must insist: God is cruel," he said. (Michael Novak. *Belief and Unbelief-A philosophy of self-knowledge* p.p.131). From Novak's perspective, "We can know that God exists, but not what he is like" (Idem. p.171). According to Novak the believers' "interests are wrongly directed." Stephen Layman argued that "There are many different reli- gious experiences, and they cannot be all reliable. Some reports contradict others" (*A Case for the Existence of God*. p. 50). This suggests that individuals' need for worship is spiritual and is met in various ways.

The desire to be well informed about true worship is spiritually realistic. Those who perceive Christianity as "mythical" tend to avoid it and make derogatory comments concerning this particular belief and lifestyle. Some of the critics have an underlying cruel intention against the worshipers of God. The atheists, for example, perceive any believer as a "myth maker." As such, the believers fail to model in order to manage and dispel the unbelievers' doubt about the existence of a loving Creator.

The idea that Christians "are supposed to be nice to the spirit of the Antichrist" (Pat Robertson, The 700 Club) is not shared by all Christians. Jimmy Carter (2005) affirmed: "We believe in religious freedom, compassion for unbelievers, and respect for all persons as inherently equal before God." The Apostle Paul counseled Timothy on avoiding "such godless chatter." For, like he said, it will lead people into more and more godliness." The difference resides in how people meet their need for worship. Rather, the focus should be on the *ultimate spiritual Model or Counselor*.

Individuals' worship customs pass on from generation to generation. The Bible states the following:

> Moses called the elders of Israel, and said to them, "Select lambs for yourselves according to your families, and kill the Passover lamb. Take a bunch of hyssop and dip it in the blood which is in the basin, and touch the lintel and the two doorposts with the blood which is in the basin; and none of you shall go out of the door of his house until the morning. . . . For the Lord will pass over the door, and will not allow the destroyer to enter your houses to slay you. You shall observe this rite as an ordinance for you and for your sons for ever. And when you come to the land which the Lord will give you, as he has promised, you shall keep this service. And when your children say to you, 'What do you mean by this service?' you shall say, "It is the sacrifice of the Lord Passover, for he passed over the houses of the people of Israel in Egypt, when he slew the Egyptians but spared our houses." And the people bowed their heads and worshiped (Ex. 12: 21-27).

The importance of Moses modeling is to follow God's instruction for the purpose of family preservation. He was demonstrating living safe. The blood passed on the doorposts represented God's promise of safe keeping for those who were present in the house. Also, Moses commissioned those present in the house to repeat this practice with the coming generations.

The "Wonderful Counselor, The Mighty God"

As I have explored and used several therapeutic models, I came to realize that the evidence of expected change in therapy is grounded in the notion of self-efficiency. There is a considerable amount of theories and research that emphasize self-efficacy as the evidence of change in individuals. William R. Miller and Stephen Rollnick (2002) stated, "Within motivational interviewing change arises through its relevance to the person's own values and concerns." According to these therapists, "expectations about a person likelihood of change can have a powerful effect on outcome, acting as a self-fulfilling prophecy." In addition, they say, "A general goal of motivational interviewing is to enhance the client's confidence in his or her capacity to cope with obstacles and to succeed in change." Leake and King (1977) found that "If you expect that change will occur with your client, your expectancy of change will influence their behavior."

According to Leake and King, "A counselor's belief in the client's ability to change is a significant determination of treatment outcome." In the same token, Cousins (1989) found that "helping efforts are more successful when the helper believes in the client's capabili- ties." The purpose is to find practical ways to solve the problem. When a counselee set a goal in counseling, and this goal is far from being achieved, the counselor on the case often places a request for more time from this client's insurance company toward achievement of his goal. The essence of this procedure has nothing to do with assessing the counselees' spiritual needs toward a life-changing experience. The refusal to accept one's limitations is due to pride and self-love when our reality is faulty, our lives will continue to be faulty. Peel concluded, "If living a quiet life of personal peace and prosperity is more compelling to us than following Jesus, we will be unwilling to put our lives on the line" (p. 73). René Descartes argued that human beings can be erroneous. Peel added, "We don't have to be the best, but we do have to give our best" (p. 65). The pursuit of empowerment, in spirituality, takes place through divine intervention that pride and self-love cannot be compromised.

The fact that Jesus Christ is a "Wonderful Counselor" is attested in building a relationship of trust. Thomas Joiner wrote, "There are two components of a fully satisfied need to belong: interactions with others and a feeling of being cared about." Believers in God have shared powerful testimonies regarding their interactions with God and the divine care that they have received. People who have been in a relationship with God through His son Jesus Christ have personal strength and resources as that they surrender to God.

How traditional counseling differs from spiritual counseling? One needs to attain a level of awareness of Christ's modeling and counseling. Regardless of one's religious standpoint, there are good lessons about Jesus' spirituality that are always useful. Jesus clarified the discrepancy that exists in the religious principles, namely "an eye for an eye" (Mat. 5:37). All of us, whether religious or nonreligious, have made rules that are advantageous to ourselves or to a group of individuals, yet detrimental to other people. Revenge is a classic example of how people are spiritually limited to love unconditionally. Christ warned against the danger of seeking one's own justice and encourages forgiveness over revenge and condemnation.

In an authoritative manner, Christ declared, "You have heard that it was said..., but I say to you. . . ." This way of loving is out of the ordinary and served to upset the religious leaders and their followers. Jesef Pieper's writing on loving in real life revealed an often-asked question about loving: "What does it means to really love another person is such a question?" Pieper expressed clear reservations on loving unconditionally. He said, "The fact remains that to love a person does not mean to wish him free of all burdens." In light of how Jesus Christ has modeled love, there is more than mere emotion; there is an act of *will*. Through the ages, Jesus Christ has set the importance of distinguishing between emotion and will. Emotion is tied to excitement, attachment, and repugnance. In will, there is choice to love as recommended by God or the opposite of the choice of loving, which is hatred. In regards to the will in loving, one of the limitations of human capability to love is that we are likely to love those who first love us. In many cases love is increased when it is recip- rocated. Love may exist in the simple form of wish. Christ's unique way of demonstrating love and compassion has inspired humanity. He performed countless miracles to all in need with no exception of race, color, religion, or intellect. This ultimate counseling involves the fact that human issues cannot be solved without interventions from God.

It is to reconstruct human life that Jesus ranks sin as the greatest spiritual issue as evi- denced in His counsel: "If your eye causes you to sin, pluck it out and throw it away, it is better for you to enter life with one eye than with two eyes to be thrown into hell of fire" (Mat 18:9). The remorse and the desire for repentance that follows sinful actions are man- aged under Christ's counseling. In many occasions Christ forgave sick peoples' sins instead of healing them: "Your sins are forgiven" (Mat 9:2; Mk 2:5; Lk 5:20). There is one true interpretation of why, on certain occasions, Jesus forgave the sick rather than healed them. It was to empower them to draw a line and forget the past and start again with a new vision and give a new meaning to life. What a vital, dynamic, and powerful way to help someone solve problems. It is true that "We are inclined to forget what we should remember and tend to remember what we should forget."

From my experience in psychotherapy, individuals may be severely distressed by the burden of their guilt. One of my female counselees, Loria (now age 50) was feeling so worthless. At the age of 35, she engaged in sexual acts with a 17 year-old teenager. Loria was prosecuted and served a jail sentence of 5 years. She stated that when she goes to a job interview, despite the fact that she provides a detailed story of her past, she is hired and later fired at some point." Loria's fear of being rejected by people in society has led to spiritual disturbance. Her guilty feelings fueled inadequate self-confidence created mental confusion and dysfunction. When asked on what occasions she "hears voices," she responded, "This often happens when I am feeling bad about myself." Loria stated, "I don't want to get close to anybody." The moment I get close to people, I want the relationship to be honest and open, and then I disclose to them about my felony. I feel that if I don't tell them up front, it would be a betrayal on my part. " Counseling sessions she had demon- strated her inability to be rooted in reality. Contrary to traditional counseling in which "the client is the expert," Jesus Christ is the center in a spiritually oriented counseling. When I got the knowledge of her belief's system, I reached the conclusion that only God through Jesus Christ is able to perform a miracle in Loria's life.

Loria needed redemption. She needed to know that she could not help herself and that her guilty feelings cannot be resolved by her own resources; only by turning to the ultimate spiritual Counselor. I gave Loria a short supplication prayer to read:

> "Dear God, I acknowledge that you are the Almighty God. Please hear my prayer. I need you because I am empty and troubled inside. Give me refuge and peace. I want to change and I need a new life. Help me believe in you as my Redeemer. I now have strength, Amen.

This prayer was given with instructions to read each morning for 7 days until next session. Loria was open to acceptance of this prayer. She recalled earlier in her life her father's belief in God and how he shared his faith with her. Loria stated that she felt a sense of comfort at the introduction of the prayer (living with trust). This prayer had a spiritually positive impact on Loria as evidenced by her weeping. Through the weeping, Loria revealed how attending church after her wrong act made her feel; she felt uncomfortable and ashamed. She continued to weep and stated, "I feel shaky." Although Loria was shaky, she continued her daily activity of prayer. Loria exhibited living with will by accepting her present discomfort knowing that she would benefit, her prognosis would change over time.

Jesus Christ is the ultimate spiritual Counselor because of His absolute power to free human beings from all burdens (Mt 11:30). The Psalmist, David who benefited from divine guidance said: "I bless the Lord who gives me counsel; in the night also my heart instructs me (Psalms 16: 7). Davidian counseling has its roots in freedom from the burden of guilt engendered by sins as evidenced in his claim: "Cast me not away from thy presence and take not thy Holy Spirit from me. Restore to me the joy of thy salvation, and uphold me with a willing spirit. I will teach transgressors thy ways, and sinners will return to thee (Ps 51: 11-13). David's bondage to internal disturbance resulted from his wrongful thoughts and acts. That's why David counseled that you should "cast all your burdens on the Lord, and he will sustain you. . . ." David's trust in God had flourished and became stronger: "I am like a green olive tree in the house of God. I trust in the steadfast love of God for ever and ever" (Ps 52:8). As a spiritual counselor, David acknowledged: "The Lord made known His ways to Moses" (Ps 103:7).

In the problem of "sin and disease," Jesus revised people's judgment of the sick. The Israelites associated individuals' diseases with the severity of their sins. The major sin of pride is that the sin of self-righteousness was unknown and religiously accepted. Given that sin increases the insecurity of self, individuals who bear the burden of guilt often feel outcast, and are too weak to claim God's assistance, especially in a prejudicial society. J. K. Rowling affirms: "It is our choices that show what we truly are, far more than our abilities" (Readers Digest. Jan 2005. p.65). Moses who felt disqualified to persuade the Pharaoh about God's plan of redemption for the Israelites was empowered by God Himself. His lack of confidence in God's mission was evident in the fact that he was raised in the Pharaoh's kingdom. Second, he had speech impairment (Ex. 4:10). Moses' inadequate self-confidence was relevant in his statement: "Who I am that I should go to Pharaoh" (Ex 3:11). I want to focus on the fact that Moses' sense of inadequacy is a classic example of God's expectation to intervene in peoples' life in respect to their will to surrender.

Jesus Christ counseled us about being in submission to God and in conformity with His plan, which is to accept the unique alternative to redemption through forgiveness of one's sins. This therapeutic model is not self-centered; it is rather a remedy to human suffering and uncertainty about tomorrow. Moses, as well as Jesus Christ, set before humanity the implications of their choice to obey the law of God. Moses as well as Christ demonstrated that "a religion is a way of life, not just a set of beliefs."

An analysis of ten suggestive points of an article, "Live a Life in Balance" reveals the difference between traditional and spiritual counseling. The outline of this article includes: (1)-Cultivate an attitude of gratitude (2)- Choose to be happy, (3)- Be proactive, (4)- Smile, (5)- Laugh, (6)- Play, (7)- Practice healthy habits, (8)- Be giving, (9)- Be forgiving, (10)- Have faith. Tara Marie Segundo backed up her "15 steps to getting the life you deserve" with a "favorite quote" from George Eliot: "It's never too late to be what you might have been," (Best Body. May, June 2006 p.36). This article carries a missing piece of the puzzle. What we notice here is a decline of gratefulness to the Creator. I point this out simply to show how reasonable recommendations and suggestions may discard the spiritual needs of human beings. One may have one or several significant reasons or desire to achieve personal goals and adopt a different way of life. However, there is one genuine and reliable spiritual cure – acceptance and devotion to God.

Speaking from the standpoint of traditional counseling, Tara M. Segundo advised to "Live the life that you want, and don't make apologies." I would not say that living life with no intent of apology is evil, but I would say that such a way of indulging in pleasurable activities is not spiritually safe and uplifting. Jesus Christ did not have a moment in life that He decided to live the life He desired. As such, His lifestyle confirmed His statement, "I am in the Father, the Father in me" (Jn 14:11). C. Stephen Layman (2007) argued, "A perfectly good God would be opposed to evil and would want to eliminate it. An almighty God would be able to eliminate every instance of evil (p.178). Layman concluded, "We can freely choose to devote ourselves to God only if we have a significant reason and/or desire to adopt a different way of life" (180).

Realistically, the goal of living a "life in balance" is not achievable in self-sufficiency. This type of spirituality is inclined to the belief that one can do all things without divine assistance. Our modern era lies also in the fact that we have lost sight of the primary rationale that there are burdens and moments of tribulation in life that are beyond our capability. There is an increased risk of harming self and others. Humans beings need help and love that are divine. Let us pass on the matter of living our lives without a sense of having to apologize for the mistakes or errors committed. There is a type of counseling which fosters self-centeredness by denying the fact that "We forecast what may be good, not only before God but also before man" (2 Cor 8:21). Spiritual counseling prepares the counselees to live worthily with the ability to judge and carefully examine what kind of decision and action may lead to true happiness. Bonnie L. Krneger (in the rubric "Cultivate an attitude of gratitude") states: "Studies tell us daily gratitude exercises result in higher levels of enthusiasm, determination, optimism and happiness," without saying to whom or to what gratitude is due. Under the rubric "Choosing to be happy" the author emphasized: "Every moment of our lives is a choice and every choice we make has a huge ripple effect." What I am strongly suggesting is that gratitude should have a direction. As such, gratitude without direction is meaningless. Gratitude can be taught, it helps to keep a positive perspective to which gratitude is due. For example, a parent who grants ice cream to a child expects to be appreciated when that child say "thank you" to the parent. This fosters a closer bond between the giver and the receiver. In spiritual counseling, we encourage people to be grateful to their Creator, so their spirit will be open to greater enlightenment and spiritual fulfillment.

From a spiritual perspective, the Apostle James declared, "If any of you lacks wisdom, let him ask of God, who gives to us all liberally and without reproach", and that He will daily provide guidance to any person who requests it, and that He will give courage, fortitude, and will power to any person who requests these qualities (James 1: 5-6). Throughout history and even today, Jesus Christ empowers people for the sake of having a spiritually healthy life: "You will receive power when the Holy Spirit has come upon you; and you will be my witnesses" (Acts 1:8).

Empowerment is helpful to those who are in a state of ignorance about their *spiritual deficiency*; it correlates with the fulfillment of one's need for redemption. The second step in benefiting from this fundamental option is the acknowledgement of one's oppression by demonic forces. Jesus provides recovery from sinful deeds that are due to addiction or spiritual captivity. Individuals who are tormented by their wrongdoing and have a desire for repentance may be freed from their spiritual captivity and have a renewal-of-mind experience. It is at this crucial point that spiritual empowerment is of great importance. When Jesus Christ said: "Apart from me you can do nothing," He meant for us to "live a life in balance" – through a sincere and growing relationship with God, our Creator – the only attractive alternative to elevate the ethical standard to the highest level of morality. It is a spiritual provision available to all, especially those who are sincerely driven to improve their spiritual lives. With this type of spiritual counseling, there is an attitude of no-defeating mentality.

The Apostle Paul, whose mind was renewed on the way to Tarsus, was so strongly persuaded by this encounter that he determined to become a counselor after his life-changing experience. This is evidence of divine intervention that led to empowerment. His insight and modeling were evident in his statement: "I can do all things in Christ who strengthens me" (Phil. 4: 13). As a matter of fact, he wrote to the Philippians: "…Brethren, whatever is true, whatever is honorable, whatever is lovely, whatever is gracious, if there is any anything worthy of praise, think about these things. What you have learned and received and heard and seen in me, do; and the God of peace will be with you' (Phil 4:8-9). The Apostle Paul could not make this powerful proclamation on his own.

Dean Ornish, MD in his book *Love and Survival* wrote, "It is our vulnerability that makes us lovable, that allows other people to feel safe enough to open their hearts to us. What we are really looking for is not approval but intimacy, acceptance – which comes from vulnerability not from perfection" (p. 206). As we have seen, Moses and David had to reach a point of vulnerability before having an experience of divine empowerment. In the case of the Apostle Paul, he was chosen by God in a way that he did not expect. He was on a violent course when traveling to Damascus. He was stopped abruptly by the light of God and blinded (Acts 26:14). After this, he became humble and bore the fruit of repentance. This explains a *delusion of self-sufficiency* that could change drastically by God. It is clear that God wants humankind to rely upon Him. God's way of counseling fosters dependence upon His plan of redemption leading one to a life of fulfillment and freedom.

Spiritual counseling clearly offers models that are not boastful of their own spiritual attainment. Given the complexity of religion, the fundamental expectation of spiritual counseling is not to serve one's own interests or doctrine, but rather to "bear fruit that befits repentance" (Mt3:8 LBV). This "fruit of repentance is evidenced by the individuals' disposition to overcome evil. When they do so, they give reverence to the One who has empowered them to think, feel, and decide to do right things; for, "In Him we live and move and have our being" (Acts 17:28). This is what we term as the *divine empowerment adherence*.

There are myriad examples that illustrate how Jesus Christ taught about ways of experiencing a spiritual renaissance. When Christ counsels "not to resist one who is evil. But if any one strikes you on the right cheek, turn to him the other one also..." (Mt 5: 39 LBV)), He knew that humans are free to choose a course of action, but to weigh their planned actions with God's love and fidelity in providing justice. This counsel is similar to what Christ said, "Love your enemy and pray for those who persecute you" (Mt 5: 43). This is an outstanding teaching that compels us to love the ones who previously cursed us, accused us for no reason, hurt and/or harm or killed our loved ones. My personal understanding of this counseling is that "loving one's enemy" without divine empowerment in not achievable. René Descartes, a French philosopher, understood and honestly expressed his viewpoint regarding limitations of human modeling. He established firmly that humans can be erroneous:

> I have no right to complain because God, having put me in the world, has not wished to place me in the ranks of the noblest and most perfect being. I indeed have reason to rejoice because, even if I do not have the power of avoiding error by the ...method, which depends on a clear and evident knowledge of all things about which I can deliberate.

In the course of a divinely oriented counseling, the participants should hold an attitude of repentance for wrongful act – confession of theses acts lead to repentance. As in the ages when penalty for sins was forgiven through offering of bestial sacrifices, John the Apostle counseled: "If we confess our sins [to Him], he is faithful and just to forgive our sins and cleanse us from all righteousness" (through prayer) (1 Jn. 9: 9). This is the therapeutic model that enhances a healthy relationship with God and with our neighbors. It does not reflect the experience of the "Life that we deserve," but rather a quality of life for which we are disqualified – it gives a taste for joy and for eternity. David, after his sinful act, he repented, by exclaiming: "Restore to me the joy of your salvation and grant me a willing spirit to sustain me (Ps 51:12).

The development of *spiritual counseling* coincides with the existence of humankind. This counseling addresses God's love for humanity. God wants us to be aware of our sinful nature and of His sufficient grace. Before Christ came to earth, God communicated with His prophets to relate to people the reality of their serious delusions that cause them the distress of sin. This form of counseling is the most effective and most reliable as evidenced by Christ's promise: "I will be with you everyday, until the end of the world" (Mt 28:20). In John 10 verse 10, Jesus Christ, not only counsels about discerning the good from the evil, the true from the false, but He also prevents us from the t*raps of temptation i*n a way that had never been done before. The solemn responsibility of a spiritual counselor is to counsel others about the "hidden treasure." This notion of "hidden treasure" was introduced by Christ Himself in the following terms: "The kingdom of heaven is like a hidden treasure in a field, when a man finds it he hides it again, and then in his joy he goes and sells all he has and buys that field" (Matt. 13: 44 NIV). This statement helps envision the brand new divine kingdom that will be established in replacement of this despondent worldly system.

As spiritual counselors, it is important to know that all individuals would accept this message that a "brand new kingdom" will replace this vanishing present world. Some may say: "It is God who made the world; I did not believe that He would destroy it," and so on.

The greatest temptation is to diminish the conviction of God and to make void the power of God within spiritual counseling. Common sense believes that "there will be no brand new kingdom" and tends to take Jesus Christ for a fictitious character. This type of situation and others requires the spiritual counselor to claim God's power in assistance through prayer. By doing so, the counselor models submission to God's sovereignty and guidance. When someone prays and asks God to show Himself powerful in time of personal weakness, God answers! The "Spirit of Truth" makes a clear difference between the two forms of counseling. "When the "Spirit of Truth" is absent, there is no moral com- mitment (Jn. 14:17). The idea that the "world hates the light" is embedded in blasphemy against Jesus Christ, and all forms of allegations against the spiritual counselors. As a matter of fact, the world hates those who maintain a truthful belief in the face of ongoing contradiction that causes people to ignore and turn away from their spiritual reality. Individuals who are morally committed always speak and behave in a way that is based on strong principles. This is what leads to an *inevitable confrontation* between those who are committed to principles and standards of good behavior and those who have the least regard for morality. Confrontation here may not result in open offense from are person to another, but rather a subtle tension due to beliefs and values (relative to money, sex, power, for instance) that are not shared.

When the counselor and his or her counselee have distinct views regarding a core belief, the likelihood of confrontation is imminent. People, in general, get frustrated when their philosophy or vision of life is not fully accepted. A response to a manifest reservation to a person's belief system could be: "I've got to stop talking with people who do not share my belief and with people of different religions."

In summary, spiritual counseling differs from traditional counseling in showing the importance of divine guidance through a new-birth experience. A spiritual counselor provides a safe environment for an open and honest communication with the counselee(s) on the effects of trusting God and His promises. The plan of redemption is evidenced by Jesus Christ who has empowered believers to understand the reality of God's care for essential spiritual growth. Once the counselee knows that God is in control of what is going in his or her life, he or she will be receptive to His wonderful plan. Jesus Christ, the ultimate spiritual Counselor teaches three central reasons to claim the *Spirit of truth* from God who is the Creator: 1) Because He is the Creator (of everything in the Heaven and on earth), 2) Because He is the Savior, 3) Because He is the Judge of humankind. A recommendation to true worship comprises the acknowledgment of the undeniable day of worship as stated in the Ten Commandments (Ex. 20: 8:11), which day of worship is not to deny or to assert its "abolishment" (Mat. 5:17). In this context, John, one of Jesus Christ's disciples said: "He who says I 'know Him,' but disobey His commandments, is a liar, and the truth is not in him" (1 Jn. 2: 4).

Modeling in a Marital Relationship

The term *marital modeling* refers to the mutual influence that is taking place in a heterosexual couple. The quality of thoughts, feelings, and behaviors in a relationship of two different-sex partners determines the *spiritual reality of the couple*. By spirituality of the couple we mean mutual understanding, sincere enthusiasm, and moral commitment, or the opposite.

I recall having a conversation with a friend who, a month before his wedding, opened the Bible and jumped on a verse describing "strange women." He felt that this was a message from God. He became ambivalent about his future commitment to get married, because the woman that he chose to marry did not share his same beliefs. My explanation to him was that individuals should commit in marriage to those who share the same faith and belief. Similarly, the Apostle, Paul advised: "Do not abide with strangers under the same roof." Although, the Apostle Paul wrote to the Christians Hebrews about "Not to forget to show hospitality to strangers," (Heb. 13:2), chances are when two different - sex partners are cohabiting, their spiritual disparity causes one to be a "stranger" to the other. What would be the spiritual implications of spiritual disparity in a couple?

There are always "great surprises" in a union of two heterosexual partners who do not share the same value system. It is understandable that in a marriage of individuals who share the same beliefs relationships can still be problematic. Some spiritual indications of a problematic marital union are in extreme change in speech and behaviors of one or the two partners. This includes *spiritual indelicateness* marked by a lack of sensitivity to the feelings of the other partner. Duplicity in speech and behavior is explained by the fact that, at time, a partner may be polite and caring; at other times, this partner may be rude and uncaring. When, for instance, a married person raises concerns such as, "I have a disrespectful wife/husband," it is because of spiritual disparity that exists in the relationship.

A way to consider obstacles to positive modeling is to look at pride involved in a heterosexual marital relationship. The majority of marital issues can remain unresolved due to pride. By definition, a boastful person "speaks with excessive pride about his/her own accomplishments, talents or possessions." It is important to understand how infidelity in marriage (i.e., failure of living with trust, living with will, living fair, and living safe) may compromise the relationship till its ruin. There are three wrongful acts that may cause a partner to feel disappointment in a relationship to a point of contemplating divorce: stealing, cheating, and carelessness. Placed in a context of spiritual disparity, it can be the case where a partner discloses his/her sexual infidelity to the other partner, which disclosure may engender a brutally shocking reaction by the hearer.

The partner who openly admits his/her defeat in one or several areas of life (living with trust, living with will, living fair and living safe) may do so due to remorse that is derived from his/her fear of divine reprisal. Due to fear of rejection, this partner earnestly unveils his wrongness and, desperately begs for forgiveness and longs for reconciliation. If the partner to whom confession is made is boastfully insensitive, the likelihood for reconciliation to take place is least. Emotional outbreak or scolding due to remorse of the wrongdoer will do little to cure the situation. The resented partner would reprove sharply and is prone to abandon the relationship. As he or she is spiritually incapable to care for and accept love from the other partner, under many circumstances, he or she may allude to the wrongness of his or her partner.

The cheater or stealer who is sincere and eager for being forgiven and seeks to safeguard his/her marital union is modeling love. The prideful partner who is unconcerned about his/her partner's insistent quest for forgiveness and safeguard of the relationship is said to be cynical. A cynical person is, basically, "scornful of the motives or virtue of others." This irreconcilable partner is, there- fore, not positively modeling commitment to marriage vow.

Beside breach of trust involved in stealing and cheating, another aspect regarding failure of marital modeling that one needs to look at is the effects of expectations carried into marriage. Often, individuals get married with a variety of wishes and goals that cannot either be achieved or are merely impracticable. Expectations prior to marital union predict the severity of a *crisis of expectation*. As we demonstrated, a faithful partner feels betrayed due to sexual infidelity on the part of the other partner. Such unfortunate event that brings con- fusion, worry and panic is likely to create serious disappointment in the faithful partner to a point of losing the meaning and purpose of his marital commitment. Disappointment that engenders confusion, worry and panic may become irresolvable and develop into a crisis of expectation, which is a chronic spiritual disturbance (CSD).

Infidelity in a marital relationship is an intolerable sin. A partner's complaints according to which "I would never, ever thought that my husband/wife would cheat on me" followed by various sorts of reactions (act of condemnation, aggression, and/or of indifference) are evidence of disappointment. The act of cheating, in this case, fails to meet the complainer's expectation of having a sexually committed partner. Regardless, the fact that an individual is jealous or not, "kissing another person" when one is in an intimate relationship can be worrisome to the other partner witnessing the act (eye witness or thru video clips). From the Cosmopolitan magazine (Aug. 2004) we quote:

> "As long as you're in an intimate relationship, no matter the level of inti-macy, kissing another person is infidelity. The best way to make that call is to ask yourself if you would be hurt by the same actions (By May, 28). Another commenter said: "If you make a commitment to someone, you shouldn't want to do anything romantic with anyone else. That just shows a lack of respect for your partner" (By Natasha, 19).
> And the third comment is that: "Doing something that could affect the health of your boyfriend is just wrong. You could easily bring home something like herpes after swapping spit with a stranger" (Sarah, 26).

We demonstrated that an effective marital modeling is a free-hurt relationship. Positive marital modeling that we have stressed is embedded in the concepts of living with trust, living with will, living fair, and living safe between two heterosexual partners. When a partner fails in one of these areas of life, the likelihood for a marital relationship to be troubled is obvious. The safety issue resulting from cheating on one's partner is evident in sexually transmitted diseases (STDs), namely AIDS that have killed millions of people every year. The infidel person has disturbed feelings associated with confusion, worry, and panic. The betrayed partner loses the meaning and purpose of his commitment to a point of being chronically spiritual disturbed. In both cases, positive modeling cannot take place. Jack Alexander argued, "The key part of integrity is not only trying to do the right thing, but also having the humility to admit when you mess up." Due to a breach of trust, the "betrayed" partner may undergo a crisis of expectation that may bring feelings of resent-ment causing him/her to remain unmoved to the partner's confession of wrongness and longing for reconciliation.

Chapter Eight

ASSESSING UNCOMFORTABLE AND DISTURBING FEELINGS TO SPIRITUAL COUNSELING

Human emotions have spiritual functions and results that can positively or negatively impact the individual's existence. The quality of a spiritual life is associated with the nature, strength, and duration of individuals' feelings. Feelings that are uncomfortable can not only negatively impact the individuals' personal life; they can also impair and destroy their relationship with God and other people as they deteriorate their disposition to benefit from other people's care, love and counsel. At a time when deteriorating interpersonal relationships are construed as a serious threat to family and society at large, let us put in focus the spiritual effects of resentment, jealousy, guilt, and dejection which can pose resistance to counseling. We will explore effective counseling to people who suffer like spiritual disturbances.

Feeling of resentment in focus

A fearful experience may be so intense that the emotional impact may result in a chronic spiritual disturbance (CSD). Resentment is an uncomfortable, strong, and long- lasting feeling. This could be the case of someone who is disappointed in a relationship or a system (religious, political, or administrative) resulting in alienation with the other person or the system to a point of developing a grudged feeling.

The duration and strength of this feeling is what makes it different from a mere feeling of dislike. The "original pain" serves as the background for the speakers' complaints and concerns - making the person vulnerable and weak to a point of continuing life against logic.

Resentment like the other feelings gives a choice of alternatives. These individuals persist in thinking, speaking and doing things even when they are contrary to their best interests. Someone who resents may say: "I know if I have to survive, I simply have to steel myself against such a traitor or such traitors." This catastrophizing idea was no doubt a sign of extreme worry. More than anyone else, these individuals expect their complaints, expressed concerns, and opinions about the identified traitors(s), to be valued and highly respected.

No feeling can be more irreversibly strong than resentment. The question is how can normality be returned to life of someone who has resented for a long time? This feeling generates a dogma that rests on innocence, integrity, veracity, and justice. It is the sense that they want to have everything under control and that nobody can persuade them to strive for impossible goals. Individuals with this chronic spiritual disturbance can easily distrust anyone who find it hard to accept the rationale for their discontent and indignation - which underlies their obstinacy. Their dogma (a belief that is held unquestionably and with absolute certainty) about being "treated in ways that they do not deserve" is the basis of their distress and resistance to being counseled; when someone is telling them, for instance: "Your offender(s)'s behavior is excusable." To this they may angrily react or simply invoke silence. They may also reply, "Are you telling me somebody who commits such a serious offense deserves to be forgiven!" A typical response can be: "Your point is absurd, and I don't think it is worth my attention." Sarcastically, they may reply, "Your point is so trivial that I don't know whether to be angry or to laugh." The central need of a person who is full of resentment is to persuade self and others about the veracity of their claims. They are driven by the conviction of being "right" which urges them to persevere in the defense of their rights. In dealing with the idiosyncrasy of this spiritual personage, there are some techniques that can help individuals with resentment.

Feelings of resentment are evidence of an unexpected event that throws individuals and their world views into a state of total confusion. A retroflexion of their "bad luck" is often introduced by "I would ever think this would have happened to me". This pattern of thoughts is the spiritual basis of a straightforward feeling, which is resentment. Their inability to think and feel otherwise confirms this crisis. Spiritually speaking, any unexpected life event can be the source for a crisis of expectation. A person may consider a dif- ference of opinion (about politics, religion...) to be a means of improvement by stating for instance, "Given the challenge that I endured, I vow to become a more persuasive speaker." Another person may perceive the same intervention as the most provocative and insulting, which may cause him or her to interpret the criticism as an insidious or a "diabolic" attempt to derogate from his or her own influence and prestige;, which is for him or her intolerable. This individual may develop a feeling of repugnance toward the intervener. Drastic changes may occur in this person's life in conjunction with correlates his (*taedium feeling* from Greek bitterness) that may evolve into a *charam feeling*, which inspires violence. The resentful individual may become foolishly bold or recklessly daring to a point of harming his opponent(s). Wishful death of the offender(s) may be lived in secret and, eventually become a public matter. The majority of their responses reflect their fear of vulnerability. When in a conversation, for instance, the name of the offender is mentioned, is not surprising to hear them reply: "Does this person exist?" Basically, what they mean is that "I wish he, she, or they were dead." In a simplistic way, they mean: "Life for me would be better and safer if these persecutors existence ceases."

Along with the avalanche of false accusations, defame, lies, and silence of complicit, a significantly spiritual outcome of a long-lasting resentment is cruel intentions. These and other like statements infer that the life of someone who is resented can be critically affected by cruel intentions. Cruel intentions are evident when the resented person starts being dependent on the non-existence of the identified "enemy" or "enemies," which may be powerful enough to lead to hostility.

Thoughts that derive from resentment reveal the two most important characteristics of a cruel intention: *the prediction of evil* and *the wish for evil* to one's offenders, which is for some is an "exclusive mission." Individuals who have cruel intentions are strongly persuaded that the other party deserves censure and they may impulsively harass and/or launch attacks to injure them. Sex, which is a common way of showing affection, may become for a resented person a powerful means to express anger and hostility toward the reproved sexual partner. The resentful dependency on the non-existence of their offender(s) may prevent them from expressing natural sympathy. When, for instance, the resentful person senses the need to sympathize with the afflicted person (who was a friend, a co-worker, or family member) who hurt them, they may do so in a superficial manner.

Their suspicion that somebody is in the business of forcing forgiveness on them may result in the rapport with this person being overwhelming and aimless, simply because they may stop seeing in this individual someone who is promoting their best interest. They may be so disappointed with counseling that they may no longer continue with the helping process. One should keep in mind that the need for caution and delimitation can be expressed in various ways. As a matter of course, they may perceive their counselors as "traitors."

Tentative Techniques for Counseling Individuals with Feelings of Resentment

Desmond Tutu (2007) declared, "A time of crisis is not just a time of anxiety and worry.

It gives a chance, an opportunity, to choose well or to choose badly" (p. 25). It takes a great deal of consideration and patience to persuade someone with feelings of resentment about going back to normality of life by revisiting their thinking patterns and decisions.

Active listening and reflection of feeling: Due to persistent "indignation," the resented person is not looking for someone to reason with them, but to naively give credence to the rationale of his or her feelings. One of the major concerns often reported by someone who has a grudge issue is: "People don't listen to what I am telling them," or "They do not believe me." After listening to their grievance, a counselor can show consideration to their pain by saying, for instance: "You are telling me that you are feeling betrayed because of the level of trust that you invested in a friendship with. . . .(the name of the person/group of people), and right now you are seriously concerned about continuing with that relationship. Is that right?"

Being perseverant: To persevere is "to continue in a given course in spite of difficulties and obstacles."

Given that resentment is a long-lasting and enduring feeling, one should commit with patience to counseling individuals in this spiritual condition. It is crucially important for counselors to know that they should not rush people to take action by changing the way they are feeling. Without a spiritual readiness, the unthinkable will remain unthinkable, and the unlovable will still be disgusting. Expectation, in counseling someone with resentment issues is something powerful. A counselor, in this context, may be tempted to do and say things in order to prepare the counselee to feel differently. The counselor may do something to make the counselee's life better and persevere in attendance, such as being there for them and listening to meaningful complaints and concerns. This means that the counselor (he or she) when facing firm resistance or when confronted with the derogatory, will remain focused and perseverant in counseling.

This technique of persevering in spiritual counseling will not allow this particular counselee to remain a passive victim, but rather it will help the counselor assess exaggerated opinions and stigmatization of the individual or group of individuals held by the counselee. What these counselees may find especially meaningful is the way their counselors are able to relate to their complaints and concerns. Because of this they may find it stimulating to share more and more about their feelings of resentment. Without reaching the appropriate time for suggesting (internal and external) in regards to the devilish actions of their "betrayer(s)," any such suggestion may be viewed as a violation of their "intrinsic rights." A reaction to this rushing initiative is when they say, for instance: "I hate when people cannot understand me!"

In regards to getting significant cues about the emotional readiness of a resentful person about any proposal of "forgiving one's debtor," there are three spiritual parameters to consider: 1) the counselee begins to enjoy counseling; 2) the counselee is paying attention to the counselor when speaking, 3) He or she stops seeing the helper as a critic.

When the counselee is found spiritually ready, help him or her explore the specifics of forgiving: By focusing on the facts of the speaker's life, it may become possible to grasp his or interest, ambitions, goals and needs. Skillfully, one would be able to start to define some priorities that would actually ease their perception of the "identified betrayer." The goal of collaborating in the process of changing the complainer's negative perception into a more positive one is to convey understanding and sympathy regarding the potentially devastating effects of their disappointment. One may start saying, "It is terrible what you went through, I really feel sorry about what happened to you," and then add, "I understand that this person deserves retribution. Is that what you're thinking?"

It is almost impossible, in a culture that constantly makes 'punishment of one's debtors" a rule of thumb, to instantly change the perception of someone with grudged feelings. Counselors should continue investing time in listening and be attuned with the hurtful feelings before embarking on the process of telling them "what is good about forgiving." Attempt to evaluate the counselees' disposition to explore this fascinating concept of friendship by asking the counselee to talk about sensations they experienced when things went well with the "infidel." This technique of retrospection may be found to be intriguing and could be refuted by the counselee. A possible reaction to this invitation is: "Please, I don't want this betrayer."

When evaluating the readiness of someone with resentment for forgiveness, one of the best ways to reduce the risk of being cast off is to incorporate the concept of forgiveness in an atmosphere that is safe and familiar. The counselor may take the approach of getting the counselee to imagine what changes he or she would like to see in "the betrayer." A good try may be: "I don't want to make you feel uncomfortable by asking you if you want to be in touch with this 'betrayer' again, my question is: Are you sure that this person can change?" The following question does not contradict the generally accepted fact that individuals who resent others tend to have a predominant fear of recurrent mistakes. To convey awareness of this fear, and to evaluate their readiness to forgive, the counselor may ask whether it is a good idea to stay away from the "dangerous person" and pray for him or her. The question related to this approach is: "What is your opinion about the speech on 'praying for those who persecute you'" (Mat. 5:44). Again, remember this biblical recommendation may serve to irritate if the person is not spiritually ready. One of the smoothest responses that one may get is: "Now, you are talking about religion, aren't you?" Following this response, the counselor may ask, "Do you think that only God can forgive?" If the answer to this question is positive (i..e,"Yes I believe so"), the spiritual counselor may invite the person to explore forgiveness through a different perspective, meaning through God's perspective.

Processing the Internal Conflict of doing God's Will and the Urge for not Letting go: In so far, we have seen how individuals' feelings of resentment can prevent them from seeing the truth to live a much fuller life. A very significant way to assess their need for God's intervention is to ask how they manage to survive when thinking of all the evil that happened to them. The way to redirect these counselees' attention away from their pain is by letting them see the necessity to learn a new language - the language of love. The fact is, with grudged feelings, people image "There is no such things as loving an evildoer!" A way that they corroborate this reality is by saying: "I am not God!" As such, the idea of loving may be a sudden bad news. The idea is to lead them from a victimization mentality (that prevents them from taking any positive action) to being a survivor's mentality that will empower them to believe in the supernatural intervention for forgiving their debtor's iniquities.

A survivor's decision is clever and calculating in that it enhances the awareness that the desired change may never happen unless they give up their pain and sorrow to God's care. If the counselee shows interest in the word of God, one may teach them the importance of building a relationship with God by saying, "When a crisis arises we have to find out what God's will is. The greatest part of this life is not only the conscious aspect of it but the maintenance of this relationship."

Emphasis of the meaning of forgiveness: It is right, and it is fitting in counseling that individuals' feelings be recognized for what they are and correctly appreciated. This involves knowing when they are comfortable and uncomfortable. The rationale of getting an exact meaning of "forgiveness" is that the urge for retributive punishment that stems from feelings of resentment coincides with a crisis of expectation. In order to help recover from this uncomfortable feeling, the individual need to understand the error of his ways when it comes to trusting people.

Because of breach of trust, many individuals express a desire to forgive but not to reconcile with their offender(s). The background feeling motivates them to an idealistic goal set of being at peace with their conscience by total forgiveness. Spiritually speaking, there is no possibility of reconciliation without total forgiveness. Individuals who are spiritually incompetent to earnestly forgive their offender(s) have argumentative speech about their partial forgiveness, which they perceive as balanced and sincere. They often brag about their "high-rank spirituality" by "forgiving Mr. /Mrs. so and so despite long-suffering of their harm." At this point, one may seek to uncover the true meaning of "forgiving" by asking: "What can you do that would convince your offender(s) that you have forgiven him/her/them?"

Forgiving, literally, means "to pass over an offense and to free the offender from the consequence of it (*The American Heritage Dictionary*)." When talking about physical and emotional effects of forgiving, Rick Agrasci, M.D. explained: "When you forgive someone you feel warm and more relaxed, you sigh and breath more easily, you heart feels warm and melty, your blood pressure and heart rate drop, you may even cry." Most importantly, Dr. Agrasci said, "Through forgiveness you once again experience the love that is the essence of your relationship (New Age Journal). This last sentence underscores the spiritual aim of forgiving that the Christians learn and endorse.

When the problem of abuse is raised, the spiritual counselor does not confront the speaker's true feelings, but shows empathy and sympathy by saying: "I understand how painful it is for you to suffer all this." If partial forgiveness sounds perfect, the following question can be asked: "Do you think, some day, you will be able to have a frank conversation with this person about how you have felt about what he or she did to you and what you would like to see change?

Putting-under-God's care counseling: When a counselee realizes that there is no better alternative to a life-changing experience than surrendering to God. The spiritual counselor may reinforce this truth of life by saying: "No man knows the truth, nor will there be a man who has knowledge about how another human being thinks and feels. For, even if he were to hit by chance upon the whole truth, he himself would not be aware of having done so, but each forms his own opinion." The aim of reading this to the counselee(s) is to make known that "the truth itself is known only to God who sees all over, thinks all over, hears all over, and whose knowledge is absolute." Another way to stimulate the counselee's choice to decide in favor of the recommendation of "forgiving one's debtors" is to ask for comment on the biblical verse: "We must obey God rather than men (Acts 5:29)." This passage has a causal explanation, and even which through people may be well-meaning, that still have no spiritual power to make the desired change happen. Nevertheless the counselor should rely on the counseling model that consists of *putting the counselee under God's care*.

The counselor ought to give his counselee enough time to prepare what we call an *outstanding date with God*. At time, the counselor's recommendation of God's guidance may appear superficial and stupid. One may have counselees who do not, apparently, understand the importance of looking at God's assistance in difficult times. For someone who heard about God (by going to church when he or she was a child) and knows where the real power lies, he or she may desire and seek after God's regenerating power with uncomfortable feelings. These individuals are more likely to testify that, "I lived my life doing what I wanted. Right now, I am willing to give in to God my sorrow and my pain." The reality is that this person may start seeing his problem of grudged feelings characterized by incapacity of being receptive to other's consideration and of loving from God's perspective. This may conclude, "Only God can change the way I am feeling." This shared information is pertinent to steer the speaker in the right direction – doing the will of God.

The counselor should also reassure the counselee about the wisdom of his decision by saying: Forgiving for the sake of God consists of giving someone a gift with no regrets, a gift that this person does not deserve. The counselor's words of encouragement could be: "As you begin to show kindness to others without exception, you will be set free from feeling of disappointment. You yourself will be empowered by the Holy Spirit to show more kindness, more often." The counselor may ask the counselee to repeat the following prayer:

Father God,

Forgive me for all the times I tried to do things on my own. Forgive me for not trusting you to take my burdens from me and place them under your care. You have been giving me countless opportunities to demonstrate how I rely on you. Today, I need your help more than ever. Send me the Holy Spirit to fill my heart with unconditional love and courage to forgive all my debtors. Lord, help me to keep my eyes on you as I am forgiving. . . . .(the name of the person).. Show me how to increase my trust in you for the outcome. Give me the wisdom to believe in your omniscient ways to defeat my future enemies. In the name of Jesus I pray you.

A Spiritual Exercise toward Total Forgiveness: Carrie Boom's popular statement was biblically inspired: "You are never as free as when you forget your enemies." Given that a spontaneous switch from an uncomfortable to a conformable feeling is spiritually unfavorable, individuals who resent should, go through the spiritual process of *resumption*, and *restoration*. The role of the spiritual counselor in this exercise is to encourage the counselee toward: (1) Awareness of their uncomfortable feeling, (2) Understanding the effects of this particular feeling in their overall life, (3) Facilitate the desire to relinquish the uncomfortable feeling, and (4) Decide the most appropriate alternative that will make the desired change happen.

Once the counselees' perception of the offender(s) or evildoer(s) has been improved, evidence of resumption is seen in a clear desire to look for an intermediary toward restoration of heir broken relationship. To process a desire for change expressed by the counselee, the counselor can elaborate in the following terms: I remember that you used to take everything that was said to you as nothing but criticism and contempt. Now, it seems to me that you are willing to be a different person. What have you learned for the past two weeks that has inspired you to change the way you see people who harmed you? The concept of restoration refers to the spiritual renovation that occurs in an individual's emotion - changing from resentment and an uncomfortable feeling, to a conformable feeling i.e., love. One may recall that "One's overall emotional responses were based on one's disappointment and horrible pain that led one to a very significant fear of being victimized again. You may have been reluctant to trust anyone who did not go through your painful experience. Now, however, you want to go from an antagonistic perspective of the "betrayer" to a more mer- ciful relationship. Is that correct?

Counseling for "Forgiving one's abuser" from a Christian perspective

Those who were physically or sexually abused and have not recovered from their abuse may become resentful toward their abuser(s). As we saw, resentment or grudge locks every alternative for recovery out, including the counselor. The reasons for not forgiving are deeply human and may be irreversible. Let us take a few examples that cause individuals not to forgive their "abusers": a person who murdered someone's child; or someone who steals the complainer's wife and finally ends up in abject loneliness are all examples. Other examples include individuals who are smeared and whose reputations are shattered by extensive and spiteful lies.

The spiritual principle of *forgiving one's abusers* is to be taken as beneficial in regards to the spiritual outcome of being at peace with self (living safe). Before this happens, individuals are fixated by the idea of revenge and, therefore are spiritually unreceptive to a sound alternative. `Such persons are easily irritated when they do not get what they desire - reprisal. Given that such people are often annoyed, and feel misunderstood by the counselor that runs contrary to their need for revenge, the role of the spiritual counselor is to effectively communicate an understanding of their *underlying message* of revenging the abuser by saying: "What I hear you saying is that you have no power to get back into this relationship and there is nothing that you can do trust this person again. Is that right?" Spiritual counselors have to keep in mind that the primary need of an abused person is

to feel safe. I have counseled under certain circumstances individuals, who stated that they would do everything in their power to set up a trap for their foe, to cause them to lead a life on edge. I, also, counseled individuals who felt severely persecuted based on suspicion of eventual future attacks by their enemies. These two examples corroborate the fact that, the abuser, as well as the victim of abuse falls short of peace within. The guilt of the abuser and the disappointment of the abused often have constraining influence in seeking peace of mind.

When an abused person is trusting to another's advice or spiritual orientation, we must recognize and process his or her craving for justice. Confronting the victim's feelings may be interpreted as a lack of justice. Christians however, assimilate the concept of "Perfect justice," which constrains them to seek God's forgiveness. Granley Morris is the tenet of this concept; here is his explanation: "Perfect justice means I shouldn't suffer punishment for someone else's sins because anything I suffered would be what I deserve for my own sin" (Forgive us our sins. p. 1). The common practice of punishing someone for his misdeed is grounded in moral judgment exercised in deliberations. For the majority of people the person who is punished is generally understood to be for the wrongness done. This rationale that governs punishment of all kinds of misdeeds contrasts with the authentic Christian's perspective.

When helping a victim of either physical and/or sexual abuse, counselors should engage the victim in critical thinking in which freedom and causality are reconciled. They should expect, on the part of their counselee, an incompatibility between their perception of God and their want of internal relief. A typical perception of God is expressed in a grievance such as, "It's not fair that God asks me to forgive such a horrible act!" Following this objec- tion, the spiritual counselor may say, "You recall how much you cared about this person, which may be the reason why his/her behavior hurt you so much in the first place!" At this particular point, the profoundness of God's love is to be explored by the victims of abuse. The spiritual counselor needs to bring the victim of abuse to an understanding that our sin led to Christ's humiliation and death, and yet He unconditionally loves every one of us. We are, of course, concerned to make them know about the cruelty of Christ's abusers by stating: the Son of God was slandered, shredded by instruments of torture, reduced to an object of shame, publicly humiliated, robbed of every speck of decency for our sins and still loved His abusers. Granley Morris, who is a spiritual counselor, argued, "The dif- ference is 60,000,000%! Like me, you are unable to imagine how your sin against God is so many times worse than your abuser's sin against you, but you can accept it as fact" (*Forgive us our Sins*. p. 2).

Living fair in the context of Christian redemption entails forgiving others' offenses in regard to God's demonstration of forgiveness. Christians accept that none of us is worthy of forgiveness, but by grace our penalties have been forgiven (Rom 3:24; Eph 2:8). Once this reality of a *gracious God* is grasped, the counselee will take delight in knowing that God is in the business of taking care of all victims of abuse. The victim's expectation may change by realizing that the purpose of forgiving people is not solely to force them into mending their ways, but to model love in light of Christ's teaching. Spiritual counselors can process counselees' desire to overcome trespasses by pronouncing a word of blessing as quoted, "May our Lord Jesus Christ himself, and God our Father, who loved us and gave us eternal comfort and good hope through grace, comfort your hearts and establish them in every good work and word (2 Thes. 2:16).

Many believers and non-believers know either the entire or an extract of the Lord's Prayer: "Forgive us as we forgive our debtors..." The meaning behind this prayer is that we are not forgiven until we consent to forgive our offenders or abusers. Believers must understand that forgiveness is a condition of being on good terms with God who promises forgiveness in return. This causal condition for "forgiving one's debtors" is completely essential to the process of (1) changing perception of the abuser, (2) forgiving the abuse, (3) and gradually forgetting the wrongful act. It is humanly hard to forget a willful misdeed, but the idea that "a rational being is capable of understanding the error of his ways is punished" may help in forgiving the evil doer. The Christian perspective of forgiving one's abuser can spiritually empower the abused person to overcome rancor. This motive to forgive is clear and effective in numerous testimonies. The spiritual counselors can encourage their voluntary choice to forgive their debtor(s), which particular choice is capitalized upon enhancing a spiritual breakthrough. As the counselee begin to show kindness to his offender, he or she will be set free from feelings of under the burden of grudge. It is helpful to let this person know that "By this choice of letting go, you will find yourself being empowered by the Holy Spirit to show kindness more often."

Here are the steps in helping individuals experience total forgiveness; in order to get over a serious mistake on the part of someone that was trusted. The counseling process leading to this spiritual growth stands for BATES:

(a) Believing that we all can make mistakes.
(b) Acknowledging the differences in individuals' worldview.

(c) Testifying about the positive spiritual effects of forgiving in the life of the ones who forgive including oneself.
(d) Expressing that forgiving one's offender in a free-choice to allow God's powerful intervention to change the way one feels.
(e) Stressing how other people are delighted when one's broken friendship or love is restored.

An example of Immediate Spiritual Counseling an Individual with Feelings of Resentment

On a Friday night, I met with a young man who had been married for three years and we were conversing about his trust in God. He said to me: "I remember when you told me earlier that God whom you committed to has not changed." On that night, I invited him to sit in my car so we could talk more. He started telling me how his relationship with his wife had deteriorated. The first thing he told me was "I am lonely." Then, he proceeded to describe to me what kind of treatment he had received from his wife that he loved so much. On some occasions, his wife hid his keys, and he had no way out to talk with somebody. That same night, he said, his child brought him the keys and felt delighted to have a chance to talk with me. According to him, his wife's primary expectation was for him to turn over his paycheck every week. His greatest disappointment was related to his wife's threat not to have sex with him any longer unless he agreed to give her his full paycheck. He felt so betrayed and afflicted that he could not help cursing his existence. As a matter of fact, he said, "My life has no meaning."

During the entire conversation he kept on telling me how he sincerely loved his beautiful and well-bred wife with whom he has two beautiful children; and yet she behaved as a prostitute. He was irritated to such an extent that he declared, as he jumped out of my car that, "I will kill myself," or "my wife." Immediately, I understood that his life was threat- ened. I drove to the backyard, as I parked the car, I asked him to open his car window and asked him to continue the conversation because I did not like the abrupt way he ended the conversation. Based on his own words, I could see how much he loved his wife. I told him that God had a plan for each of His believers, and that he was not going to defeat God's plan. I also told him, "Suppose you met someone who went through all kinds of turmoil, and by the grace of God has overcome it, what would you say?" Then he told me that he did not intend to divorce his wife, even though he felt deceived by her behavior – acting like a prostitute. I said then, "You love your wife, at the same time it is painful to deal with her expectation of having sex with you on the basis on a paycheck. How do you think you might solve this problem?" He said, "If I give in she would let everybody know that she had bested." I added there is another problem: you don't want people to know your weak- ness, and yet you say you love your wife and your family. How often do you pray? I am urging you to be thankful to God that he has given you the understanding of how things are supposed to be in a marital relationship. Because of this knowledge and understanding neither suicide nor homicide conforms to God's way. You will be lost if you even think of doing such evil to yourself. I urge you to knock at God's door and ask Him for strength and endurance. So much so that I will pray for you, and call you since I have your phone number."

Jealousy in focus - *Understanding the spiritual nature of jealousy and how this feeling impacts the individuals' spiritual life*

I know a 25 year-old male co-worker who was overwhelmed by feelings of jealousy. On a Sunday morning he went to a Christian church, and at sunset he knocked at his fiancée's door and entered her house and horribly stabbed her. He was condemned to life in prison. The answer as to why he went to church before he committed the crime remains unanswered. The Bible gives a powerful illustration of jealousy. In the Song of Solomon jealousy is described as "cruel as the grave: the coals thereof are coals of fire" (chap: 8:6).

Jealousy is an irresistible feeling and demeans our coping strategies. Spiritually speaking, it is the need for connection that is met in a very frightening way. Therefore, when jealousy overtakes love a great imbalance exists between the fear of rejection and the need for connection. Jealousy, as such, can lead to malicious talk and evil motives. I read a story of a man who was so jealous of his girlfriend that his existence became dependent on her. His reactions consisted of going crazy about every "little thing," his girlfriend reported. He expressed his disappointment by hitting his head against the wall, or swerving the car at high speed around the city, and even threatening to kill himself. An indication of how deeply jealousy rendered him vulnerable was that when his girlfriend told him that she was going to leave him, his response was: "I am going to die and it will be all your fault." It turns out that jealousy can so strongly impact an individual's self-confidence that his life and soul will be in jeopardy. His fear of rejection caused him to call his girlfriend "horrible names" and told her "the whole world hates her." In addition, he pretended to be sick without explaining to his girlfriend what the problem was. It is obvious that he had been using his 'sickness' as an excuse to gain attention and affection from his girlfriend. In point of fact, he did not want to have x-rays for he thought they would cause him more health problems.

As do other types of feelings, jealousy closes the jealous mind to advice and wise counseling. The jealous are not spiritually ready to consider how their interlocutors feel and think. The lady in that story was eager to help her boyfriend solve his health problems and reported her unsuccessful attempts to help him: "I love him so much, but he refuses any kind of help or ideas to improve things to the point where bringing them up just start more arguments. " On the internet forum she asked "What can I do to help him get healthy and stop this madness?

First, let us understand jealousy from the spiritual perspective of the human need for connection. There is a correlation between jealousy and consciousness. One of the major negative influences of jealousy in people is that it makes them unconcerned with others' problems. This reflects the fact that the reasoning ability of a jealous person is not guided by their True Conscience. They speak and act beyond what is reasonable and just. In a sense their judgment and accusations of their "betrayer" are stereotyped.

In interpersonal relationships, jealousy is an uncomfortable feeling that brings about inadequate self-confidence. In regards to this spiritual condition, the jealous person may develop cruel intentions in relation to their deception. Due to the predominant fear of being rejected by the other partner the jealous becomes very protective and emotionally fragile. As the notion of living a trusting and fair existence with others is lost, they may unconsciously harm the partner perceived as a "betrayer." The most important disturbing experience is the loss of the one they love. As such, this loss is the primary source of an inadequate self-confidence. This makes a jealous person prone to suspect they have a rival. People who are jealous live a life of debt, meaning they are short of trust and safety. Their reflection pattern may beget a number of the related physical manifestations: difficulty falling asleep, daytime sleepiness and headaches. At time, the rewards of feelings pride and self-love may bring them to an intended act of cruelty without having any guilt.

Like the lady in the story above, who affirmed that her boyfriend got "crazy about every little thing," Nicole's experience did not differ much. Nicole told the story of how her "boyfriend tried to kill her." Nicole who met Joe the in summer explained why, because of her boyfriend's jealousy, she couldn't spend time with her family and friends. "I started losing my friends because I never saw them anymore. He said if I went out with them that meant I didn't love him," she explained. She also complained about "spending so much time doing Joe's home work," which caused her to pass from an A student to failing. She also reported multiple physical assaults by her boyfriend, Joe who strove to make her believe the unbelievable. Here is what she said: "I remember one exercise was to discuss how our boyfriends talked to us. I explained how Joe said that if he didn't love me he wouldn't hit me" (Teen Magazine. Spring, 2007. p.102 & 103). This evidences that the jealous are eager for others' attention and consideration. In order to profit from such atten- tion the jealous may become mindlessly violent.

This blundering fear of rejection negatively impacts the jealous' normal spiritual life - it renders life intense and disturbing. This fear gives way to response that is unconscionable, meaning behaviors are actions that "are not restrained by conscience." This is the reason the jealous' fear of rejection causes a *utopia of ownership* in that he or she may violently react when they realize they are losing control over the relationship. Analogically, a jealous person is compared with a Roman soldier who is deprived of his shield (which his passionate love); he ends up suspecting his girlfriend who has caused distress.

In the next paragraphs we consider some aspects of spiritual counseling for a jealous person, in reference the above examples.

Counseling a Jealous Person

A jealous person considers himself or herself betrayed. "Feeling betrayed," as expressed by someone, is the most relevant component to an impending crisis. Therefore, the individual who is likely to spiritually advise a "betrayed person" is the "traitor." The question is how and when?

It is a challenge described in the Bible as follows: "Wrath is cruel and anger is overwhelming: but who is able to stand before jealousy." Does it mean that there is no way to be helpful to a jealous person? For the purpose of finding efficient spiritual techniques to counsel a jealous person, let us now consider why that person is spiritually threatened. The major problem of jealousy is in the automatic response. In other words, jealousy always triggers anger, which gives way to emotionally driven impulses. The jealous cannot avoid spontaneous reactions such as blaming, yelling, and hitting. They are unable to restrain their emotions and talk calmly, like telling the truth with love. In a love relationship, it is inappropriate and insulting to say to a jealous partner: "Don't be jealous," or "There is no reason to get jealous." These words would aggravate them.

The individual with a grudge whom you are committed to help is not always capable of giving a clear description of what causes him to feel guilty. One must remember that behind jealousy there is an unmet need, which is the need for connection and a deep fear of rejection. The jealous person who strives for connection needs first to be reassured that he or she is not an "unwanted person." Therefore, when a jealous person weeps, the tears have a double meaning: "I do not want you to forsake me," and "I want you to assure me that you are not forsaking me for another 'person'" (of the opposite sex). This pattern of thought suggests the individual falls short of his aspirations, which is to do always the right things in order to keep a healthy rapport with other people.

The jealous may lose their spiritual capability of managing their shame over negative events of the past and get involved in mindless acts. Suppose a lady left her boyfriend alone to go dancing with another man, the boyfriend might feel ashamed by ruminating end- lessly: "I shouldn't have been alone at that time of night." He becomes violent toward the person who caused him such overwhelming loneliness. This is a typical interpretation that reflects the need for self- preservation, which is referred to as a *survival interpretation*. It does not entail feelings of doing something wrong, as in the case of guilty feelings; rather the person who "betrays" him makes him feel despised, rejected and ashamed.

Here are some ways that the so-called "traitor" can persuade and reassure the "betrayed": He or she may ask: "What makes you think that I had an affair with somebody else?" After hearing the response one may proceed by saying and asking: "I know you have a right to think that. . . .so, what can I do to take all those suspicions go away?" Not suggested is the use of the following typical questions that display a lack of empathy, such as: "What is that you are really afraid of? "What do I need to do to make this situation safe for you?" Such questions can be asked of oneself, not to the "betrayed" one. Remember that a jealous person is very sensitive to any form of comment or question. There is no need to say that if the partner is a true traitor no attempt of counseling is possible. In a heterosexual relationship, loving two partners at a time poses a moral dilemma that creates a chronic spiritual disturbance within the unfaithful partner. There is a core belief one must avoid, that excuses infidelity and generates jealousy in the other partner, such as: "My relationship is so solid and trusting that we can experience other relationships freely," or "My partner is so satisfied with me and our relationship that having other partners will not threaten the bond we enjoy." This is spiritually risky, and such individuals are not qualified to counsel the jealous person in matters of trust. It is devilish to think "It is good to make a person jealous."

A so-called "betrayer" can help his or her jealous partner by telling the truth to eradicate the on-going suspicion. It is risky to tell lies to cover a fact and think the problem is solved. Many lovers lie about their true feelings for each other, the feelings they have for others, and their level of commitment, and so on. Some individuals save their biggest lies for the one they "love." Spiritually speaking, there is no intimacy in such a stratagem. Because of such misleading behavior, the person who lies cannot be a successful counselor to the jealous one. Their attempt to solve the problem may make matters worse; they fail to assure the "betrayed' person who becomes further misled once they know it was simply lies. On the whole truth telling is the effective response to any form of jealousy, especially when the person recognizes the fact that you were telling the truth, for you may then persuade him or her about living in trust.

Jealousy is caused by spiritual distress and needs to be resolved with a spiritual approach. It takes a lot of assertiveness and commitment, not pride and aggressiveness, to help a jealous person. A jealous person may stop being jealous in response to his or her partner's skill in communicating a new philosophy of living. Spiritual counseling by a so called "traitor" may succeed in persuading the partner about living in trust, living safe, and living well. Some people may find living with a jealous partner exhausting, but they may do a better job than professional counselors. Their involvement is intense because the unresolved outcome of the jealous one affects the jealous as well as the person toward whom jealousy is expressed. Partners who are accused of being "traitors" should be confident in their decision to save the relationship. When they are in doubt they bring much anguish to themselves and make no progress. The following thought is of significance in assessing jealousy that could be normal or spiritually destructive: "Occasionally, jealousy is natural and can help keep a relationship alive, but if it becomes intense and irrational it can be very destructive" (bbc.co.uk).

Let us consider a case of a jealous person who is insufficiently self-confident and develop thoughts of committing suicide. This could be one of the crucial moments in counseling a jealous person. This displays "inertia" or a resistance to change. This indicates that *taedium feelings* may give way to strongly negative thoughts by putting the anima in danger. Since the threat to harm self is eminent, the spiritual counselor has to humbly seek divine assistance. Prayer is the essential means to deal with such spiritual urgency. Here is an example of reflected prayer that a spiritual counselor can say when facing suicide threats. One may ask the person to repeat after you:

Lord!

You know my heart! I am so oppressed on all sides that I quite often want to end my life! Life has become hopeless and I see no way out.
Lord Your word says that my body is Your temple and as such I have no authority over my life and body. Yet Lord I am unable to resist this suicidal tendency. Strengthen my heart and remove all suicidal thoughts and any attempts I have made to take my own life. I acknowledge that Satan is a thief and comes to steal, kill and destroy. I now choose You Lord Jesus, as my Master who came to give me life and give it abundantly.

I renounce all my harmful thoughts and I crave Your forgiveness for nursing such thoughts. Thank You for Your forgiveness that allows me to forgive myself. I believe that my times are in Your precious hands and that there is always hope in Christ. Thank You Lord for taking over my soul, my body and my life. In Jesus name I pray" (Prayer Tower Online).

At work, I was putting in some late hours one night, when a young lady knocked at the door intent on making confession to me, which I did not expect. She said to me:

Co-worker: Can I tell you something? I cheated on my boyfriend."
Me: How did that happen?
Co-worker: He's been in jail for 1 year. Should I tell him, she asked.
Me: How do you think he would react if he knew about it? Would he become mad and violent towards you?
Co-worker: "I think so," she replied.
Me: What brought him to jail?
Co-worker: Because he violated the terms of probation.
Me: May be you should wait until he gets out of jail.

Me: Also, it has to be at the right time, and be careful with the way and means you would tell him.

After this brief conversation, the young co-worker shut the door and left. Because I know what it takes to get jealous, I called on her to be cautious whenever she decided to break the silence on her betrayal. One should always bear in mind that the spiritual results of jealousy can be detrimental due to development of *shammah feeling*. I understand that she felt the need to confess to someone, but at the same time she needed to do it the proper way so as to avoid harming herself and her boyfriend. It is evident that I encouraged her to tell her boyfriend the truth of her breach in faith, and she was willing to do so. The reason I advised her not to confess to her boyfriend while he was still in jail is because he is certainly not ready to hear any news of that sort.

Feelings of guilt in focus

Individuals acquire their own sense of what is right and wrong, as they grow up. When individuals think, behave, or feel in ways that violate their conscience, their guilt takes a very strong control on their meaning of life and behavior. Unresolved guilt makes intense the fear of spiritual burden in preventing the individuals from enjoying life with a peace of mind. This peace of mind may forcefully be acquired by an induced-clear conscience by which individuals justify their own actions, thoughts, and feelings. One should keep in mind that guilty feelings not, only, condemn wrong doing, it can produce an in-depth spiritual change in the individual's life. Due to guilt, one may engage in many kinds of activities to alleviate the emotional burden created by the guilt.

The following supports the existing contrast between a judge who declares someone guilty and the actual guilty feeling that the individual may experience:

When a judge declares the accused to be guilty before the law, the judge is describing the offender's state; the offender's condition. The judge doesn't know how the offender feels, and may not care. Undoubtedly a judge pronounces many offenders guilty who do not feel guilty at all. Still, we all agree it's appropriate for someone who has done wrong to feel guilty. It's appropriate for state and feelings to match up. When people who are guilty also feel guilty, their guilt (feeling) is called "real guilt." (Sheila M. Harron, Ph..D. *Concerning our Guilt*. p. 1).

Exercise: One of the professors in the Masters program of Mental Health said: "A guy whose wife had an affair went to the Mental Health Program because he was afraid he might hurt his wife. He's never been violent before. He started drinking 14 glasses of booze a day 9 to 10 months before he took the road of abstinence. Based on this man's decision, what was the feeling experienced?

      a- Humiliation
      b- Shame
      c- Guilt

Counseling how to deal with feelings of guilt

Only a spiritual being can have a reflection-based interpretation of his or her erroneous speech and conduct. To effectively serve an individual who is experiencing guilty feelings, the spiritual counselor must assess the remorse and the induced self-blaming. In helping a person burdened with guilt, the first thing to consider is the *utilis* (money, sex, power, fame, and fun). In light of the person's commitment to the *utilis*, one may understand the difference in vision of life engendered by moral judgment. The aim of counseling is to help this person have a reflection-based interpretation of why they are feeling the way they are. In order to help overcome internal disturbance created by guilt, the counselor should understand and address, not only concerns about the error committed, but also the nature of reality of the most accurate predicament for guilt.

Like falling in love, guilt is a very subjective experience. In our judgment of human conduct, we often are alarmed by the foolishness and gravity of the error committed and that we end up making forceful expression of adverse judgment that might turn out to be detrimental. At all times, guilt is a learning opportunity for the person who experiences the guilt in relation to a specific *utilis* that stops being enjoyable. When a causal explanation is given to such a spiritual experience, a successful reflection is produced on one's wrongful act. What gives rise to an increasingly disquiet spirit is not the same for everybody. When, in a very gentle way, the burden of guilt is approached in terms of cause and effect, the need for redemption becomes clear and gives a profound sense of responsibility. Guilt is clari- fied as the basis of spiritual empowerment to move forward through realization of what is important in life. Let us now look at some techniques that are consistent with the helping spiritual process of individuals who are feeling guilty.

Bringing the counselee to a high level of awareness of his wrongful act: Self-awareness is the first step in helping a heartfelt-guilty person. Certainly, the individuals burdened with guilt are likely to be aware of the wrongness of what they did. The technique to an effective awareness is through *retracing involvement in the act*. There is a difference between knowing that an act is wrong and being engaged in revisiting and specifying the exact responsibility. It is not for the purpose of forcing people into seeing themselves as "bad." This interviewing strategy is to help a counselee acknowledge his or her vulnerability and enhance his or her understanding of the spiritual consequence for standing for one's values. I previously pointed out how impressed I was by Loria's awareness and insights of her wrongful act, which, honesty, I acknowledged, and for which I showed consideration on several occasions. The most obvious aspect of this 59- year old woman was evidenced by her statement: "I am feeling guilty. It's my fault for having sex with a 12 year-old boy." To enhance her understanding of her definitive involvement in the sexual act, I assisted her in touching base with what she had done in a way to entice the 12-year old man. A per- tinent way that I helped her retrace her wrongful act was to ask her two questions: (1) "Can you tell me how your relationship with this boy had developed?" (2) "At what moment in your life (when) did you decide to have sex with a 12-year old child?" To these questions she replied: "At first, he was reluctant. Along the way, I did all I could to make myself look as a teenager. I started acting out sexually and allowed him to touch me in sexualized ways." My counselee's means of tempting the boy is consistent with Miller William's explanation of "the role of value" when he said, "Values can play a role in increasing confidence." This helped Loria realize the presence of an intention and choice for the adultery act.

Another method of facilitating awareness of guilt is called *disquieting the True Conscience*. It consists in sharing personal and/or others' experience of guilty feelings. The process of *disquieting the conscience* could be confrontational when, for instance, someone argues "Drinking makes me feel more relaxed and forgetful of this stressful world" and a counselor intervenes: "You are telling me that you feel more relaxed during and after a drink. How did you experience such relaxing moments?" "Aftermath, did you get sick?" When using this technique, the spiritual counselor must carefully pick an audio and/or written message that would have a stimulating effect on their individual's True Conscience by enhancing a reflection-based interpretation. A way to prevent heated confrontation is to take one or two paragraphs of appropriately wise counsels from a book or magazine that contrast the counselee's viewpoint or lifestyle, and give them to him/her to read. The choice of the article(s) depends on the raised issue. Based on the previous example, the spiritual counselor may introduce the method by saying: The following is an example of a writer's viewpoints on "Quitting smoking." By reading this you will form your own objection or acceptance of the author's opinion. Please read it and tell me what you think:

> "Quitting, in many cases, requires an act of bravery, a leap of faith. And it calls for a hard look in the mirror. Is five pounds worth risking your life for? Is it worth jeopardizing the health of those around you? If your vanity still isn't strunk, think about combing your hair after chemotherapy; envision wrinkles creeping over your face where the skin is still smooth. Does the company of cigarettes seem too hard to give up? Think about your children,

mourning and missing a mother who died prematurely from lung cancer or heart disease. (Oprah Magazine, Feb. 2002. Why Are We Still Smoking by Dorothy Foltz-Gray. p. 108).

After reading, the counselor allows the counselee a few seconds for him or her to think and formulate opinions about what he just read. The following paragraphs are from "Our Daily Bread" magazine, which might be helpful in disquieting the TC of a counselee who is resented against one or several offenders:
"I don't even like her"

> When Missy started her new job in the factory, she was determined to let her light shine for the Lord. But soon she knew it wasn't going to be easy. Brassy, defensive and crude, Louise ridiculed everything Missy did. When Missy tried to befriend her and tell her about Jesus, she was rejected. Louise said, "I tried that. It didn't work."
>
> Missy asked God for help. She open her Bible to John 13:34, "A new commandment I give to you, that you love one another; as I have loved you." So Missy kept trying to show love. Bur all she met was hardness. After a particularly rough day at work, Missy open her Bible and cried out to God. Again, her eyes fell on John 13:34. "But I don't even like her!" Missy complained.
>
> One day Louise sat beside Missy at break and said: "You are the only person who cares." Then she poured out a story of heartache and trouble. Missy put her arms around her and they became friends. Louise attended church with Missy and, after a struggle, open her heart to Jesus. – Dave Egner

The absence of intention to explore the choice of a wrongful act committed lessens the possibility of pursuing counseling and the desire for repentance. At this point, the person who shared feelings of guilt might become resistant and start arguing: "I did not choose to do so," or "I was enticed and dragged into it…" This person's denial of intention or choice prevents distress generated by guilty feelings – a self-induced-clear conscience is a natural defense of retributive punishment by guilt Assisting counselees in self-awareness entails a reflection- based interpretation of the error(s) or wrongful act(s) toward an improved quality of life. Thanks to this particular counseling technique, the spiritual counselors would help their counselees reach a level of awareness of the impact of cigarette nicotine, grudged feelings in their life and other behavior and life issues.

Clarifying the cause and effect of guilty feelings: Guilty feelings can be so powerfully retributive that they devoid individuals' attempts to keep their misdeed private. On a radio station, I listened to a young married woman who was in tears as she was disclosing about her guilt resulting from "a one brief adultery act." The counselor met her at her level of thinking by saying, "You succumbed to the temptation, Ha-a!" When the spiritual counselor asked that woman "What are you afraid of?" she responded, "I am afraid of losing my family, my home and my husband." She admitted that her involvement in a sexual relationship outside her marriage was inappropriate. The impact of guilt, like the impact of stress, decreases the strength of will, which is a spiritual condition that causes disordered reflection and includes confusion, worry, and panic. This young woman's account of responsibility was pragmatic and brought her into a constantly worrisome state of mind to the extent that her desire for having an intimate connection with her husband is disrupted. She can easily get panicked when she is approached by her husband.

Guilt plays a crucial role in an individuals' need for self-assurance in what they believe to be meaningful in life. In similar cases and others where individuals violated their internalized standards of behavior the role of the Educated Conscience (EC) is to impress upon the person's Mind the badness of what he or she knew to be bad without the desire to seek counseling and the appropriate therapy. These individuals become confused about themselves and their moral values, and if their disordered reflection remains unresolved, a chronic spiritual disturbance (CSD) will evolve.

An individuals' sense of inadequacy due to the work of the EC is evident in worrisome expressions such as, "I will never feel whole again," or "I will never be the person I used to be." When the problem of freedom from guilt is raised, the counselor should clarify that individuals who break their commitment to marriage and have sex outside marriage often feels likewise. By this explanation, the counselee will come to realize that the internal dis- tress associated with his or her adulterous act is a normal spiritual experience. By doing so, shame that tends to be prevailing with guilt will weaken. The likelihood for a person highly committed to moral values to feel guilty and seek counseling is greater than for those who have no concerns about morality. Also, the former may become more chroni- cally disturbed than the latter.

A planned guilt predicament: The purpose of helping someone who is feeling guilty is not to point to the immoral quality of a certain deed, or a certain kind of behavior. It is rather directing them toward an in-depth understanding of the choice he made that causes him or her the infliction of pain and deprivation. The individual who is willing to honestly elaborate on when and how the wrongful act happened is likely to collaborate with the helping spiritual process. After actively listening to the presenting problem and asking questions that help complete awareness of the wrongful act, the spiritual counselor may ask: "How did you come to know what you say or did was wrong?" When questioned about her life after a jail sentence, Loria's socially reinforced fear was obvious when she said, "A probation officer, one day, told me the homicide kills individuals once, but, in my case, the victim is still suffering." Loria was aware of social rejection because of her shortcoming: "No matter how much I prove myself to society, "she said, "they have turned me down."

The truth about an individual's need for redemption is that Jesus Christ should be at the center in order for this need to be fulfilled. Dr. Cooper stated, "Helping others improve their health is without question very important to me. But an even greater privilege is telling people how Jesus Christ made my life complete." People may think of other ways to live through their feeling of *contrition*. Nevertheless, the basic role of a spiritual counselor is to facilitate reflection-based interpretation of *God's plan for human redemption*. It is important to explore several aspects of the counselee's assumptions about God who is the Redeemer. There are at least three indicators that coincide with negative changes in attitude that may be noticed when God is mentioned in spiritual counseling: (1) When hearing about God, the counselee's interest in counseling may decrease as evidenced by a lack of motive to talk about personal issues, (2) When hearing about God, denial of the problem surfaces, and finally, (3) A decrease in the desire for change in one's beliefs and value system.

Cooper's straightforward counsel to people in order to fulfill their need for redemption is that: "You, too, can be made complete simply by inviting the Lord into your life" (Buckingham. 1999. Power for Living). A Christian spiritual scholar summarized counseling based on godly guidelines as follows:

> It is as simple as this - put your problem in God's hands. Allow your thoughts to rise above the problem so that you look down upon it, not up at it. Test it according to God's will. That is, do not try to get success from something that is wrong. Be sure it is right morally, spiritually, and ethically. You can never get a right result from an error. If your thinking is wrong, it is wrong and not right so long as it is wrong. It is wrong in the essence it is bond to be wrong in the result (Norman Vincent Peale, 2005, The Power of Positive Thinking. p. 171)

The main purpose in helping someone who is feeling overwhelmed by guilty feelings is to train the true-felt guilty person's mind to the acceptance of God-pleasing ways. This includes restitution and restoration. Spiritual counseling should not be confrontational. It should emphasize the individuals' freedom from guilt (it may be experienced as God's reprisal which is above human power) – only God can forgive sin and redeem. As was pointed out earlier, techniques of secular counseling carry the idea of empowering the counselees to be more knowledgeable of self so they would make informed decisions. The main focus of spiritual counseling is truth oriented. A heart-felt guilt individual for example, will be spiritually ready to listen to the ultimate spiritual Counselor for redemption and healing. This counseling emphasizes *the necessity for effective care of one's guilty feeling* and other serious issues related to sins. In summary, the techniques of helping someone who is truly feeling guilty include:

1- Building a spiritually enriching and trustworthy relationship with the counselee.
2- Listening attentively to the presenting problem and asking questions in a non-judgmental way about the feelings.
3- Helping the person retrace the source or origin of his guilty feelings – by encouraging him or her to sort out personal responsibility in the behavior or act.
4- Capitalizing upon the necessity for effective care of guilty feelings – in light of God's plan of restoration and redemption.

Dejection in focus

In times of trouble, individuals are inclined to experience dejection. Dejection is a spiritual condition associated with a long-lasting *teadium feeling*. After a tragic accident leading to physical disability, a degenerative and fatal illness, a significant loss (death of a beloved person, or of riches), or any encountered failure, an individual may become silent and morose. It takes some time to get to this point.

Everyone acquires a definition of success in family and society. Often, our growing success prevents us from seeing the reality of the downcast side of life. The reality is that it is in such moments of enthusiasm, and great avidity, the unexpected strikes, causing a crisis of expectation. The austerity of unexpectedness in life may cause discouragement and, eventually, irremediable despair. Someone who is reflecting over his present distress or misery has a *taedium feeling* (i.e., melancholy) that dominates his entire life and is said to be dejected.

No one ever doubted the fame of Mike Tyson. In light of relevant statements made by Tyson concerning his disappointments in life, there is a way to believe that this famous boxer has endured a crisis of expectation. Tyson's social achievements fail to satisfy his hope to live delightfully. In an interview, Mike Tyson acknowledged that fame and praises gained from society were vain pursuit: "People put me so high, I wanted to tear that image down," he said. He declared, "My life has been a waste" (USA Today. June 3, 2005.p. 2A) - a statement that is contrary to honor.

This American boxer showed distress and profound despair when talking about his broken relationship with his wife which caused him to be "confused and humiliated," he said. In addition to his worrisome relationship, his spiritual disturbance derived from "shat- tered finances" and a "reputation in ruin." All of these losses led him to a state of dejection as evident in his statement: "I'll never be happy," and "I believe I'll die alone. I would want it that way." He depicted himself as a "sad, pathetic case." He plainly stated, "I'm really embarrassed with myself and my life." His expression, "I just want to escape" has a sui- cidal connotation that needs to be under watch. Tyson's spirituality epitomizes the criteria of dejection.

Suicide from a spiritual perspective - *suicidal thoughts stem from the state of dejection*

Dejection may lead to *incredibilis* and *inedicabilis*, meaning a situation that is unbelievable and inexplicable. When someone thinks and/or says: "Nothing in the world can bring me the joy that I had in life," this infers that the speaker fails in the areas of living with trust and living with will. Spiritually, this individual may block out happy memories and respond to them with confusion and annoyance. Individuals with a facile conscience, an obscured conscience, or an induced-self conscience, who were determined to make a difference in their life (regardless if it is immoral), may start being discouraged with the way things are. These conscience variants often generate a prototypic reflection: "I am rich, I am prospered, and I need nothing" (Rev. 3:17). The likelihood that an individual with unrealistic expectations may be dispirited or dejected is greater than for someone who is leading a life of simplicity.

From a spiritual standpoint, suicidal thoughts arise due to *impugnation* by the True Conscience. This internal impulse takes place in the thinker's Mind (the Seat of Spiritual Interpretation) and abruptly inspires a desire for self-improvement that does result in a successful reflection. This inspiration is spiritually unproductive because it does not allow engagement in the right course of action. The TC impugns when it radically opposes detrac- tive thoughts that feign reality.

An individual's inclination to suicide is not to be considered as a disease. This spiritual condition affects the perception of self and feelings in ways that are radically complex. Because the thinker cannot stand the truth about their true self, the individual's ill will to harm self is characterized by a sense of failure that is perverted. Failure for this person is unacceptable and creates anguish that, under certain circumstances, generates internal voices that persistently recall particular moments of failure. At time the thinker may start feeling desperate. Given that this individual may fail to persuade himself (or herself) otherwise, his or her reality of themselves and their lives may become seriously distorted. The path of annoying self that goes along with *taedium feelings* may lead to significant worry: a condition in which the individual may be panicked to the extent of losing intense self-control. As we pointed earlier, when a person is dejected, he or she may be prone to self-injury. This type of emotional development is due to *sharam feelings* – These persons' disappointment redefines their meaning of life and their future: a condition in which the two elements of the Mind, both the Educated Conscience and the True Conscience become welded together as a unit. When energy of the TC and the EC's are confluent, meaning flowing together, the point of conjunction of these spiritual energy creates a state of *confusion* - there begins all spiritual disturbances.

Infertility may deter the individuals' purpose of living with trust and with will. This incapability of procreating can be attributed to *infelicitas* the idea of being stricken by a "bad luck," or a misfortune. An individual or a married couple may go through discouragement, sorrow, and grief, because of the incapability to procreate. To better understand suffering resulting from infertility, I would like to begin by offering a sharp connection between conscious awareness of wrongdoing and the instance of suffering and loss it brings to infertility. We use the connotation, *evil passion or immoral value commitment*, in reference to the individuals' constant distraction from their True Conscience. This consideration infers that an infertile person may be suffering from awareness of sexual wrongdoing for which he or she is responsible.

The spiritual burden created by infertility is real and can significantly cause a great deal of suffering. The *taedium feelings* of this person progressively ruin his or her self-confidence, when mentally revisiting "bad things" that one did, namely abortion. It is clear that a woman who is highly concerned about getting pregnant and has tried for years to have a baby may feel guilty about the life taken away from the aborted child. When, for instance, this woman goes to public places and sees pregnant women and when she learns about other women's pregnancies she is prone to exasperate. A sterile woman declared, "I can recall many miserable moments I spent in waiting rooms filled with glowing pregnant women" (*Focus on the Family Magazine*. April 1989. p.2).

Regardless of their trust in God's existence, individuals who are deprived of their power of procreation tend to attribute their misfortune to "God." In their grieving process, these individuals may adopt an austerity toward God and downcast His justice by saying: "God has been unfair to me. What did I do so wrong to be treated by God like this?" This mark of rigor expressed toward God is noticeable when, for instance, they hear about friends who have had children become pregnant again. These "unfortunate men and women" become furious when they read newspapers and watch television reporting on child abuse. They may argue, "I deserve these children more than these abusing parents or care providers!" Increasing feelings of disappointment, shame, and guilt involved in infertility (due to either biological deficiency or operative), may generate serious distress in life.

Dejection may impair the individual's ability to solve new and relatively complex problems. The spiritual basis is that these individuals do not concern themselves with exploring their strengths; rather, they have frequent reflection-based interpretation of their weaknesses. Due to fear, a dejected person may contemplate suicide. We have distinguished fear that allows individuals to function in life (i.e., *functional fear*) and fear that cause individuals to think and act confusedly and make stupid mistakes i.e., *blundering fear*.

Vulnerability that includes fear of death, fear of tomorrow, and fear of recurrent mistakes, infers that individuals are naturally creative in finding ways to overcome obstacles to success. Dejection may cause a lack of the empowering spirit. These individuals may never entirely overcome their potent fear of failure to a point of becoming pessimistic (their sense of living with trust and with wills is absent). Their meaning of life and their satisfaction in life deteriorates. The individual's fear of tomorrow is blundered. This person has a screwed perspective. They become spiritually uncreative in problem solving when it comes to controlling fate or destiny. This is a person who cannot find out what is needed to get involved and move forward in life. This impairs the individuals' wish for living by a series of intricate "Why" reasoning. A typical reasoning is: "Why should I spend so much energy creating a friendship that would not make me feel any better." Another example is that:

"Why should I wake up, dress myself and do things that are meaningless." The worst that could happen is when the need for self-preservation is dissolved due to a blundered fear of recurrent mistakes. The dejected person devotes a great deal of time and energy revisiting the errors committed, and becomes disappointed and hopeless. Buckingham argued, "If you possess a strong belief theme, you have certain core values that are enduring" (p.88). So to speak, the individual who wants and seeks to cease living is spiritually lacking "belief theme."

As we demonstrated, expectations that are unrealistically grounded are likely to provoke an intense breakdown in life. In recognition of how powerful individuals' concept of living with trust and will can be, we can say that a spiritually complex disturbance increases in direct proportion to the individual's cumulative self-confidence. Pride is the bedstead of any spiritually damaging experience. The greater the pride (due to exaggerated trust in self), the greater and damaging is the individual's disappointment in life. This explains the correlation between human fear management and the *crisis of expectation*.

Adequate self-confidence is not to be confounded with self-sufficiency and pride. An adequate self-confidence gives the individuals the energy to realistically move forward with life; rather, the individuals' errors of judgment increases in proportion with pride, which enhances the likelihood of being deceived. These individuals may be unable to persuade themselves about their own philosophy of living – the need for self-persuasion or for self-assuredness is negated. In the absence of meaning of life, the thinker cannot fail to have successful reflection on needs and the strategies to fulfill those needs. An instance of need that progressively fades away is the need for self-preservation.

Spiritually Counseling a Person who is Dejected

As of with guilt, spiritually counseling a dejected or suicidal person is based on history and examination. The first step is to assess the counselee's energy level by asking scaling questions, such as: On a scale of 0 to 10 - where zero, you are no longer capable of doing things you used to do and 10 you are energetic to do as much as or more than you used to, how would you rate your energy level? A second question can be: Do you think you are capable of keeping up with the help needed at this time? Spiritual counselors must avoid using the word "fear' in any phase of counseling. Throughout the process, the counselor and the counselee gain a better understanding of how much spiritual energy is in effect, how the counselor may help toward restoring trust that makes life important and meaningful. It is a good step to be aware of whether the counselee cares about his or her physical welfare as reflected in his or her interest in eating, drinking, and sleeping. In facilitating a retrospective analysis of experiences that were positively meaningful to the individual, the main strategy consists of getting someone focused on the positive aspects of life following abandonment, the loss of a beloved one, financial burden, or multiples losses. This spiritual counselor may ask, "Could you find me some reasons to be grateful? In addition, one may inquire for "Something for which you are grateful to God?" Following a loss, one should avoid downplaying the counselee's grievances; a spiritually normal process to an afflicted person is to assist in self-persuasion about a brighter tomorrow with blessings and love.

Meaninglessness of life can be addressed by asking: Could you tell me a few things that you are used to doing and that you no longer enjoy? The loss of courage (physical and emo- tional) is interwoven with inadequate self-confidence. One important question in assessing the individual's concept of living with trust is: What is the most important lesson you have ever learned about being responsible to yourself and other people? A typical question that aims at evaluating the individual's concept of living with trust is: It seems that you are determined for excellence in everything, what is the worst that could happen if you decide that you are not going to try anyhow? Another question may be: What difference would it make in your life if you were to entrust again your potentials? Also, one may ask: From your personal experience can God be trusted again?

As spiritual counselors, we need to keep in mind that, in moments of sorrow, individuals are likely to feel hurt. As their pain increase, counseling tends to be unwelcoming. Instilling hope is the key strategy in counseling individuals who are perplexed in life or when facing a tragic life condition of a beloved one. Let us take, as an example, somebody whose mother is suffering from cancer and this person is worried and anxious to grasp the latest information on cancer treatment. The counselor may, by careless comments, fall short of meeting this counselee's legitimate expectation. A careless comment could be: "The most reliable research findings confirm 'cancer is incurable.' " Such inadvertent affirmation will, certainly, have negative effects on the counselee who is eager for getting the necessary cure for his or her suffering mother. James J. Lynch, PhD stated, "Loneliness is a killer." To assist in overcoming feelings of despair, counselors should instill hope to those who have the need for self-assuredness. Dr. Siegel, on his part, argued, "To me, the worst thing a doctor can do is tell a person he's going to die. For one thing, it's a deception. There's no way anyone can predict with any certainty the course a disease will take in an individual. Secondly, it's the quickest way to make that patient another statistic." When talking about the impact of statistics in medical prognostics, Dr. Siegel called our attention to the fact that:

> The doctor's dilemma is statistics. If statistics say that nine out of ten people die from this disease, most physicians will tell their patients, "The odds are against you. Prepare to die," I tell my patients, "You can be the one who gets well. Let's teach you how. I am not guaranteeing immortality. I ask them if they want to learn how to live (*Healing Power of Emotion* - The Complete Guide to your Emotions and your Health. p. 540)

Spiritual counselors must tell their counselees what exactly they need to know, but in a very inspirational way. We can say, for instance, "None of us knows the future. The future belongs to God only. There is hope for those who believe in God in the present life and even when they might die. I know individuals who were diagnosed for a terminal disease, but they survived because of their faith in God." At this point, the spiritual counselor may convey commitment to counseling by saying, "For your mother's sake, I think continuous search would be helpful as we will continue to pray for your mother's healing." And the counselor may emphasize, "Sometimes when something is lost, something bigger replaces it." This "bigger thing" is *faith* that is the pinnacle of living with trust. These points of view and others may be very different from the counselee. When the counselee and you disagree on something, every detail will seem significant. Remember, spiritual counselors must clarify in light of the Bible – in this case Job's experience is a good fit.

Another aspect of counseling someone with dejection consists of helping in regaining courage after the loss of a loved one. Under such a circumstance, spiritual counselors should be aware of the fact that nobody knows their counselees' pain and sorrow like they do. The various fears that someone is experiencing over the loss of a significant person is comprised of the fear of the unknown and the fear of the invisible. This is a time more than ever to be an active and sensitive listener; then, restate what you heard in a very gently way. An example of rephrasing what a grieving person said is: "I heard you saying that you are feeling so overwhelmed by the loss of your 'father' that you are wondering whether you would survive." Following this restatement, the counselor may add, "I don't want to criti- cize or judge your thoughts that emerge from how you are feeling now. It is good to know that it is worth continuing with life. Even after this terrible loss, I know you can find ways to make life enjoyable. Your friends, co-worker and kids (if this is the case) will benefit from your courage to live up."

Habits developed because of a missing person are significant factors in weighing the spiritual burden created by the loss. The idea is to carefully question grieving people over their loss. This is recommended to avoid questions that may dramatize the lives of the counselees. The most intriguing aspect of counseling a grieving person is to ask him (or her) to tell about the *utilis* (a meaningful object or person). A way to do so is by saying: "I know how painful it has been for you to think and talk about what you missed because of this significant loss, and you have desperately cried because of what happened?" To place the impact of habits in a context of a spiritual burden created by a loss, we refer to a report by *Time Magazine* on a soldier's wife who died in Iraq (June 2003. p. 29): Chris Coffin had promised his wife Betsy to "be home for his birthday." The day Betsy was informed that her husband had been shot, she became dejectedly disoriented in life: "Every night," she said, "when I walked the dog. I would stop and talk to the star. The dog was so con- fused; she could tell I was talking to Chris, but she couldn't see him." In similar grieving moments, the afflicted person remembers the agreeable moments that they had with their loved ones. In the Time's article, Betsy recalled her habit with the deceased beloved hus- band: "I miss doing the laundry with you helping me hang it out."

Suicide bombing – *assessing and spiritually counseling a potential candidate to a suicide bombing*

Suicide is a worldwide phenomenon. It occurs in all cultures, nationalities, groups, and professions. According to researchers, there are categories of individuals that are subject to an increased risk of suicide. The numbers of individuals who attempt or commit suicide have expanded every year. The "World Health Organization" reported that there is a "global mortality rate of 16 per 100,000." In addition, they said: "In the last 45 years suicide rates have increased by 60% worldwide. Suicide is now among the three leading causes of death among those aged 15-44 of both sexes. Suicide attempts in the world are "up to 20 times more frequent than completed suicides (www.befrienders.org/suicide/statistics.htm).

Suicide bombing in the Middle East and other parts of the world unveils an outstanding means to expressing beliefs. There are two ways to possibly grasp survival interpretation of a candidate of suicide bombing. First, the *share of belief* that renders life meaningless; second, their fear of death manifested as an evil passion.

This culture despises death. There is a strong religious and political commitment that makes suicide bombing an *evil passion*. Robert Pape, an associate professor of political science at the University of Chicago specializing in international security affairs wrote:

> Suicide is absolutely unnatural; it is an aberration in creatures whose instinct is to survive. It is not easy to override that instinct. But just to add another dimension to our survival instinct, think of what you know about mothers. Is it the case that protection of her young is primary? It is not difficult for us to imagine a mother who sacrifices herself for her child, we can understand that. But can we imagine a mother of two small children ready to

commit suicide for a cause? (Robert Pope. *The Myth of the Suicide Bomber* Retrieved from www. rense.com/general67/suicc.htm. July 12, 2012).

From the *Guide to Understanding Islam*, we quote: "The point of the bomber isn't suicide - it is to kill infidels in battle. This is not just permitted by Muhammad, but encouraged with liberal promises of earthy rewards in heaven, including food and sex" Retrieved July 20, 2012).

Culture makes suicide bombing possible (education pertaining to living with trust). Time magazine reported the following: "These days Palestinians celebrate the suicides in news- paper announcements that read, perversely, like wedding invitations" (TIME, April. 15, 2002). This article pointed that: "Children in the Middle East play a game called 'Being a martyr' in which the martyr buries himself in a shallow grave, the job of the bomber is to reward the surviving family with cash bonuses and health benefits." If these children become candidates to suicide bombing, their True Conscience will ineffectively prove wrong to their intention to harm. Their Educated Conscience will drive them to be aligned with the group of people who are supposedly defending a "good cause." The unrealistic expectation tied to suicide bombing was clarified by many candidates. A candidate to suicide bombing argued, "Every time a man ends tragically his life; he will find himself in the midst of a dozen virgin women."

Following her son's involvement in a raid, the mother interpreted her son's act by saying: "My son is now a symbol of Tunis. He gave his life so we can have freedom" (Time. Jan. 2012). For this woman, her son achieved an act of great significance. This woman's meaning of life debases the principles of living with trust, living with will, living fair, and living safe. We have good reasons to suppose that the candidates to suicide bombing have had no successful reflection over their need for self-preservation, which is one of human spiritual needs. As a mother she reasoned in opposition to her desire to see her child growing and caring for her. This woman's survival interpretation of her son's violence is an indication of her evil passion.

Such desire to "live in the midst of virgin women" is not innate; it is the outcome of a socially reinforced fear. Spiritually speaking, a candidate to suicide bombing is manipulated to a predictably wrong action by denying some alternate paths through life.

Knowing that "martyrdom in battle is glorified by their religion," these candidates are spiritually conditioned by an erroneous concept of death e.g. "Killing for Allah to avoid hell." The tenacity and harshness with which the candidates expose their impetuosity as evidenced by their willpower, arrogance and by, what we call, *argumentum*. They feel compelled to present the "facts and the truth" no matter how offensive they are. A candidate to suicide bombing denies human values characterized by trust, will, fairness and safety for self and others.

How, as spiritual counselors, can we help a candidate to suicide bombing? Our presence in a room with a suicide bomber is a golden opportunity to listen to someone who likes all facts about himself (or herself). On the wall facing the entrance door and above the counselor's head a poster may contain this motto: "*Freedom is the ability to make decision. Wisdom is the ability to make the right decisions* (Brice and Stan. p. 57). I recommend that the first session be centered on the free will issue. This infers that the spiritual counselor should expect resistance and eventually aggressive reactions on the part of this particular counselee. The presence of free will should not detract the counselor from the concept of manipulation that is in line with suicide bombing. In the prospect of helping this candidate predisposed to cruelty, spiritual counselors should demonstrate kindness, gentleness, and tenderness which can be a persuasive way to teach humaneness. This technique baptized *merciful modeling* can have significant impacts on the candidate. Notice that we emphasize that the sessions with suicide bombers must be held on an individual basis. Two security officers and an interpreter (in a case where the candidate does not speak English) need to be present at the interview setting. An introductory statement can be: "I am glad that you come to talk with someone who has a different worldview from you. I am persuaded that we are going to spend a good time talking." A way to reassure a suicide bomber is to say: "Thanks again for coming to the first session. Unlike some people, I am not going to impose my views on you. Feel free to share your opinions with me. And I promise you everything that you share here will remain highly confidential." These introductory statements will allow no discomfort with exposing their beliefs, concerns, and grievances.

The main purpose of counseling a potentially suicide bomber is to foster wellness through conscious awareness of needs. This may lead to *heated confrontation*. The rationale of *inevitable confrontation* is supported by the fact that "The laws of nature are immutable and eternal; for injustice, ingratitude, arrogance, pride, iniquity, inacceptance of persons, and the rest, can never be made lawful" (James Rachels. p. 58).

Although confrontation may be out of the counselor's control, spiritual counselors should, tactfully, use techniques to serve problem resolution. With tact and wisdom, the counselor decreases the likelihood of hurting the counselee(s) by effectively managing frustration and anger. The rule of thumb is that spiritual counselors must avoid inviting anger through provocation. This counselee may feel provoked to anger by being constantly crossed or nagged by questions starting with "Why…?" or "How is that…? These types of questions tend to disturb their disposition to pursue counseling. One should avoid questions such as, "Why do you plan to kill yourself and destroy the lives of many? Rather one may efficiently articulate, "I know you have decided to end your life in a way that seems agreeable to you, tell me how you are going to do so."

Here are a few questions that are appropriate, but likely to produce confrontational reactions on the part of a candidate of suicide bombing:

- Could you tell me how your family members described their feelings when they learned that you are a candidate to a suicide bombing?
- What do you think would be beneficial to your children: being alive or dead?
- How many people do you know who died and are still famous?
- How would you feel if the day you decide to go ahead with your plan, suddenly you notice a significant other in the crowd?
- Have you noticed people who are close to you were in pain?

Purposefully, when listening to people, one should pay close attention to their underlying fears and needs that are present in every single declaration. Many blundering fears and the absence of correlated needs that drive individuals to be suicidal and homicidal are to be carefully assessed. When in a case of candidacy to a suicide bombing somebody is highly confident to distance self from relatives, friends, co-workers, and others, starts nourishing cruel intentions to a point of contemplating suicide and homicide, the fear in effect is a blundering fear of rejection with a devoid need for connection. Due to this spiri- tual disturbance, the grace of desiring and seeking after relationships disappears. From this understanding, we can concentrate on the facts that might help the person come up with the realization that there is a vital need that is despised and discarded. As of people who are involved in assisting others in committing suicide (euthanasia) the external and internal pressure of the candidate to suicide bombing to choose death deters reasoning whether or not the act is supported by a "good will of mercy." As we quote, "The argument from mercy says euthanasia is justified because it provides an end to that" (Rachels p. 190). "That," in this statement, stands for horrible pain due to a terminal illness.

Let us explore a few techniques that aim at increasing the reasoning ability in a candidate of suicide bombing. The first technique to consider is metaphor. A metaphor is, by definition, "A figure of speech in which a term is transferred from the object it ordinarily designates to an object it may designate only implicit comparison or analogy" (The American Heritage Dictionary). Here is an example of metaphor: A man who was working near a well fell by mistake into the well. People who were passing looked into the well saw the man and made a variety of comments: "This well is bottomless; there is no way that this person will be rescued out." Other people said: "How careless it was for someone to slide into this well!" or "Only a low-altitude climber can succeed in this rescue." This act-of-mind metaphor will help discover the alignment between the counselee's core values, intentions and actions.

The idea of living fair and living with the will to convey fairness are in focus. Suppose the candidate who listens to this metaphor does not show any concern for helping the man in need and finds "ok" that the walkers did not spend any effort to rescue the man - these are signs of insentience. A chronic lack of sensitivity to the feelings or circumstances of others disables a candidate to a suicide bombing to make decisions and live by the direc- tion of his/

her True Conscience. Lehcher (2009) was right when he said, "Before we can sympathize with the feelings of other people, you have to figure out what they are feeling" (How we Decide. p. 180). A candidate to a suicide bombing has no emotional capacity to sympathize with a suffering person. The contrary stands for a good sign of spiritual improvement.

Another technique is in the attempt of disquieting the candidate's True Conscience. One should read a true story of a candidate for suicide bombing such as: A 14 year-old Grace Akallo who was kidnapped from her Ugandan. Here is what the young lady shared:

> We were forced to kill people. It's really hard to say, that's what we were forced to do. We were taught that 'killing was natural' they just give you a man. The man just comes and takes you away. Once I fainted, and the rebels buried me alive because they thought I was dead. Not long after that, I was raped. God was with me. I stayed in the bush for three days. No food, nothing. I was surviving on soil," We are tired of arms. We have been fighting for 20 years pouring blood. (Boston Herald. April 26, 2006. Children being abducted…p. 7).

If there is no reaction whatsoever to this story telling or the alike, one may ask: "How does this exercise help you understand the extent to which some people may be forced to think and do what is contrary to their core beliefs?"

What should one do when the candidate shows extreme temerity, meaning he or she becomes reckless, bold and unreceptive? At this point, the spiritual counselor should remain calm and observant. Such reactions are significant in that they help identify the trend to violence, which can be used to build up, in proper time, skills of problem solving.

Spiritual inversion is a technique that aims at redirecting a candidate to suicide bombing toward an interchange of vision of life – a worldview inversed in order. It is difficult for someone who is so highly committed, like a strong-minded candidate to suicide bombing, to cease contemplating being "in the midst of the virgin angels." In proper time, the spiritual counselor can proceed by sharing Jesus Christ's life history: "2,000 years ago, a little boy was born. The day of his birth, three wise men brought Him precious gifts. Regardless of His compassion and the miracles that He performed on the lamed and the sick, He was tortured, put to death and hung among two evildoers (one on each side). Because of His outstanding way of modeling love, many people have accepted His teaching and counsel. Because He was indeed resurrected from the dead, He is alive and many believers have chosen Him as their Personal Savior. Before He ascended to heaven, He promised all His believers that He will, some day, come back and He will raise those who died to everlasting life. One thing that is worth mentioning is that Jesus' believers have a specific mission of hope that is comforting to the suffering and despaired. Also, healing the physically and emotionally wounded, sharing the alternative of resurrection for those who are alive and will die from a natural death or diseases, introduces a series of benefits as opposed to a suicide bombing.

Increasing the will of taking control over negativity in life: This technique is simple. In every session a spiritual counselee can ask the counselor to repeat once, after him (or her), the following statement:

> I am now aware that I must love myself. Therefore, I am willing to develop peaceful and loving relationships with myself. When I begin to improve on focusing on the positive about myself, I will create love and a peaceful self, I will start seeing other people differently, and then I will respect them, value the individuals they are, and show them love.

At the end of the second repetition, the counselor can proceed with: The statement that you just repeated is to help you (1) Remember the times you have felt good about yourselves and how well your life was going, (2) Remember the time when you were in love and for those period you seem have no problem (Hay. p. 77). More particularly, for someone who is worried and at times get panicked, emotional response to this exercise may include: weeping, confessing, and feelings of guilt. The idea is not to precipitate the counselee to think as if "There is nothing good with him" or "he or she is not good enough." This exercise can help the candidates to realize the serious impacts of affiliation in an organization that promotes thinking and acting against their will. This positive self-affirmation training guided by the counselor aims at initiating a new pattern of reflection about self and others in replacement of the old ways of criticizing self.

Spiritual counseling provided to a candidate to a suicide bombing lasts 45 minutes or one hour. A counseling moment may be terminated before the suggested timeframe when, for instance, the counselee becomes irreversibly resistant or decisively walks out of the room. When this happens, the spiritual counselor must try to ease the process of termination by calmly ordering the security guards to gently escort the counselee on his or her way out. If a candidate to a suicide bombing goes through the 10-session program, the recommendation is not to separate him (or her) from the rest of his organization but to follow-up with an anger management group whose attendants are individuals who were suicide-bombing candidates.

Chapter Nine

HUMAN SEXUALITY AND SPIRITUAL COUNSELING

When we talked about the negative impacts of society on human spirituality, the choice of a sexual lifestyle is not excluded, which choice may be conflicting with the individuals' True Conscience. When we take an honest look at our life, there is a way to say that all of us, at one point in life, have made difficult and negative decisions that are mostly or completely out of our control. We distinguish three aspects of sexuality that go along with love as designed by God - the union of a male and a female character: (1) eliminating solitude, (2) propagating children, and (3) preventing immorality. A way to understand how se*xually-ill orientation d*evelops is consistent with the loss of trust (or of faith) in the universal truth concerning marriage leading to a strong aversion (*taedium feeling*) toward heterosexuality. When one's feeling towards marriage causes a feeling of antipathy, the pursuit of any aim, goal, and dream that is sexual may lead to something insidiously dangerous to self, family members, and society at large.

Political and religious leaders who believe in marriage seem to be losing the authority to convince the sexually-ill oriented to relinquish on their choice. In the United States (US), the executive and the legislative branches are divided on the issue of banning "same-sex marriage." Several newspapers issued between May and August of 2006, in the United States disclosed very strong controversies on the issue of same sex marriage. The Boston Globe, reported: "President Bush invoked the Massachusetts Supreme Court yesterday in calling on Congress to approve a constitutional amendment banning gay marriage, telling a group of religious leaders that the 'most fundamental institution of civilization' is in jeopardy because of activists" (June 2006). President Bush, the US Republican president released a bill for amendment at the first of three days of the congressional debate to re-define marriage to cast the homosexual union down.

The president in a speech at Eisenhower Executive Office Building alleged: "Our policies should aim to strengthen families, not undermine them" (idem). His conservative message on the consecrated union was clear when he said: "Changing the definition of marriage would undermine the family structure." The American leaders and many others who believe and attempt to preserve the heterosexual marriage are motivated by their moral obligation to oppose the growing same-sex movement. Many observers are astonished at how things have been going on the quest of changing the primary definition of marriage, regardless of the courageous standing of the American authorities and other people who believe and are committed to marriage as a standard of living.

Individuals whose need for connection is not fulfilled through a healthy love relationship may end up having horrors and distress. From a spiritual standpoint, the fear of rejection enhances the need for connection which brings a source of contentment and gratification. When this fear is blundered, the individual cannot seize the opportunity to repair a wrong in order to safeguard the connection. Metaphorically, a man who seeks to get rid of his dog puts it in a box and throws it away into an ocean. The "dog thrown away into the ocean" symbolizes the deprivation of that which makes us distinctly humans i.e., love. Realistically, somebody ever deprives self of what is meaningful to him unless he or she is suggested or manipulated to do so. The absence of love in life coincides with isolation.

Isolation is the seating of spiritual disturbances. When isolated, individuals spend a good deal of time in worrisome reflection. Anthony Storr wrote, "Isolated children often invent imaginary companions." An individual's life that is deprived of love ability causes this person to suffer from intimate relationship with a partner of the opposite sex. The man, in the above metaphor, was emotionally numb or insensitive when he decided to get rid of his dog by saying, for instance, "My dog is much happier from being in a free environment and breathing fresh air." People have been driven to find the "right person" for the most perfect heterosexual relationship. These individuals may not accept the reality that even the most long-lasting and closest relationship can have flaws and disadvantages. When a relationship does not go as they expected they are inclined to have a crisis of expectation. When we say that individuals may be engaged in be *sexually-ill oriented*, this concept carries the idea that, following a deceitful heterosexual relationship, an individual may become creative in exploring other sources of fulfillment in the need for connection. This person may fail to appreciate his place in a society of heterosexuals. Like the man in the metaphor who gets a new meaning of a "true love" for his dog, someone who reproves mar- riage may seek to plead his or her case by convincing people to acknowledge the impor- tance of the sexual choice he or she makes. The rule of thumb is that loving, caring, and nurturing are the bases of fulfilling one's need for connection. A spiritual counselor should agree that with these individuals there is a gap between (A) acceptance of marriage and (B) their actual sexual choice. One way to resolve the tension created by their sexual choice is to move the counselee from point B to point A as we are keeping in mind that

"God actu- ally created sex as a means of enjoyment, and it was given as part of a solution to man's loneliness" (McLaughlin. p. 85).

For an essay assignment on gender differences, I emphasized the likelihood of adolescents to sexual orientation which I discussed in this class. I wrote:

The spiritual work toward self identity may be challenging to a teenager. Teenagers, often, face identity crisis that brings severely emotional distress and the need for a variety of coping strategies to overcome the psychological, emotional and spiritual outcomes. Thus, sexual orientation can generate a great deal of depression. Bartel. B. (2006) says, "Today's teenager is going into a world that they've never experienced. They are attempting things and doing things that they've never done" (p. 89). This statement is coherent with sexual desire that a teenage can have with an individual of the same sex and eventually attempt to sexually connect with this person. This starts a different brand of lifestyle. The questions are: How do adolescents get fascinated with this new-world sexual lifestyle? How do they succeed in managing the emotions and attitudes by the demand of their gender role?

I added: It takes a lot of emotional distress for changes to happen in sexual identity. It requires serious efforts to adjust to the gender role that pertains to these changes. In my culture and many others, parents experience the joy of giving birth to a "boy" or a "girl." This is a parental standard expectation. In modern societies, pregnant women may undergo a medical test to identify the sex of their carrying baby (either male or female). Furthermore, parents raise children in regards to their gender. I remember growing up and going on vacations in the countryside. As a boy I often begged somebody to relay messages to my mother in town to send me balls to play soccer. I imaged how upset and shocked my mother would be if she was told that I wanted her to send me either "skirts," "lipstick," or other female-product types. Her reaction to me would have been, "I know I gave birth to a boy, how you dare ask me for female stuff!" She might have expressly come to the countryside and physically assaulted me. As I commented on the visual aid, I said: The video that we watched in class allowed me to view the level of emotional distress that teenagers have been going through because of sexual orientation.

On the video, a teenage black lady declares: "I can't stay home; I don't have support within my family." Freddie, 16 years old male, one of the video characters, confided: "I was quiet about my sexuality, I could not tell anybody. I continue holding this secret. Eventually I said, 'I am gay.'" This young man who faced his siblings' misunderstanding regarding his sexual choice said: "My older brother could not understand what being gay means." Here are a few comments that the professor made on this essay:

Comment #1: "All of the major health organizations have issued statements that homosexuality is a normal variant of human sexual expression; those include the American Psychological Association; the American Psychiatric National Association; the National Association of Social Workers; the American Counseling Association and many others."

Comment #2: "You are giving your opinion which is not supported by scientific evidence."

Comment #3 (following the conclusion): Raymond, if we all work to end such stigma, these young people would grow up to be much more psychologically healthy."

Many adolescents who claim a certain sexual orientation grow up in heterosexual families. They therefore acquire family values that correspond with this lifestyle. Previously we emphasized how adults and parents should be accountable and consistent in modeling for young people. This includes avoidance of mixed messages and a lifestyle in order to preserve children from emotional distress. Inversely, L. B. Silverstein and C. F. Auerback viewed the "Male role model" as a myth. To support their assumption, they argued: "Many gay people are gay because they wanted to be fathers." They gave as example a young man who became gay and "desperately wanted to be normal." According to this story, Tom who got married was saved from being gay, but continued to be tormented by the reminiscence of his past sexually wrongful acts. The idea that "Tom as father is still open gay male even though he is a married man" is inconsistent with an upward spiritual experience.

Based on the following statement, it is obvious that these authors held firm conviction about heterosexual parenting that they perceived as a failure: "Trying to conform to a single version family is not just doomed to failure, but unnecessary." Their antagonism was more outrageous when they said: "If people attempt to conform to idealized myths, they are making the difficult challenge of raising healthy children even more difficult." John Burroughs, on his part said: "A man can fail many times, but he isn't a failure until he begins to blame someone else." Tom, in this story, makes a difference in how he responded to his distress caused by his sexual orienta- tion. The authors, however, blamed the heterosexual mode of parenting children.

From a sociology book, homosexuality is defined as "an individual's preference in terms of sexual partners: same sex, other sex, either sex, neither sex (Lips, 1993). The term, "orientation" itself implies liberality. The term, *sexually-ill oriented* refers to individuals who are involved in erotic pleasure that makes it hard for them to persuade themselves about the choice of lifestyle they make. In figuring out whether homosexuality falls into the concept, sexually-ill orientation, the utilitarian argument deserves our attention. This argument is elaborated as follows: "Any action or social policy is morally right if it serves to increase the amount of happiness in the world or to decrease the amount of misery. Conversely, an action or social policy is morally wrong if it serves to decrease happiness or to increase misery" (Rachels. p. 192). The degree to which sex becomes a creative way of fulfilling a need for connection is relevant to the individual's expectation of an ideal relationship. Someone who was deceived in a heterosexual relationship may abandon any hope of having intimate attachments with an individual of the opposite sex, with the risk of embarking upon relations that are guilt inducing.

Homosexuals react to worry as if it were persecution. This *kind of torment* makes it hard for them to persuade themselves about their choice(s) and deal peacefully with cul- tural differences. Challenged by their spirituality, the gays and lesbians plan and organize public protests that are mostly violent. The way society appraises love and intimate relationships contributes to their doubts about their lifestyle with an amplified fear of rejection. Homosexuals form suspicions of discrimination on the part of the heterosexuals that they label as "homophobic." It is not right to deny people freedom of choice.

It is obvious that the homosexuals' involvement in promoting happiness through validity of their choice is not spiritually healthy. Rosenberg C.S.W. argued: "Sexual acts for these people are not gratifying experiences but an endless obsession that leaves them feeling degraded and full of self-loading" (SELF p.30 Apr, 1996). When talking about the deficiency that homosexuality involves, Kluckhohn (1948) and other commenter stated; "Because homosexual relations do not permit reproduction, no record exists of a society that favored homosexuality to the exclusion of heterosexuality" (Ford & Beach, 1951; Greenberg, 1988). Homosexuality is a deviation from the divine plan of procreation, because only a man and a woman can become a mother and a father.

Christ said, "I do not come to judge the world" (Jn 12:47). As spiritual counselors, our part does not consist of judging anybody, but to guide or redirect in a gentle and compassionate manner. The spiritual counselors should not violate the individuals' rights. In a due chance to counsel the sexually-ill oriented, the first thing is to allow them to talk about themselves with no interruption. There is a way of determining whether a sexual orientation is a manipulative or a deliberate choice. A question significant to this determination can be: What does it mean to you to be a gay (or a lesbian)? The subjective version of the answer to this question can be the gateway to learn about some more advanced experi- ence including feeling judged and rejected. To find out how they are facing societal chal- lenges, one may infer and ask: "We should note the possibility that people might differ very strongly with most of us. What is your view on differences of sexual orientation?"

Harriet Lerner in the "New Woman" magazine encouraged one of her correspondents to free their distress by saying, "It is a better sign that you can observe your own acts of decep- tion" (July. 1998). An individual who is sexually-ill oriented has a polarized vision of life - their meaning of life is dubious. They can, internally, sense being judged for their choice, but their sense of moral judgment may not lead to a successful reflection on the necessary decision to experience peace inside. In a program of Masters of Psychology Counseling, a student who was presenting on "gay activities" used flags, logos and lifestyles. To this the classmate, I asked: "Could you give me your opinion on the fact that some gay people have sought for repentance?" The class atmosphere became cold; everyone was silent waiting for an answer. The presenter was honest to reply, "It is true that some gays and lesbians realized that they do not fit the movement and gave up." This latter question sounded very complex. It raised a genuine real issue, an important one, i.e., the desire for repentance that a gay or lesbian may have.

In a relaxing moment, a spiritual counselor may ask a homosexual: "What do you think makes God smile?" Such a question appears simplistic. Penn and Teller argue, "A viewer has only so much attention to give, and if he is laughing his mind is too busy with the joke to backtrack rationality." Contrary to Penn and Teller who revealed the secrets for manipulating the human mind by making them laugh, this question is a way to primarily assess the person's belief in God. Second, it can insinuate if he or she is aware that God has moral values to pursue. Finally, if he or she is willing to win over any sinful temptations – all of this makes God smile. The spiritual counselor proceed with: "I know the following is a challenge, but let us put it this way: Let us, together, figure out what would please God and then figure out the extent to which we can commit to do so." This technique, if implemented after building a counseling rapport with the person, is a non-judgmental and effective way to generate in him or her some kind of reflection-based interpretation of self and personal relationship with God.

Jesus Christ said, "Those who are well have no need for a physician, but those who are sick" (Mat. 9:12). As demonstrated, sexuality has spiritual backgrounds. Sexuality is correlated with feelings experienced during and after sexual acts. A spiritually healthy bond is secured by a heterosexual marriage. Having "safe sex" before marriage does spiritually warrant a level of satisfaction. This is not free of emotional distress. On a radio-broadcasted spiritual counseling, a caller shared that she had been addicted to sex for two years. This caller said (having a talk with his sister regarding their mother's addiction to valium), "My mom was addicted to valium, I start seeing where the roots are," he said. Thus, the caller tried to associate his sexual addiction with his mother's past problem. The spiritual counselor did a good job by clarifying: "Your mother's problem of addiction to valium may have nothing to do with the decision that you made later in life." This answer was an effective way to break up the caller's efforts to conceal the real source of the problem. Furthermore, the spiritual counselor asked, "What happens when you try to connect?" The caller's answer to this question was: "I don't know how I have to feel." Another caller who was a young lady told about her boyfriend who was willing to get married one day and have children, yet she was struggling with impulsive thoughts of homosexuality. The spiritual counselor started by saying "We all have been struggling with these types of sinful trends," and suggested the lady should encourage her boyfriend to look for counseling sup- port for his pitfall mindset.

Let us look at pedophilia. The word pedophilia comes from Greek *paidophilia* – "paias" and "philia", meaning "love and friendship." Greek poets coined this term as a substitute for "paiderastia" (pederasty). It implies sexual interest of an adult primarily toward youngsters. This passion may drive individuals to promote child pornography, child prostitution by means of the internet and or in facility. There exists what is called, "Pedophile Activists." These people strongly advocate "social acceptance of adults' romantic or sexual attraction to children; social acceptance of adults' sexual activity with children; and change in institutions of concern to pedophiles, such as changing age-of-consent laws and mental illness classifications" (Wikipedia.org). "Tough Love Solutions" affirm: "When a society cannot agree on what is age-appropriate sexual behavior, when no limits or values are expressed, then sexual behavior becomes a personal choice from the smorgasbord of life. The cheapest and easiest values prevail. Sex becomes sensational and children become sex objects" (p. 97).

The question is how young is too young for an adolescent to be sexually involved with an adult. In the view of some experts, five years younger than the adult is too young. It is reasonable that post adolescents are physically mature to get married. An adult of 25 years old who has sex with a twenty-year old adolescent needs to be looked at from a different perspective. It is a sign of evil passion for an adult to have sexual activities with a young person. Pragmatically, an opportunistic offense against a child constitutes a breach of trust that a child suffers. In this particular context, a question to open the conversation is to say: "Have you ever heard about pedology?" A possible answer to this question could be "No I don't. What is that?" The spiritual counselor may provide the following definition of Pedology" by saying, "According to the American Heritage Dictionary, "Pedology" is "the study of the physical and mental development and characteristics of children." To a counselee who said having a child or two or more children, one may ask, "Of these two children, who is liked best, is it the child who gains greater attention and more privilege from you than the other ones?" This spiritual exercise aims at helping the child molester to see clearly what he/she did not see before. Other ways to get the pedophile into a signifi- cantly insightful moment is to ask: "How much do you know about the age group?" "Could you, please, share with me this knowledge?" In a lapse of seven to ten minutes of silence, one may obtain some tears, which is spiritually valuable to cure. Even a single sex crime perpetrated against a child is condemnable. It is an evil passion that requires a realistic- acceptance approach.

Incest involves sexual contact, inappropriate touching, or sexual penetration involving people who are genetically related, meaning descendants of a family. It refers to sexual involvement between a father and daughter, a brother and sister, and the like. A victim of incest may undergo a chronic spiritual disturbance (CSD) if the emotional distress is not resolved. Often this victim is intensely traumatized by continuous threats on the part of the offender(s). The victim of incest is in a spiritual state of incertus which involves uncertainty, doubtfulness, and perplexity. The taedium feelings upset her need for connection – it is an abhorrent type of feeling. Often the victim becomes speechless for fear of losing the offender's esteem. Manipulation is the key concept that corroborates the reactions of the victim. This supposes that a victim of incest was involved in a sexual act against his or her will. An experience that is physically and emotionally agonizing in such a way that it may keep the victim from trusting anyone. Trusting becomes the major spiritual barrier to the victim of incest. As we quote, "You are free to love only after you are free to trust" (Stephen C. Paul. Gary Max Collins. In Love. p. 48).

Now, how can a spiritual counselor succeed in mending the wounds of a victim of incest? As spiritual counselors, our first job consists of helping a victim of incest break up the shield of silence, by allowing him or her to unmask the reality. The role of the spiritual counselor is to confront the pattern of reflection disorder concerning *disqualification of being loved*. This is a strange feeling that needs to be respected, and can be addressed as follows: I know the kind of person we are now has a lot to do with what we had done in the past. In your case, you did not do anything wrong. I want you to be certain that you did nothing wrong. Nothing!"

Definition helps makes conscious decision because of the awareness that involves. An exercise of *definition* and *contrast* can help clarify and exclude all the faulty possibilities. As such, the spiritual counselor can gently open a dictionary and invite the counselee to look at the difference between the two words: "Offender and Victim." The importance of this exercise is that the counselee will deduce that he or she did nothing wrong, the blame should be on the offender. The technique of "empty chair" can be used as: Look at this chair. Now, imagine that the person who hurt you is sitting on this chair and you are going to talk to him or her. If there is a prolonged silence, the spiritual counselor may invite the counselee to repeat after him/her: "If you love me as you are assuming, why in the world you hurt me so bad." The other technique associated with the previous one is to give an opportunity to the victim to transfer the burdens of his/her guilt to the offender. This technique is baptized as *burden transference*. Thus, the spiritual counselor assigns a journal to the counselee for which he or she will write several times: "Of course, there are moments in my life that I failed doing the right thing. This particular event that has brought me feelings of shame and overwhelming guilt was not my fault. From today, I am transferring the burdens of my shame and guilt to you (name of the person) who physically and emotionally hurt me." By these three techniques (definition and contrast, the "empty chair," and burden transference), the spiritual counselor is involved in identifying the guilty and easing the emotional burden. It is when the burdens of irrational guilt vanishes that the victim will stop blaming self and gets the understanding and responsibility to forgive his/her debtor(s).

The advanced stage in counseling a victim of offense is to assist this person in *trusting again*. It is a fact that the emotional impacts of incest can be more severe on certain children and adolescents than other. Some of them may be so distressed that they may become incapable of trusting anyone. One of the simplest ways to address the dilemma of "trusting again" is to prioritize "forgiveness" over "trust." The rationale of this method is that the problem is so painful that the victim would be incapable of perceiving accurately the idea of trusting someone who has caused so much suffering. This trust issue will, eventually, be resolved after the goal of forgiving is attained. In the chapter "The cleansing power of forgiveness," Don Colbert wrote, "Forgiveness enables a person to release buried anger, resentment, bitterness, shame, grief, regret, guilt, hate, and other toxic emotions that hide deep in the soul and make a person sick" (p. 163). This knowledge may serve the counselor as premise to this intervention: Given that you acknowledged you were victimized by someone of greater power than you and that you transferred the guilt and shame to this offender, let us look at the definition of "forgiving." From the American Heritage Dictionary "forgiving" is the synonym for "granting pardon without harboring resentment." The idea is that someone who is willing to pass over a mistake is likely to trust again the offender and other people. For this purpose, the spiritual counselor can intervene: In the beginning you told me how painful it was to believe in this horrible thing that happened to you. And, you were very concerned about trusting this person who violated your will. Apparently, your incapability of trusting this individual has caused you to mistrust all people. Let us look at this problem of trusting from a different angle, that is the angle of forgiving.

The following question aims at checking on the person's readiness for this spiritual advent: "Do you think that you are emotionally ready to pass over your offender's trespassing?" If the person requires further clarification: "What I mean is, are you willing to free the offender from the consequences of being treated as the 'devil.'" The counselor's task of teaching forgiveness would be much easier if the counselee is a believer in God. Jesus Christ is the perfect model of a forgiver. As it is for resentment and anger, forgiving goes along with attitude and impression. The question, "How do you want this person to know about your desire to forgive him or her?" is equivalent to "How would you be suc- cessful in communicating and demonstrating that you are forgiving the offender?" The last thing to do is to pray for the counselee to achieve his goal of forgiving his/her debtors."

What if an adult is a prostitute? As the other described sexual ill-orientation, prostitution is a vivid example of sexual liberality, meaning involvement in sexual activities out of regulation of one's True Conscience. The following is a testimony made by a young prostitute, Katia who came to realize that her life was in jeopardy:

> I could not believe for a moment that AIDS really exists, up to the day that one of my friends was hit by the surge of the enemy. Already, when I was 17, I had affairs with many men simultaneously. From one Hotel to another, I traveled to all the big cities in those years, always looking for the best affairs. Prior to the illness of my best friend (she who initiated me in this business), I did not want to hear talk about AIDS and offering condoms was considered an insult to my person. And today, I am aware of the spread of the disease, due to our ignorance, our fight of the humiliation, which accompanies this illness in the society and our incredibility, she said with pain (www.panosinst.org/Island/IB38e.shtml).

This testimony shows three spiritual dimensions of prostitution: confusion, an inadequate self-confidence, and an obscured conscience. Prostitution has three features: financial security, happiness, and sexuality. One of the indications of obscured conscience is a lack of center of awareness of one's spiritual needs. In this case of prostitution, Katia's need for self-preservation was lacking. Prior to this shocking event, she was practically insensitive to the true meaning of life. She found insulting, the use of "condoms" by her customers. We know that Katia had been suffering greatly because of her friend's loss. Katia's death of her friend from AIDS persuaded her about the importance of self-protection. She became more fully aware of this lack, which is the desire to stay healthy. The story of this young prostitute does unveil a need for redemption. To get a sense of her concepts of living with trust and living safe, one may ask her: "Katia, have you ever tried to compare the time you were truly in love with these present periods of your life?" Such a question may bring an insight of her lack in order to live the life she really aspires to. A typical question that can inspire the need for redemption in any sexually-ill oriented person is: "Is it possible for you to really feel secure when you have some concerns about your lifestyle?"

Chapter Ten

PREVARICATION AND SPIRITUAL COUNSELING TO PREVARICATORS

Etiology of lying – *an understanding of the causes or triggers to lies*

Prevarication is a spiritual disturbance characterized by deceitful speech and manipulative behavior for personal gain. A prevaricator is a chronic liar in that this person is prompted to evade the point in the question and engages in counterfeit. Given the prevailing belief that lying opens opportunities to life, fear of contradiction of these individuals car- ries the inability to deal with uncertainty. Given that a prevaricator stretches, distorts, per- verts, hides or conceals the truth, this person may claim to have said the truth, though, in fact, it is deceit. Such reaction reveals a fear of rejection. To a great extent, someone with this spiritual disturbance has reflection disorder that keeps him from achieving a desired goal and solving a possible solution.

The prevaricator gains a sense of safety in lying. The entire process of lying brings a temporary relief. This spiritual condition is characterized by a pattern of survival interpre- tation of opportunities without a second thought. In normal situations, fear of contradiction brings concerns about self and/or the decisions or choices previously made. It involves that a prevaricator depends upon the outcomes of a given lies. A prevaricator, for fear of being contradicted, goes from lies to lies. They are gainsayers. Failure of lies begets much more sophisticated ones. Their inability to discern causes them to rely on the correctness of their own judgment and competency of their own powers. When they feel uncomfortable after telling lies (in order for them to regain an internal comfort) they often aggrandize their ignominious defeat. When a prevaricator is confronted by the evidence of truth, they may appear astounded, and then declare to be false any presented evidence.

They use conterexamples and facts to disprove others' hypotheses on their weaknesses and past failure.

The rationale of recurrent lies is *meo voto*, meaning "according to my own wish." On revealing David P. Abbott's secrets of manipulating the human mind (an Omaha magician), Penn and Teller commented, "Nothing fool you better than the lies you tell yourself" (Smithsonian. March, 2012. p. 31). In a prevaricator's mind, the Educated Conscience (EC) creates a stream of falsehood that surges over the True Conscience (TC). When the EC overrules the Mind, the ongoing spiritual activities create confusion in the person's mind as evidenced by a loss of clarity and a lack of center of awareness. This person senses no obligation to tell the truth and to act truthfully. This is a way of saying that every action a predicator takes aims at serving his or her personal interests. Nevertheless, the well-known consequences of a prospective action is denied or ridiculed.

An *alibi* aims at *faking the reality*. One of the greatest *alibi* that liars use is "nobody is perfect," which indeed sounds reasonable. Another alibi is "I have no reason to lie." Remember a manipulator is also a liar. And lying is a means of manipulation. A typical "but message" is characterized by a good intention followed by some reservations. With serious intent to insult, a liar may say: "I hope this does not insult you, but. . . ." As they are saying and doing things that are likely to upset their interlocutor(s), a liar may state: "I don't want to upset you, but. . . ." In fact, a potential prevaricator forms his or her initial opinion before he or she even has the capacity to honor a promise. Whenever someone disregards intentionally one or several principles of living with trust, living with will, living fair, and living safe, what occurs is purely alibi.

There is a need to look at the achievability of some specific vows. A person, with the intent to deceive a love partner can speak and act falsely or evasively. A vow could be: "I adore you. I will love you for ever." Another romantic vow is: "I can't stop thinking about you. I don't feel complete without you next to me." What may happen is that when like promises fail for any reason, another typical alibi that is likely to happen is: "Your absence screwed me up." "I was not mindful enough to imagine how I would make such a mistake." Three hypotheses establish an individual's likelihood to utter such lies:

1- The more one is egocentric, the more one utters lies about self.
2- The more a personal goal is unrealistic, the greater is the worry and the dissatisfaction with life, and the greater are chances to persistently use alibi.
3- The least lack of knowledge and trust in Jesus Christ enhances vulnerability to lies.

We have identified four significant domains that help to account for the etiology (the origins and causes) of lies:

1- Circumstantial Lies (CL)
2- Institutional Lies (IL)
3- Power-positioning Lies (PpL), and
4- Grudge-induced Lies (GiL)

Circumstantial Lies (CL): There are moments in life that are more tedious than others. The desire to meet a standard of living and the energy invested in reaching a goal may increase the possibilities for lying when situations are getting wearisome. The fears that make us offensive and the ones that render us defensive when facing obstacles are distinct. That's because the energy level associated with certain fears provokes worry and panic that leads to lies. One lies due to fear of vulnerability, fear of failure, fear of rejection, and fear of recurrent failure. There is a great sense of comfort that follows lies that permit a detour to a challenging situation and appeases the core of the issue within self.

Contrary to circumstantial lies that are automatic or impulsive, *premeditated* lies have practical purposes, which is the avoidance of retribution. The individual who seeks to avoid punishment, precontemplate ways to succeed in self-defensiveness. In so far, as human beings premeditate on the consequences of their bad behavior, they tend to conceal the truth or lie about what they did that creates the problem. An example of premeditating reflection is: "If I have to cover my wrongdoing, I should go from step A to step B, from C to D, and so on." Worry associated with self-defensiveness increases the individuals' likeli- hood to fail in covering their trespassing. What happens is that as one is obsessing himself or herself over covering up lies by other lies, disappointment and deception are on the line. Fear of abandonment, for instance, may engender premeditating lies toward fulfillment of one's need for connection. With no intent to stereotype, premeditated lies are very common in politicians who strive to inspire their potential voters to offset the usual ways in which they process information concerning "betterment."

Institutional Lies (IL): There exist, in the world, institutions and organizations that hire people for marketing and salespersons. Those institutions have pre-established ways to persuade customers with no second thought toward investment (of time and money). The internal drive to secure tomorrow (fear of tomorrow) with riches was found to be a key incentive of this worldwide practice. While a sense of community is a positive way to build confidence in self and in God, some religious, political, and/or economic standards, seem to be detrimental to people's self-confidence building by the recognition that their leaders violated their trust and naiveté. Often, people who are ignorantly determined to spread forgeries have no clue that they are doing something wrong. It is when government, after due investigation, closes the company due to fraud that some of them do come to the realization of their counterfeit.

Some religious beliefs may be the cause of the individuals' divergence from the truth. There are religions which are established in a system that support a *prevaricating common sense*. The Apostle Paul understood that in a God-and-human relationship there should be no "darkness." As he said, "This is the message we have heard from him and proclaim to you, that God is light and in Him there is no darkness at all. If we say we have fellowship with Him while we walk in darkness, we lie and do not live according to the truth" (1 John 1:5–7). Individuals who are living in accordance with a religiously wrong doctrine are spiritually misled and are enslaved by the dogma they are professing. Some religious doctrines constitute the doorway to confusion. The notion of "living by grace and/or by law" seems to perpetuate the dilemma of discerning the truth among the Christians. Religious leaders that take a stance against the law are engaged in intensive efforts to dissuade their followers about the ground rules of living with trust, living with will, living fair and living safe consistent with an improved quality of life. That's because as religious leaders they have the responsibility to model faith, justice and love in all aspects of life. By preaching or teaching that the Ten Commandments are obsolete, they are contradicting themselves and not earnestly engaged in helping their disciples concerning their need for redemption.

The Apostle John considered clergymen who encourage others to deny the spiritually positive impacts that the Ten Commandments of God have had in human lives are "liars": "He who says 'I know' Him but disobeys his commandments is a liar, and the truth is not in him…He who says he abides in Him ought to walk in the same way in which He walked" (1 John 2: 4-5). From Schumacher's perspective, "When there is so many gods, all competing with one another and claiming first priority, and there is no supreme God, no supreme good or value in terns of which everything else needs to justify itself, society cannot but drift into chaos" (p. 509) To help overcome confusion created by institutional lies, spiritual counseling may include the following outlines:

- Helping to acknowledge that God is the Creator as He has made provision by which all His human creatures should abide.
- Reading aloud Exodus 20 in the Bible and Mathew 5 verse 17 as a way to empha- size the invariability of the Ten Commandments.
- Jesus Christ, the Son of God observed the Sabbath - including all the command- ments, and finally,
- Imploring God's grace to understand the necessity for complying with all divinely therapeutic means.

Power-positioning Lies (PpL): The temptation to lie may be associated with the individuals' will to get or maintain power. To these individuals, social influence is the vehicle that brings happiness. The pursuit of power is correlated with socially reinforced fears such as, fear of failure, and fear of rejection, when blunder causes a lie. In other words, individuals who feel disapproved, disliked, hated, or rejected by society may be driven to compensate their lack by faking the true self. In a context of these reinforced fears, individuals may lie about their achievements that include their job status, their marital status, and/or their career.

When talking about abortion, James Rachels argued, "Human beings are tempted to enjoy exercising power over others. . . ." This leads us to the consideration of the moral sense of human power. In the same way, parents, teachers, supervisors, CEOs may cause their subalterns (children, staff, and directors) to feel compelled to use stratagems (i.e., false promises) to compel them into compliance with their expectations. It is obvious that individuals who suffer from the *malady of power* are excellent in manipulating or lying to others because of their power position. Their potentiality to manipulate may turn to be disappointing when the truth is unveiled. This spiritual matter is of fundamental importance in that the manipulator can easily become disappointed when confronted by evidence of their lies and rebellion on the part of their prey.

Prevarication may lead to *power entertainment*. When two individuals are in a power position and both are eager for taking control over an institution or a group, it is likely that one is engaged in "bearing false witness against" the other, which is a sin according to Exodus 20 verse 16. Imagine a married woman becomes an officer in a church and is highly esteemed for her moral commitment by the church members. Suppose, this woman had an extra-marital affair and gets pregnant, and the explanation provided on her aborted baby is dubitably diversified. The story told about the child's death may be done in variously complicated ways. Here are a few things that this woman might say in order to convince people about her "unwanted abortion:" To one person she may say, "I fell down from climbing last step of a stair which caused the death of my carrying baby." To another person she might say: "I was about to go downstairs to draw water from the well when I missed the very last step." In the event somebody approaches her to tell her what was heard, by saying: "I was informed about the incident of your falling when you were going downstairs to get drinkable water," she may respond by embarrassment, weeping, and, eventually, gets irritated. Maintaining influence in church is for this woman the *peak priority*.

This woman's zeal to go to church and exert her leadership as if nothing had happened is conceptualized as *power entertainment*. All attempts to take away her reputation are critical. As she strives to conceal her immoral act, anyone suspected to tell the truth about her will generate a wide-range of reactions on her part.

To the church members who approach her on the issue, this woman may speak out with a feeling of pride and arrogance; she may swear, calumniate, bear false witness, defame, and/or make mockery. The likelihood of having cruel intention is significant. It is reasonable to conclude that the death of an aborted baby is a sad and guilt-induced event; power entrainment unfolds the woman's efforts to safeguard her reputation as evidenced by her concealment of her wrongful act. Her reactions to obvious obstacles constitute the other side of eagerness for power that is power exhibition – a demonstration of being in full force or execution.

Grudge-induced lies (GiL) refer to a strongly emotional disturbance due to worry and panic created by past offense(s). Individuals seek and become friends, are bound in partnership and romantic relationships with those who have values that are similar to their own. When their relationship goes wrong, they tend to have strong negative feelings toward one another (i.e., abhorrent feelings). It usually involves a vague suspicion that the offender may assail again. The pattern of thoughts associated with these feelings provides the basis of derogatory expressions against the betrayer or the offender. The friend who was "betrayed" may become seriously resentful.

The Greek word that best describes resentment or grudge is "pikria" that stands for acridity (esp. poison). Grudged feelings produce an enduring tendency to think, feel, and behave in a constantly unfavorable fashion with respect to the inflicted evil. An example of irritation stemmed from feelings of resentment is when someone says: "I did not deserve that." The most recurring reflection disorder about past injustices (*retroflection*) gear to the thought: "This was one of my worst moments in life," or they may start their complaints as: "What a humiliation for me when someone. . . ." Mental processes of the kind are likely to enhance capabilities of revenging a specific "unjust act." These individuals may become extremely rigid and pitiless in blaming, cursing, and accusing their offenders. In pursuit of revenge, the person who was hurt tends to respond to evil by evil, which includes character assassination and false accusation. This corroborates the rationale of grudge-induced lies.

Counseling techniques and skill building exercise to withstand temptation to lying

In our construct of spirituality, individuals may have needs that are unmet and seek gratification of a specific need by intellectual powers. Given the emphasis that we put on a truth-oriented therapy, spiritual counselors should get a clear mental impression of the counselee's source of dissatisfaction [due to unmet need(s)] that has caused his or her dependence on lying. The purpose is not to rush blaming nor deterring a chronic liar (a prevaricator), but the "shame of lies." The best attitude of the counselor is to stop, look and listen. The counselor has to look for the intention behind the story. Often, a lie is allied with two or more contradictory messages. Decisions to lie seem to be determined by specific needs, fears, and feelings to which one needs to be paying special attention. Someone may say: "I remember when my grandfather died. His death was such a burden for me that I was unable to eat, or go to work for months. I could not believe that his death could have been so agonizing to me. " In this case, the two following questions help illuminate the dilemmas that lie in the story telling.

These questions can serve as a reality check. After actively listening to the story telling, one may ask: "How old was your grandfather?" Second, "When were you sick, after the funerals? Which person assisted you?" When lying, individuals do not carefully evaluate the information provided. Some hypothetical questions can help clarify why the emotional burden resulting from a severely old person may not be as heavy as grieving from the loss of a young person.

Another benefit of hypothetical questions is to determine the extent to which the death has caused dejection and how distress associated with dejection (if any) was managed. When the scenario of emotional impacts is given, the speaker may disregard the reality that people with depression need either family support or medical intervention. The answer may be such as: "For 5 years, I was living away from my mother, and my sister was not married, but I learned to love my grandmother who lived in the countryside." To the same extent, a mother who said constantly to her little daughter "I love you," but yells and screams at the child who accidentally breaks a glass; this mother is, in sight of this child, likely to be viewed as a "liar."

The spiritual counselor should seek after *clarity of purposes*. Instead of asking a counselee if there is an area of his/her life where he/she wants to redirect his life, the center of attention of a spiritual counselor is to be on the fear-and-need factors that can be used as premises to further understanding and questioning. In the previous scenario, for clarity of purpose, one may ask: "You just told me about the kinds of feelings you experienced when your grandfather died. What was the purpose of calling your boss and asking for several months off work when you need the money to pay your bills?" Multiple unsuccessful attempts to commit suicide are instances of prevarication. Obviously, this person is not in an eminent danger to die by suicide but is alarmed about his surroundings around a particular fear and need. In many occasions, someone may state, "I tell her I will kill myself if she doesn't let me leave" – a statement that may be a mere stratagem to scare the partner.

The speaker's fear of vulnerability here is blundered due to ignorance, confusion, and the stupidity (serial suicidal attempts) involved. A way to find out the purpose of 'these acts" is to ask a *metaphoric question* such as, "How heavy is the dresser when you are pushing it against the wall and no one comes to assist you?" Such a question aims at evaluating the level of self-trust without others' aid. The speaker in the previous example demonstrates a need for connection in relation to his fear of rejection or of abandonment that is blundered, as shown. These techniques: seeking clarity of purpose and metaphoric questions spare the counselor from asking difficult questions, notably: "What kind of things you want to see happen in your life to decide not to lie any longer?" Another difficult and embarrassing question could be: "Have you ever felt an impulse to put someone else down in public or even to shirk responsibility and blame someone else for your failings?"

Praying God's attributes is a skill building exercise that can help a prevaricator. The issue of self-trust that gives rise to recurrent lies is due to impossibilities and hopeless situations. The kind of prayer that the spiritual counselor teaches is an important part of spiritual skill building.

We cannot guarantee that our help will cause people to be faithful to God, but we can teach them how to trust and claim God's attributes. This could be for the counselee the beginning of a new start in a relationship with God. They may need to know what prayer really is and the benefits and grace of prayer. Typically, it is always good for someone who feels rejected to seek refuge in God. A resentful person who is engaged in speaking evil about their offenders may not turn to God and pray His attributes due persistent bitterness created by the evildoer(s). Together, the spiritual counselor and the counselee will explore whether the prayer request is a realistic and achievable goal.

If the counselee verbally consents to praying God's attributes with humbleness, the counselor should teach the basics of prayer: 1) Prayer is honest and private conversation to God, 2) Anyone who believes in God can turn their concerns into prayer (concern of being betrayed, concern of being unable to trust again, or your most important challenge in telling the truth about yourself and others). The prevaricator has to acknowledge the incredible spiritual and emotional benefits of telling the truth to God about the propensity to utter lies.

To help build confidence in God's attributes, the counselor may let the counselee read the following (quoted from *Busy Woman's Guide to Prayer*):

Jehovahnissi: "The Lord My Banner." "His banner over me is love" (see Exodus 17:15 and Song of Songs 2:4 NJV and NLT).

Jehovahjireh, meaning "The Lord will Provide." He knows our needs and provides for them (see Genesis 22:14 KJV and NLT).

Jehovahshalom, meaning "The Lord is Peace." He gives us inner peace (see Judges 6:24 KJV and NLT).

Jehovahraah, meaning "The Lord is My Shepherd." He promises to lead and guide us, to speak to us, and show us what direction to go (see Psalm 23).

Jehovahrapha, meaning "The Lord Who Heals" (see Exodus 15:25-27 NASB; Psalm 103:3, 147:3; 1 Peter 2:24).

As Cheri Fuller (2005) suggested, the counselor may ask his or her counselee to choose one of these attributes to incorporate into his or her weekly prayer. Some counselees may find this exercise helpful and pray in faith as they proclaim God's grace, which experience is likely to be reiterated. Other people may view it as time consuming, boring, and even worthless. These responses are similar to several instances of spiritual counseling.

Chapter Eleven

THE ETHICS FOR BEING A SPIRITUAL COUNSELOR

Individuals' opinions on a topic vary on account of cultural diversity and distinct experiences. Philosophers are not always clear about the positive effects of having consistent rules and living by those rules. In practice, spiritual counseling should avoid the dilemma pertaining to moral rules conflict. For success in spiritual counseling, there is a need to establish rules, principles, and ethical manners. In all instances of spiritual counseling, conflicts of values are to be resolved in reference to the Bible. In light of Jesus Christ's statement, "The truth will set you free," derives the golden rule in spiritual counseling that is, *one ought not to harm*. When presenting the truth from the Bible, the counselor should do it with respect and humbleness. Let us examine specific rules and cautions to be taken on the part of spiritual counseling.

A Spiritual Counselor has no Power to produce a Desired Result

There is an objective and subjective version of the principle of involvement in powerful counseling. Objectively, a spiritual counselor should be true to his responsibilities and limitations on the part of counseling. The subjective aspect is about facing the way one avoids fear and other negative emotions in the course of counseling. This concerns how one distracts from resistance and rejection, and also how one comforts self in the face of unmerited credits. What is needed here is a clear distinction between the counselor's expec- tation of positive outcomes and the results expected through God's intervention. From this perspective, when spiritual counselors see the absurdity in their way, they are unlikely to become defensive to a point of cursing and abandoning, and any other negative attitudes that may have huge impact on counseling.

The second leading idea in spiritual counseling is based on the participant's freedom of choice. Participants are free to weigh the benefits of their involvement in the counseling process and make interpretations of the presented alternatives. The problem comes when a counselor tries to exert control over the participant who, otherwise, finds it more distressing than it is in reality. Hence there is a distinction between self-conceived rules and expectations that can be used to judge other progress and values and rules that are divinely established. In spiritual counseling, it is unrelated to deny God's supernatural power to make change more in individuals' hearts and lifestyles. The term in line with God's intervention is *lucri causa intervention*, which means "intervention for the sake of gain." An attitude of humility and dependence on God can spare the process of counseling from a wide variety of misunderstanding and misperception. When confronted by questions and when presenting problems that are beyond their understanding, the best attitude and response that a counselor can provide is by saying: "For a better understanding of this matter, we need to pray to God about it."

A Spiritual Counselor must cease being Religious

As adults we were religiously and culturally trained to make other people feel guilty when they do not share same religious beliefs as us. Given the complexity of religion, spiritual counselors need to defer their personal religious beliefs by capitalizing upon the truths of life. A religious person does not value the principles of living with trust in God, fails to be fair and safe and is stubbornly unreceptive to wise counsel. This person's customs will not change overnight. Spiritual counselors should bear in mind that counselees have the right to dissent the truths of life as presented in the Bible.

Critics consider a debate on religion to be one of the most provocative issues of our time. To avoid tensions due to a difference in religion, it is recommended that the spiritual counselors refrain from speaking and acting on behalf of any religion. The idea is strongly advanced that religious people will fail to gain the attention of their counselees on the truths of life, by excessive talking about their religion achievements, as they feign weak- nesses of this or that religion. We have to think in terms of benefits not just philosophy. The way a religious person lives his or her life is entirely different from the life a simple person. The Apostle Paul ceased being religious in that instead of using constraining influence for the sake of his philosophy, he honestly acknowledged, "…the evil I do not want is what I do" (Rom. 7:19). `In the initial meeting with a counselee, one may ask him or her to briefly speak about his or her religion preference if he or she has one. The spiritual counselor can kindly emphasize, "I know how much your religion means to you. However, we are going to spend the next few precious moments not in exploring or discussing certain religions, but rather what is in our best interests – how much God cares for you and me."

A pertinent incident of how someone's religion can be a threat to someone else was reported by Boston Herald. The headline was about a man who killed his wife due to complaints about exposure to "too much religion" on the part of his wife. The question raised by the reporter was the following: "Did too much religion made him kill?" (Boston Herald on May 22, 2006). We learned that this man who repudiated his wife's religion hammered her to death. The man's cruel intention, prior to his homicidal act, was brought to the readers' attention through the statements of the victim's church members and her neighbors. A church member stated, "We knew of the challenges she was having." A family's friend confirmed, "He did not like her religion." (pp.7). It is obvious that the woman's religion became a source of nuisance to her husband that caused him resentment and the homicidal act. From this report, our deduction is that some individuals' perception of a given religion (or of all religions) is that they may be resistant and/or act aggressively toward the adepts of this religion. Thus, how people relate to counsel may be troublesome due to people's misapprehension that spiritual counseling is "merely religious."

Jesus Christ gave a classic counsel of how to handle extreme resistance on the part of a counselee or a group of counselees? We give credence to this technique of *shaking-the-dust reaction*, since our safety may depend upon it. Here is Christ's explanation: "If any one will not receive you or listen to your words, shake the dust off your feet as you leave that house or town" (Mat. 10:14). This reaction is not to be applied literally. It is a way for the counselors to avoid heating arguments and prevent harmful conduct on the part of their counselees. Turning one's back to provocation is the most effective way to show acceptance of the speaker's free will and agree with his or her right to refuse counseling.

Given that the aim of spiritual counseling is to see people improve in their personal values, a spiritual counselor can use the following phrase to introduce this possibility of religion-free counseling: "Let us diligently and enthusiastically 'seek things that are above, where Christ is seated at the right hand of God. Set our affections (or minds) on things above, not on things on earth" (Col 3:1). The benefit of making spiritual counseling a truth- oriented counseling can be traced to Jesus Christ's exemplary life and His promises. The goal is to work together with the counselee(s) toward a deeper and richer relationship with Christ.

A Spiritual Counselor must clarify in regard to Biblical References

In a meeting of two or more people, one of the most powerful and effective ways to effective spiritual counseling is to be equipped with a book of reference. All religions have a book of reference that differs in many areas. The main areas of dissimilarity of these books of reference include dietary restrictions, pre-marital sex, and justices seeking, who may to a certain extent offend normal patterns of thinking. One of the objectives of spiritual counseling is to make individuals less and less vulnerable to confusion. It is obvious that when one religion allows eating certain foods that are forbidden in another, cultural diversity of such may lead to confusion. In order to prevent confusion in spiritual counseling, one should seek to be truly relaxed and comfortable with the most recommended book of reference that is the Bible. The counselee should also consent to this reference. As we quote: "A man cannot be comfortable without his own comfort" (Mark Twain).

When considering alternatives for change that work quiet well, we understand that many truths of life cannot be grasped by common ways of discerning and imagination or as processed by traditional therapy. Commitment to the Bible, as the book of reference for spiritual counseling, can lead to real freedom and to moral growth. The Bible is particularly valuable when exploring issues related to real-life situations and the abstract. A spiritual counselor needs to use his or her own judgment concerning when, in the course of counseling, he or she may introduce the Bible. On most occasions (when traveling, when meeting people in the street, in market places, or elsewhere) one may use memory to paraphrase biblical verses. In a well-planned meeting, a spiritual counselor can skillfully introduce the Bible as such, "I know all religions have a different book of reference. I am wondering when we are meeting, in order to clarify points of discussion, whether we can use the Bible as the book of reference."

The Bible can improve the natural ability of discerning in living with trust, living with will, living fair and living safe. Because of cultural diversity, in our time, unity of trust and of interpretation of biblical counsels is difficult to achieve. At this point, one should expect resistance on the part of the counselee or counselees. Resistance of sort can be attributed to refusal to abnegate one's belief in a book of reference quiet different from custom. The counselor's task may turn to be harder in persuading the participant(s) about the fact that the Bible is a reliable book that inspires wisdom to all of its readers.

The Bible is the unique way to reflect on the gift of life and provides the exacting alternative to a life-changing experience. It is clear that only the Bible strongly emphasizes sin as the core issue of humankind. Given "sin" is a biblically centered concept, the solution for eradication of sin must be drawn from instructions of the Bible. Early influences of the Bible in individuals' lives are beneficial in that these individuals' Educated Conscience enhances their discerning ability. As of the other inspired authors of the Bible, the Apostle Paul wrote to the Romans and the other people of his time about the extent to which sin can damage self and others if is not taken care of. Paul recommended that the first step on becoming insightful of one's sinful acts is by the knowledge of the law of God. To the Romans, the Apostle wrote: "Through the law comes knowledge of sin" (Rom. 3:20). When someone expressed the need for "a better life…," the question that is worth being asked is: "What is a better life?" There is a sense in which people's decision for a "better life" may not fall in line with the Bible. Spiritual counselors can approach this need in light of the need of redemption that is compatible with the causal principal according to which a person may be held responsible for his own conduct and feel compelled to seek help. We must therefore argue our spirit governed by our conscience is the greater part of the process of experiencing this need.

In conjunction with the biblical truth that *all humans are sinners*, there is a need to clarify "a better life" in the context of the Ten Commandments. Thus, if a person has chosen to refrain from doing the wrongful act (A) and has a condition (B) that renders the decision to refrain from wrongdoing as ineffective, there will be a need for a new-birth experience to overcome this predicament. Our predisposition to sin is not an isolated case in the overall spiritual issues of humankind. This trend to sin substantiates the *raison d'être* of spiritual counseling. Charles Colson (2002) stated:

> Sinner is not some theological term contrived to explain away the presence of evil in this world; nor is it a cliché conceived by colonial hymn writers or backwoods preachers to frighten recalcitrant congregations.

Colson concluded by saying: "We are not theological sinners or honorary sinners or vicarious sinners. We are sinners indeed and in deed." If we are to think here of a choice possibly rendered ineffective, it can be a spiritual disturbance in which the individual is mentally incapable of refraining from wrongdoing. This condition is identified as *mindlessness*. This might be a person who knows he is killing someone (either with a weapon or an infectious disease) and has chosen to do so. This choice of harming others may be deliberate or excusable, due to the mental derangement that causes the person's denial of having done anything wrong. We do not need a certain test to decide whether a person was not free and so not responsible for his misdeed other than the knowledge he chose to avoid the wrong he committed. R.C. Sproul summed it up well: "We are not sinners because we sin; we sin because we are sinners."

When a counselee is skeptical of the possibility of being forgiven by God and is feeling distressed by the burden of his guilt, what is to be done? A way to reassure a counselee that God's plan of redemption underlies forgiveness of all sins regardless their gravity is by saying: 1) I understand that "Everyone shall die for his own sin, each man who eats sour grapes, his teeth shall be set on edge (Jer. 31:30); 2) God will not look to you in anger as long as you acknowledge your guilt and your rebellion against the Lord God (Jer. 3: 12-13). This truth can help one to see how precious we are in God's sight, and lead one to contemplate the practical aspect of His love that was demonstrated by Christ's crucifixion. David Laeger (2004) wrote: "Covenant was made through the sacrifice of animal prepared for eating by both sides. As they are, they were unified by participation in the body of the same animal (p. 100).

Charles W. Conn affirmed, "The more we feed upon God's word, the more we grow spiritually." A spiritual counselor must be biblically equipped to demonstrate the correlation between the effectiveness of grace and the believers' commitment to the law. Although "all have sinned and fall short of the glory of God" (Rom. 2:12), Christ still redeems and empowers all true seekers to pursue the ideal of being freed from the curse of sin that strikes everyone's dignity. God does not want anyone to be enslaved by any form of addiction (sexual, money, fame, power ...). This infers that Jesus Christ is the only "WAY" for salvation and redemption. As a way to support the validity of prophetic writings, spiritual counselors should allude to changes that powerful religious and political characters have experienced in the law of God (Daniel 7:25). The spiritual counselors may bring to their counselees' attention the historical fact that, in the year 321 A.D. emperor Cardinal Constantine amended the fourth commandment (information that can be found online).

There are times when spiritual counselors need to validate their counselee's points of view. Validation of the counselee's ideas and opinions followed by biblical recommendations can be made by use of one of the following phrases:

"That sounds like a good idea." "That's a good point."
"I think you're right about that."

This technique of validation, when used, helps increase the counselee(s)'s awareness of the reality that spiritual counseling is not grounded in the counselor's philosophy or values; the focus is rather on biblically-defined truths of life. It is true that "Ambivalence about various possibilities can be viewed in part as the experiential result of multiple conflicting values" (Miller Rollnick. p. 292). Validation is an incredible booster of self-worth, personal development, and any active participation brought to the discussion. A Practical way to encourage someone who is prompted to confess his mistakes is to say: "It seems that you are very considerate of how your actions affect your life and the lives of other people. Let us pray and study the Word of God as we ask for His guidance this process."

In sum, the central importance of clarifying by means of biblical references is to establish a collaborative process that aims at screening a point in discussion to avoid any mistake in interpretation – errors that may be attributed to subjectivity. This task of clarifying may lead to an important phase, *e.g.*, "changing one's mind" after discovering and weighing one or several truths of life. This suggests that pinpointing the wrongness of someone's habits, in light of the Bible, ought to be distinguished from some sort of constraint to obeying. The reasons for change will arise from a reflection-based interpretation of what is read, or it may come through ignoring the important work of this phase or by being concealed by excuses of all sorts. This exercise is unlike other forms of counseling as it is attributed to an out-of-the-ordinary counseling. Remember our counselees are free to decide for themselves. It is their prerogative to believe whether the Bible's instructions are truths of life or unworthy of serious consideration.

A Spiritual Counselor should lead a Lifestyle of Simplicity

Our cultural and family upbringing may render our life unpredictably complicated. A complicated life is, by definition, a life with exaggerated concerns or fears. Faulty interpretation, for example, makes one's desires and actions indiscernible. These confused individuals generate an incredibly complex lifestyle as evidenced by pride and intellectuality. Their greed and ambition are long-lasting characteristics of their complicated life. We want to point out that these individuals may have passion for money, passion for sex, and passion for power that block their reasoning ability even with the simplest life issue. Following a wrongful act, these individuals often blame other people rather than taking responsibility for their mistakes.

Let us now look at the lifestyle and conduct of a simple person. The three aspects of a life of simplicity are revealed in: (1) positive speech, (2) humble attitude toward sacred things, and (3) sincere condemnation of wrong doing. Some people's simplicity is evidenced in their integrity of judgment. A simple person, for example, is not worried about his or her reputation when making a rational stand for a fact. His or her integrity prevents him or her from getting involved in manipulative acts. He or she acknowledges his or her wrongful acts with no intent to manipulate others. The discrepancy between an intended act and the actual act itself can be explained by a variety of circumstances.

A simple person, for example, often accepts the badness of his or her conduct and does not force other people to approve his or her wrongful acts. Unlike to a complicated person, the argument and counsel of a simple person are not misleading and self-contradicting. Such simplicity shows itself quite clearly in fostering collaborative works and mediation between dissidents. The way they interpret a problem and their sincere engagement in solving conflicts is unequivocal and likely to be appreciated by the parties involved. As spiritual counselors, our aim, therefore, is to model a life of simplicity through our speech and behavior.

A Spiritual Counselor must Trust the Promise of Resurrection and Counsels in Accordance with this Trust

A spiritual counselor is committed to presenting the truth and the solution to the greatest tragedy of humanity - that is death. This major concern of humanity should be explained in a clear, correct, and persuasive manner. When a causal explanation is given about death, a spiritual counselor then establishes the truth regarding resurrection. We are, of course, concerned with knowing what is true and what is false about the doctrine of death.

The physical condition of the dead is often misinterpreted. Solomon was speaking the truth when he said, "The living know that they will die, but the dead know nothing." (Eccl. 9:5). This infers that once a person is dead, there is no way that he or she may continue communicating with living beings. At the time, Solomon was not referencing the notion of resurrection in to his conclusive statement, "The dead have no reward and the memory of them is lost" (Ibid). The spiritual counselor, however, should not condemn the doctrine of the state of the dead without presenting first the sole alternative i.e., the resurrection. To this extent, the retributive theory may be wrong regarding the prophesized judgment of the dead. As it is written:

> Truly, truly, I say to you, the hour is coming, and now is, when the dead will hear the voice of the Son of God, and those who hear will live. For as the Father has life in himself, so He has granted the Son also to have life in Himself, and has given Him authority to execute judgment, because he is the Son of man. Do not marvel at this; for the hour is coming when all who are in the tombs will hear his voice and come forth, those who have done good, to the resurrection of life, and those who have done evil, to the resurrection of judgment (Jn. 25:29).

When the issue of death is raised, and attention is drawn to reasons, the spiritual counselor must regard the counselee's argument as a normal process due to fear of death that is universal. A complete explanation of death can be given in terms of its cause and effect for humanity from a scientific point of view. It is indeed non-rational to argue that there are signs of life in the death. Erroneous conclusions such as, the spirit of the dead is reincarnated, or that the dead can interact with other human beings, depend on whether or not we believe the promise of Jesus Christ regarding the resurrection and judgment of the dead.

In the matter of persuading one's counselees about the future resurrection of the dead, what matters most is the counselor's trust in Christ's victory over death and the proclamation of His resurrection. Such knowledge is to be clarified in regards to the One who was divinely empowered to tell about His death and His resurrection (Jn.11:25, Lk.16:21). The historical fact of Christ's resurrection was attested to by 500 witnesses. There exist, in fact, two possible ways to engage in a discussion about death and resurrection in reference to historical facts: (1) If the dead are not raised, then Christ has not been raised (Cor. 15:16), and to (2) Remember Jesus Christ rose from the dead (2 Tim. 2:8).

A Spiritual counselor should be an Open–minded Person

The concept of open-mindedness in spiritual counseling is embedded in Christ's recommendation to be "the light of the world" and "the salt of the earth" (Mat. 5:14; Mat. 5:13). This account of responsibility never varies to suit the times. Through the ages, light did and must shine in the darkness, and salt has proven its value over tastelessness. There is a deterministic condition in being open-minded by reaching out with people of cul- tural differences. In the process of helping, an open-minded person is kind, merciful and longsuffering.

Tolerance is defined as the ability or willingness to accept (or tolerate) the behavior, custom, opinion or beliefs of others (*Macmillan Dictionary*). Although it may be difficult, at times, to apply the distinction between open mindedness and tolerance, spiritual counselors should know their level of comfort with certain lifestyles. Spiritual counseling helps individuals discern rightful behaviors or lifestyles as opposed to the wrongful ones, while helping them to make the most significant or right choices. As such, spiritual counselors should be fully aware of their counselees' culture, and whether their cultural differences would derange the process. This suggests that when counselors despise and feel disgusted by a particular custom or lifestyle, the most the appropriate decision is to avoid being ineffective in communicating empathy, sympathy, and acceptance by either stopping counseling or gently refer the counselee(s) to another counselor or group of counselors. The construct *realistic acceptance* prevents a counselor from compromising with some mysterious free will, but to foster a collaborative rapport toward spiritual growth. The counselor's simplicity deters him or her from judging people on the basis of their gender, prized status, physical and intellectual skills, body build, and skin color.

Being Reliable or Accountable - *an important requirement in spiritual counseling*

Trust is a core value in counseling. Spiritual counseling is a trust-building relationship. The risk of not being trustworthy on the part of counseling is critical. Human beings, in general, starve for trust. One of the greatest obstacles to successful counseling is a breach of trust. When trust is absent in a relationship, there is a risk for a sudden or complete loss of disposition to disclose private matters. A risk involved is that any explanation given and promise made will be implausible - not believable.

Trust opens the gate of communication and distrust closes that gate. In times of success and of tribulation, we often need a companion that we can rely on. Living with trust, in counseling, is not a matter of blind reliance on the helper. Disappointment due to breach of confidentiality may plunge the counselee into the pinnacle of distrust in counseling. Counseling may turn out to be a rueful experience when the counselor fails to tell the truth, keep promises, or when the rules of confidentiality are broken. Breach of confidentiality makes the rapport between counselor-counselee unproductive and leads to an eventual rupture. Under no circumstances, should individuals' private issues be revealed to anyone or institution without their consent. It turns out that a counselee may gradually lose the memory of previous benefits when this person comes to realize his or her personal information, thoughts, or feelings that were passed on was divulged. As a result of his disappointment, the individual will develop feelings of insecurity and abandon the counseling – this is the key to understanding the power of trust in spiritual counseling.

Developing a strong spiritual companionship requires skills for negotiating and renegotiating. When a spiritual counselor makes a promise and is facing the impossibility to keep up with that promise, he or she must revise the promise as soon as possible. When a counselor artfully renegotiates promises to meet at a given schedule, shows up on time, or call to reschedule, it is correct to say this spiritual counselor is purposefully trustworthy.

It is recommended that a counselor takes note during counseling and carefully plan activities for upcoming sessions. Although it may be difficult, at time, to be perfect in timing and other facets of interpersonal relationships, the idea is to be consistent and honest in providing explanation regarding inability to reach a goal. Daniel Robin argues, "If you want trust, focus on how to be trustworthy."

God is a reliable counselor in that believers in God often have their fears under con- trol (Isaiah 12:2). It is true that counselees tend to rely on their counselors' trust or faith in God. They often check on their counselor's reasons for anchoring their life in God. Given that individuals deal with adversity differently in the face of trouble or danger, coun- selors who are courageous and faithful may at such times loose ground in their convictions. Consequently, these counselors may stop being tactful when talking about God, His might, and His compassion. This shift in the counselors' behaviors and attitudes could damage the counseling process. A counselor, for instance, may confidently declared, "Prayer releases God's power and brings grace and help to us in fulfilling our needs and others'," may nonetheless be ineffective in convincing others that he or she will overcome a life tragedy. This is seen more clearly in the example of a counselor who was healthy but became sick, and his sickness led him to inappropriate skepticism. This counselor's illness here is the causal condition preventing him from counseling in a consistent manner. This can also be the case in which one becomes impecunious, e.g., having no money, poor, penniless. In this time of tribulation, the faith or trust in God that a counselor demonstrates becomes dispensable to the counselees' spiritual growth.

If a counselor is skeptical about God's ability to guide through all situations, heal all types of diseases, and forgive all sinners, then the counselor should back off from counseling and seek another counselor's support for himself or herself as well as that of the counselee – this prevents counseling from being deceptive. Being a reliable counselor requires a great deal of patience in order to assist one's counselees in taking responsibility for their life or turning to God in moments of turmoil.

When a spiritual counselor is asked, "Tell me what you think" about a particular topic and the counselor does not provide the correct answer, the counselee may begin to be concerned about whether he or she has to rely on any further counsel. When confronted by a challenging question such as, "When will be the end of the world" or "When is the second coming of Jesus Christ," the best way a spiritual counselor can handle this challenge would be to say, "I don't know the exact time," or "The Bible did not state when or how." Christ's teaching about avoidance of disappointment due to expectations placed on the counselors is to be truthful at all time: "Let what you say be simply 'Yes' or 'No;' anything more than this comes from evil (Mat 5:37). This counsel cautions against impending distrust that may result from a discrepancy between what one actually does as opposed to what one is said to be doing. Spiritual counselors should bear in mind that there is a price attributed to errors or lapses due to inattention, carelessness, and negligence on the part of counseling.

A Spiritual Counselor should use Discretion when asking Pertinent Questions

For spiritual counseling to be successful, it is recommended that counselors use discre- tion when asking pertinent questions. Some questions are susceptible to making individuals feel judged or condemned and they may take offense. Here are some examples of inop- portune questions that may turn to be offensive: "Are you married?", "Were your children born before marriage?", "What kind of job do you have?", or "What is your salary/ annual income?" These types of questions can terribly upset the counselee's disposition. In an attempt to win our counselees' sympathy it is more appropriate to ask opened-ended ques-tions than closed questions, as mentioned above. An example of these questions is: "Tell me about yourself, (your family and/or religion)?"

Nothing hurts as much as being derided in front of friends and family members. A law for a spiritual counselor is to avoid causing more pain and despair in people. Again, the focus is to be on the person's self-determination to benefit from counseling. When counseling a former murderer, for instance, it is spiritually unsafe to ask questions that can irritate. Although we believe that it is immoral to kill defenseless little babies, it is inappropriate for a counselor to bombard a woman who reveals her involvement in abortion with questions that center on the wrongness for killing. Typically, these questions give rise to worry, panic, and eventually the counselee may perceive the counselor as inconsiderate. Typical questions that begin with the words What, How, and Why give the counselee(s) the latitude to be expressive, sharing background information, feelings, and intentions. As a counselor wishes complete solidarity on the part of their counselees, he or she avoids asking difficult questions (i.e., questions that can harm). The person who is receiving spiritual guidance is the one who has to initiate sensitive issues.Making jokes and being sarcastic are attitudes that need to avoid. The reason that jokes are prohibited in spiritual counseling is because a miscalculating joke may turn to be a serious offense to the person targeted in the joke.

A Spiritual Counselor must be Impartial in Managing Conflicts

Mediation is a powerful art. The goal of mediation is to have agreement of all parties involved. Individuals who think they are right and the other person(s) is/are wrong have "good reasons" to reject any form of mediation. In the process of counseling, it is impor- tant to be aware of the fact that individuals often give reasonable explanations of their disengagement in friendship or intimate relationship. Individuals who seek mediation want to benefit greatly from having someone they can trust and have the skill in helping them safeguard an endangered relationship with a friend, a family member, a classmate, or a co-worker.

What makes individuals worried in the first place is partiality of the helper. When mediating, counselors are expected to live up to their perfect right; otherwise, individuals who are served may abruptly want to cease mediation. The first step in mediation is to inform all parties involved about the necessity for listening to all of them. This can bring a sense of impartiality in the process, as the position of all is valued and given due consideration.

A mediator should avoid any side-conversation with one person (directly or on the phone). Suppose one person insists on having a private conversation with you (the mediator); an appropriate and relevant way to respond to this demand is by saying: "I understand that you have grievances and complaints that you want to share with me, what if we wait for our next meeting to bring this issue to the table." This primal session has to be held in a quiet and closed environment with all parties involved. Preferably, a face-to-face conversation with all parties involved in a planned conference, will allow for a greater field of transaction that maximizes the possibility of exchanging and contrasting information. By so doing, the spiritual counselor diverts any suspicions from himself or herself as being partial or of involvement in gossiping or backbiting. The mediator's attendance is to actively listen to the conferees without opposing or defeating any viewpoints expressed on the debating issues.

The second ethic in mediating is to avoid *confutation*. Everyone has within themselves the power of will to confute, meaning, they have the ability to prove someone to be wrong or in error. This sort of temptation ought to be purposefully resisted when mediating. The man who says, "I do not love my wife" or the woman who say, "I do not love my husband" has good reasons to experience the absence of love. The mediator simply has to acknowledge *absence of the will to love* without exposing the speaker who is responsible for love deficiency. Disclosure of a wrongful act or "sin" made by a beneficiary of mediation, not only should be kept confidential; but also such revelation does not authorize the mediator to hold the person who confesses to be in the wrong. The goal of mediating toward conflict resolution is to get all parties engaged in the process of compromising. Every time a decision is on the line that may disappoint a conferee for the purpose of being totally impartial, one should watch over one's intervention by letting them know that, "For the sake of our discussion, let us distinguish what we might call the cause of the problem-contexts and the problem-solving strategies." Presumably, in a problem-context, the focus would be on the descriptive meaning of what went wrong among you, whereas in a context of problem-solving, the strategies to be used in solving the conflict that would be significant. In the event that a conferee verbally attacks another attendant, the mediator should re-direct the speaker by saying, "Let us tackle the important problems first and leave these passing issues to another time."

Spiritual counselors should be mindful that, despite their willingness to help resolve conflicts, they may face misunderstanding. Their tentativeness in counseling may be ascribed to being unethical and partial. Individuals may react to mediation in several ways. In an on going mediation, a conferee may speak no words, one may react to all suggestions with indifference or inexplicably turn down any suggestions with disdain or ridicule. A conferee may openly talk about his or her "indignity of having to invite a third party in debating private matters, which hurt more than physical pain." Because of inexplicability of the reason of their rejection, mediators often feel tempted to give up on pursuing mediation and can be even discouraged from engaging in further spiritual counseling.

The main purpose of contributing to conflict resolution is to persuade the dissidents about the spiritual meaning of seeking mediation in order to resolve issues related to their discord. In a conclusive statement, one needs to reiterate trust in all parties by letting them know that their disapproval of you for mediation is not final, they can still invite someone else that they think would be able to help them solve the identified problem and make it history.

To be successful in spiritual counseling the "Seven biblical counseling keys" established by the "Hope for the Heart" ministry can be helpful in summarizing the basic goals of spiritual counseling:

1. The **solutions** are not your solutions. (John 14:26)
2. The **self-sufficiency** you lean on should be replaced with Christ-sufficiency. (John 15:5)
3. The **Spirit** of Christ is your counselor, enabling you to counsel with truth. (John 16:13)
4. The **sin** of another should never be confronted with a condemning spirit. (1 Peter 3 15-16)
5. The **success** of your counseling is not dependent on how you walk out of all the answers. (Proverbs 3: 5-6)
6. The **Scriptures** will light the way as you help others walk out of darkness. (Psalm 119:105)
7. The **secret** of victory over temptation is relying on the power of the indwelling pres- ence of Christ. (Philippians 4:13) - (Hope for the Heart. 2006).

Epilogue

Spirituality is relevant in the way people think, feel and decide. Spirituality has a need for self-knowledge for healthy decisions. Spirituality has a natural drive to achieve self-actualization. It drives for self-actualization, which can be viewed in the context of fear-driven inspiration that compel people to the satisfaction of their needs. Spirituality can take place at all levels of interpersonal communication and so does spiritual counseling. Spirituality can bring about a spiritual breakthrough and regeneration, or self-failure.

Jonah Lehrer (2009) states, "The desire to avoid anything that smacks of loss often shapes our behavior, leading us to foolish things" (*How we decide* p. 77). He said that human beings fear appearing to others as making mistakes. Lehrer held that this fear causes people to do foolish things to avoid appearing wrong. On his part, Louis L. Hay argued, "There are so many ways you can approach your healing. Try them all and then use the ones that appeal to you the most" (Hay. p. 95).

In light of True Conscience and the Educated Conscience, the philosophy outlined in this book emphasizes the need for counselors to help their counselees to come to terms with life, with the values of living with trust, living with will, living fair, and living safe. These are values that originated with Christ who is the "Wonderful Counselor," and who Himself modeled these values of living in His own life and earthly existence.

This essay hoped to highlight techniques and skills in identifying the counselees' fears and needs. It also intended to demonstrate those fears as well as how spiritual counseling can be a persuasive and powerful tool when the counselor, before entering counseling, becomes aware of his or her own spiritual needs. This essay also showed how those needs can be satisfied in accordance with God's plan of redemption. This essay also pointed out that helping efforts are likely to bring about positive outcomes when the spiritual counselor is knowledgeable and lives up to this plan – it is when spiritual counseling becomes more credible. This paper also pointed out that successful counseling requires ethics, and respect for human differences.

On becoming an effective helper, one should know how people think, feel and make decisions. One should also be aware that people can suffer from disordered reflection; they can be confused, and ambivalent about who they are and what purpose they have in life. The modeling behavior of the counselor can have a significant impact on the counseling process and its outcomes. The values of both (the counselor's and his counselee's) will interact. One can see this impact in the testimonies given by a counselee for counseling received and about the counselor's consistent lifestyle. Because spiritual counselors are open-minded and believe in the ability of human beings to change, this constitutes a factor of positive impact on the counselee.

Spiritual counselors should be prepared to face possible resistance from their counselees. The reality is that some people strive to retain their belief and some tend to operate in total secrecy, or lie. Often, people are reluctant to reveal even trivial details of their lives. They aim to avoid being influenced by any other types of beliefs or logic. Their inde- pendence can pose serious obstacles to a spiritual breakthrough, regeneration, and growth (transforming of hearts and mind). From a spiritual perspective, whenever a person is inspired to go against others or goes away from others, it is an indication that the fear that naturally allows good functioning through the fulfillment of one's need for connection is blundered. This often results in human distress due to loneliness and behaviors (or evil passion) created by like internal disturbance.

Spiritual counseling removes the idea of "self-efficacy" to rely on special divine promises that guarantees success. The first promise has to do with the divine empowerment: "Do not be anxious how you are to speak and what you have to say; for what you are to say will be given to you in that hour; for it not you who speak, but the spirit of your Father speaking though you" (Mat 10:19 & 20). Another promise that guarantees the success of spiritual counseling is when Christ stated, "I am with you always, to the close this age" (Mat 28:20).

Redemption is the key concept in which one can find success in spiritual counseling. When helping counselees toward recognizing and fulfilling their need for redemption, counselors should avoid thinking about multiple options that may result in confusion. It is reassuring that for human beings to know that they can live life at its fullest, but through divine intervention, redemption becomes attainable goal. Spiritual counseling is a truth-oriented counseling in reference to the fact that "Faith in Christ is not a leap into the dark; it's a step into the light" (Our Daily Bread, May, 2008). Efficacy of this counseling is grounded in the testimonies of millions of converted Christians. In comparing and contrasting her past meaning of life and lifestyle with new-birth experience. In 1996, Sheila Field, after her second broken marriage wrote, "Jesus is the lover of my soul, my best friend and my confidant. He is a husband like no other. I've discovered that the best earthly relationship is a mere shadow of the perfect love He has for me" (Focus on the Family. Feb., 2007). This is evidence that Sheila found the truth, and a life of redemption that indicated the last stage in the Pyramid of an upward spiritual experience.

A CHECLIST FOR SPIRITUAL SELF-ASSESSMENT

This questionnaire allows you to assess yourself in terms of your Vision of life, Trends and Feelings that condition the kinds of decisions that you might make in certain situations. Answer honestly and rapidly these questions by putting T or F after reading each question. By doing so, you signify that the statement is either True or False.

SECTION SC

T □ F

1. I want to be successful in all urgent situations.

2. No one is patient enough to succeed in what they are competent to do.

3. Success never comes without competition.

4. What makes all individuals happy is nothing but praise from society.

5. There should be no regrets in the desire to succeed.

6. Rejoicing in life stands for the best therapy, since death may knock us down at anytime.

7. Life would be meaningless without a society of happiness.

8. Nothing in the world can prevent me from achieving happiness.

9. The better one enjoys life, the less one will worry about the future.

10. Why should I be different from other people with whom I share some of the same beliefs.

SECTION MgG

T ☐ F

11. Those, who blame themselves after making a bad choice, did not actually know what they wanted.

12. The reasons for my regrets are often unknown.

13. Feelings of guilt are always the result of unfair societal law and peer pressure.

14. Every thing that makes me feel uncomfortable I quickly ignored.

15. Every thing that brings a moment of happiness never brings sadness afterwards, unless one has psychological impairment.

16. I avoid feeling guilty because it makes feel weak. What I really want is to be in control of all my feelings.

17. Most of errors and mistakes people make are due to genetic or environment

18. am not ready and willing to blame anybody for not taking responsibility of their mistakes.

19. Confessing (to God) and Repentance from sin are two concepts invented by religion that do not concern me.

20. It is a wonderful feeling to identify the underlining factor (s) of one's mistakes, and forget it/them right way.

SECTION GEN

T ☐ F

21. Selfishness is the second nature of all human beings.

22. People, who help others, are those, who live in abundance.

23. One can do nothing to eliminate poverty; it is the result of idleness.

24. It is such hypocrisy to provide assistance to people after an inevitable disaster or catastrophe.

25. Assistance to the poor has nothing to do with the humanity of the helpers.

26. All, who provide charity funds, are those, who want their name listed in the world newspapers in the front pages

27. There are so many problems that involve poverty that I have thought of not wasting my money and time.

28. It is such a waste of time to counsel addicts; they will never quit their bad habits.

29. Spending two hours to help others out of one's household is a great violation of one's family commitment.

30. People do not need sound advice; what they need is a pleasurable life.

SECTION PfM

T ☐ F

31. Spending money to help people (except a significant other) is not realistic

32. People, who say "money is everything," are realistic.

33. Safety, love and survival, are all about money.

34. Money is a standard of success in all aspects of living on this planet.

35. The primary motive of any relationship is unconsciously driven by the desire to have money.

36. One may never resist to opportunity of making money by either lying or making fraud – whatever seems to be more convenient.

37. The natural sorting of strengths means others see you as wealthy as they are.

38. There is nothing I hate more than spending a day without money.

39. I am really good at setting a focus and importance on people who succeed because of their money.

40. It is incredibly rewarding to watch someone make a very quick transition from poverty to prosperity.

SECTION FORG

T □ F

41. People, who hurt others, do not deserve forgiveness.

42. Even God does not forgive all mistakes.

43. All that I do, when people hurt me, is to hate them.

44. I would never be honest with someone who treated me hard in the past.

45. I am a good teacher, but a bad listener, especially, to those, who have Disappointed me.

46. I feel secure enough to break a relationship when the fault is not mine.

47. When I am frustrated with a relationship for which I cared, I blame the other person for not being sincere with me.

48. Someone, who is quick to forgive, has a big problem of being supported by others.

49. I should not forget that when I was young, I suffered hurt.

50. Those, who say, "It does not do any good to go around hating somebody," have no empathy toward those who were hurt

51. The idea that "I can be healed from past offenses" cannot distract me from the right to confront my evildoers.

52. People are better burying the hurt deep in their hearts in order to survive their bit- terness from evildoing, because they will never be happy.

SECTION PRG

T □ F

53. God is the only one who is responsible for the evil and suffering of the humankind.

54. All suffering is from God.

55. God unjustly allows some people to suffer others not.

56. God teaches us good lessons, when lets us suffer more than others.

57. God will spread out seven plaques to destroy the world, which is no fair.

58. God did not show Himself to be powerful when He said to the Apostle Paul, after his long-life suffering: "My grace is sufficient for you" instead of healing him.

59. There is no joy (or fun), at all, in being submitted to God.

60. I think I should never be busy with doing God's will.

61. God has nothing to do with my feelings.

62. As long as I am able to master my life, I don't see any reason to pray.

63. All teaching and assumptions about God are human creative thinking that aims for personal profits.

64. The theory of Evolution makes more sense than the Creationism by a God who is eternally invisible.

SECTION PfS

T □ F

65. God has nothing to do with individual sexual orientation.

66. I am afraid that I would become homosexual or lesbian if I allow my homosexual tendencies too much expression.

67. I am struggling with having genuine romantic relationship with the opposite sex.

68. Often, I tell myself God wants me to be gay.

69. Often, I tell myself polygamy has nothing to do with being mentally healthy.

70. Watching pornography is to be taken as an intellectual pursuit.

71. I consider that one of the ways to manage one's sexual desires is to go with the impulses.

72. It is fun to decide to post on the media (i.e., the internet) the stories of interesting sexual events.

73. My focus is powerful and I do not bother to figure whether or not a particular sexual act is opposing to others' perspective of sexuality.

74. Religious people must understand that not everybody feels their urge for what they call, "sexual purity."

SECTION PfP

T ☐ F

75. When I want to gratify my needs, I just do it with certainty and might.

76. I have physical and intellectual power to lay all my enemies down.

77. Tricks that are often used to convince someone to do something in my way are outstanding.

78. I have no fear at telling the truth, when it is within my power to do so.

79. To me, ascribing "All Power" to "God" makes no sense.

80. The truth is "Humans can do all things and prevent all damages due to power."

81. It is very important to me to be efficient in convincing people to do what I want them to do.

82. In a discussion, when someone starts to debase my points of view, I use the intellectual power to help this person determine priorities and get back on course.

83. When I am in a group, I create en environment of what is predictable, which makes me the most extremely valuable figure.

84. I can now see how it is possible to acquire social recognition without actual talent.

Scale for Spiritual Self-assessing:

The 84 questions that you have answered are categorized in 8 Sections that pertain to different aspects of individual spirituality. These Sections vary in number of questions. The following gives a scale that helps figure out your spiritual strengths and weaknesses. A ratio 2:3 of True answers confirms significant weaknesses in this Spiritual Domain evident linked to the Section.

Sections / Domains	Nbr. of Questions per Section	Nbr. of True Answers (provided)	Ratio 2:3 of True Answers = Evidence of Weaknesses
SC: Social Compliance	10		6 (or higher)
MgG: Management of Guilty Feelings	10		6
GEN: Generosity	10		6
PfM: Passion for Money	10		6
FORG: Forgiveness	12		8 (or higher)
PRG: Perception and Reliance on God	12		8
PfS: Passion for Sexuality	10		6
PfP: Passion for Power	10		6

References

American Bible Society. 1970. The Bible. New York.

Berne, Katrina. 1995. Running Empty –the complete guide for chronic fatigue syndrome. Ed. Hunter house, Inc.

Branden, Nathaniel. 1995. Six Pillars of self-esteem. Ed. Publishing History.

Bruce and Stan. 2000. God is in the small little stuff for men.

Campolo, Tony. 1997. Following Jesus without embarrassing God.

Colbert, Don. 2003. Deadly emotions. Ed. The Lockman Foundation.

Copeland, Kenneth. 2001. Sensitivity of heart.

Corr, A. Charles. 1996. Death and Dying. Ed. Older Edition.

Corsini, J. Raymond. 2007. Current Psychotherapies. Ed REV.

Cousins, Norman. 1981. Anatomy of Illness Human Options. Ed. the Berkeley Publishing Group.

Dobson, James. (2007-2009). Focus on the Family.

Dolan, Jill. 2010. The Feminist Spectator. Retrieved from feministspectator.blogspot.com posted on 02/22/2010.

Eckhart, Tolle. 1999. The power of now.

Eisenberg, Leon. 2001. 50 years of Child and Adolescent Psychiatry: A personal memoir.

Journal of American Academy of Child and Adolescent Psychiatry.

Fuller. Cheri. 2005. A busy woman's guide to prayer. Ed. Integrity Publishers.

Fuske, John. Introduction to communication studies. Ed. Methuen & Co.

Gleen, Bland. 1996. The power of thought.

Hagee, John. 2009. Life's challenges your opportunities. Ed. Charisma House.

Hay, L. Louise. 1987. You can heal your life.

Houghton Mifflin Company. 1991. The American Heritage Dictionary. Second Edition.

Hume, David. 1955.

Inriq, Gary. 2005. Forgiveness.

Jeremiah, David. 2009. Making a way. Ed. Turning Point.

Jones, D. Marie. Christian, Rebecca. Eaton, June et al. 2003.Ed. Louis Weber, CEO.

Kalish, Richard. 1977. Psychology of Human Behavior.
Layman, C. Stephen. 2007. A Case of the Existence of God. Ed. Oxford University Press.
Lehrer, Jonah. 2009. How we decide. Ed. First Mariner Books.
Lynch, J. James 1977. The broken heart: The Medical Consequences of Loneliness.
MacDonald, James. 2000. I really want to change . . . .so, Help me God.
Macfarland, Charles. 1942. A digest Christian thinking.
Marcel, Gabriel. Creative Fidelity translated from French by Gabriel Rosthal.
McConnell, James. 1989. Understanding human behavior.
Martin Luther King Jr,, Valerie. 1988. America's greatest nonviolent leader in the struggle for human rights. Ed. North American.
Miller R. William. Rollnick, Stephen. 2002. Motivational Interviewing. The Guilford Press.
Moore, Pam. 2000. Finding ways through Depression. Ed. Spire.
Norvak, Michael. Belief and Unbelief-A philosophy of self-knowledge
Ornish, Dean. 1998. Love & Survival – The spiritual counseling basis for the healing power of intimacy.
Peel, W. Carr. Walt, Larimore. 2003. Going Public you Faith. Ed. Zonderman.
Paul, C. Stephen. Collins, Gary. 1995. In Love: Vision for Growth and Harmony in Relationships.
Pape, Robert. The Myth of the Suicide Bomber. Retrieved from www. rense.com/general67/suicc.htm. July 12, 2012
Puff, Robert. 2005. Anger Work: How to express your anger and still be kind.
Ramsey, Michael. 1964. Sacred and Secular. Ed. Longmans.
Rachels, James. 1999. The rights things to do –Basics readings in moral philosophy. Ed. McGraw Hill Companies.
Robin, Daniel. Trust this: Five Ways to be Reliable. 2012. Ruthven,
Malise. 2004. Fundamentalism- the search for meaning. Santrock, John. 2003. Adolescence. Ed. McGraw Hill Education. Schumacher. E. F. 1997. A guide for the perplexed. Ed. Herper Colophon.
Scott, Peck. 1983. People of the lie – the hope for healing human evil. Ed. Touchstone. Seligman, Martin. 2002. Authentic Happiness. Daedalus. Spring, 2004.
Seligman, Martin. 2004. Eudaemonia, the Good Life: A Talk with Martin Seligman. Edge Foundation, Inc.
Sullivan, Andrew. 1995. Virtually Normal – an argument about homosexuality.
Spurgeon, Charles. 1997. Finding peace in life's storms.
Stanley, Charles. 1997. The truth about failures. 2010. Ed. In Touch.
Stanley, Charles. 2008. Wisdom for the trials of life. Ed. In Touch.
Stanley, Charles. 1997. Reasons of my hope. Ed. Thomas Nelson.

References

Stevenson, Jay. 1998. The complete idiot's guide to philosophy. Stoop, David. 2008. You are what you think.

Stephen, Paul. Collins, Max. 1985. In love.

Strong, James. 1996. The new Strong's complete dictionary of Bible words.

Teasdale, Wayne. 2004. The Mystic Hours – a daybook of interspiritual wisdom & devotion. Tutu, Desmond. 2007. Believe. Ed. Blue Mountain Press.

Water, Mark. 2000. Hard Questions about Christianity made easy. Hendrickson Publishers, Inc.

Wechsler, Harlan. 1990. What's so bad about guilt? Learning to live with it since we can't live without it.

Xavier, Amador. Johnson, Anna. 2000. I am not sick I don't need help!. Ed. Vida.

Yalom, Irvin. Leszcz, Molyn. 2005. Theory and Practice of Group Psychotherapy. Persueus Books Group. N.Y.

Index

A

Ambivalence, ... 14, 23, 82, 96, 156

Anger, ... 45-49, 100-101, 141
    due to jealousy, ... 112

B

Belief, ... 20-22, 28, 97, 127
    (in) God, ... 35, 36, 89, 138
    (in) miracle, ... 21
    share of, ... 127

C

Change, ... 70-83
    desire for, ... 76
    contextualizing spiritual, ... 18
    motivation for, ... 82, 83
    obstacles, ... 70-73
    resistance, ... 70, 166
    reward of, ... 80
    stages of (in a pyramid), ... 81
    stagnation, ... 67
    testimony, ... 20

Confusion, ... 23, 28, 46, 28, 70, 98, 123, 144, 153, 166

Commitment, ... 74, 84, 113, 114
    value, ... 23, 72
    immoral value, ... 22, 123
    moral value, ... 22, 35, 40, 42
    relapse, ... 53
    utilis, ... 18, 75, 77, 116, 127

Confrontation, ... 59, 60, 117
    inevitable, ... 59, 95, 129
    heated, ... 129
    irritable, ... 60
    due to resistance, ... 61

Conscience
    variants, ... 71, 72
    facile, ... 73
    obscured, ... 72-73
    Educated, ... xi, xii, 43, 73, 128, 143-150
    self-eulogia, ... 73
    self-induced clear, ... 72-73, 115, 118
    True, ... xi, xii, 14-16, 22, 24, 79, 117, 118, 128 132

D

Death, 157-158
  See Fear of vulnerability.

Disturbance, ...70-73, 75
  chronic spiritual (CSD), ...24, 99-101,
    119, 133-142, 143-150
  indelicateness, ...97
  inedicabilis, ...122
  infelicitas, ...126
  inexplicabilis, ...23, 75
  internal, ...78, 90
  mindlessness, ...17, 155
  profligatus, ...24

E

Expectation
  crisis of, ...98, 100, 104, 124
  parents', ...85
  (in) resentment, ...102
  unrealistic, ...128

Experience
  argumentum, ...128
  born again, ...44, 45
  chronic lack of sensitivity, ...126
  cruel intention, ...101, 130
  delusion of self-sufficiency, ...94
  downward spiritual, ...13, 23-25
  exertus, ...24, 144
  incertus, ...144
  incredibilis, ...122
  inedicabilis, ...122
  learned sympathy, ...48
  meaningfulness of life, ...125
  miracle, ...21, 22
  outstanding date with God, ...105

  realistic acceptance of
    sinful nature, ...45
  repentance, ...22-23
  restoration, ...106
  resumption, ...106
  spiritual deficiency, ...93
  spiritual indelicateness, ...97
  total forgiveness (BATES), ...108-109
  upward spiritual, ...13, 23-25, 66
  utopia of ownership, ... 111
  sanus, ...24

Evil, ...94, 104
  passion, 122, 123, 127, 128, 138

F

Faith, ...35, 126
  confession, 36, 59

Fear (of)
  blundering, ...123
  contradiction, ...72, 143
  divine reprisal, ...120,
  driven inspiration, ...13
  failure, ...124, 145
  functional, ...123
  rejection, ...97, 110, 112, 130, 138
  recurrent failure, ...85, 141
  recurrent mistakes, ...103
  socially reinforced, ...128
  vulnerability
    (i.e., of death, of tomorrow, of
    recurrent mistakes), ...75, 77,
    79, 82, 123, 124, 127, 145, 153

Feeling (of), ...99-132
  abhorrent, ...161
  comfortable, ...151

dejection, ...121-127
grudge, ...103
guilt, ...77, 78, 90, 116-121
jealousy, ...112-115
remedial, ...74
resentment, ...75, 99-110, 111
sharam, ...100, 122
suicide, ...122
taedium, ...100, 114, 122-124, 133, 139
trust, ...82-83, 138
uncomfortable and disturbing, ...23, 32, 42, 78, 91, 99-132

Forgiveness, ...101-110, 140, 141
BATES, ...108, 109
Christian perspective (from a), ...106-109
exercise toward total forgiveness, ...106
meaning of, ...104, 141

G

God, ...54-57, 77-81, 87-89, 120, 121, 146, 160
attributes, ...150
Creator, ...80, 92, 96, 146
devotion (to), ...92
(our) Father, ...108
gracious, ...108
intervention, ...53, 77, 90, 151, 152
law, ...27-29, 91, 146, 155, 156
love, ...94
Mighty, ...88
Perception (of), ...108
plan, ...68, 120
trust (in), ...53, 91, 123
ultimate spiritual Redeemer, ...68, 80

Son (of), ...108
Group, ...40-50
Anger Management (AMG), ...39-49
leader's testimony, ...44, 45
role play, ...46-49
size, ...45
spirituality-based, ...45

Guilt, ...16, 76, 77, 90, 116-121, 140
burden of, ...90, 91
cause and effect, ...119
confutation, ...162
contrition, ...120
effective care of, ...121
impugnation, ...122
indurate, ...77
planned predicament, ...119
true, ...68, 69, 76, 120-121

I

Interpretation,
Mind, ...17
survival, ...73, 109, 112, 127, 128
reflection-based, ...17, 40, 45, 48, 54, 69, 116, 118, 120, 123, 140

L

Life
meaning of, ... 15, 35, 115, 122-124, 128, 136, 142
vision of, ...13-15, 17, 24, 40, 43, 44, 66, 79, 81, 85, 116, 137
Stages of improvement (upward spiritual experience), ...73-81
Agnosia – time of ignorance, ...73

Existemi - time of
    wondering,..........................16, 74-76
Nocham thelema - desire for
    repentance,.........................76-78, 92
Sanus - A life Relevant of
    Redemption, ...78- 81

Living (with)
    trust, ...41, 44, 63, 80,
        83, 93, 99, 130, 159, 164, 165
    will, ...42, 45, 66, 82, 85, 90, 97, 154
    fair, ...41, 44, 43, 80, 83, 96, 108, 154
    safe, ...41, 44, 65, 43, 80, 83, 97, 154

Love, ...89, 93, 108
    God's, ...79, 94, 107, 111

M

Manipulation, ...13, 20, 24, 85, 124,
    125, 130, 134, 136, 140

Model
    choice of,...82
    perfect, ...82
    virtuous, ...82
    ultimate spiritual, ...87, 90

Modeling
    choice of worship,............................87
    emulation,....................................82, 83
    marital relationship, ...95-97
    merciful,..125
    parental,....................................83-85, 87
    teacher's failure,.........................86, 87
    teaching of moral values, ...83-85, 87

N

Need (for)
    connection,.................45, 58, 111, 166
    redemption, ...14, 15, 40, 71,
        74, 77, 89, 166
    self-preservation,.......................75, 128
    worship,............................80, 87-88, 95

P

Prevarication (Lies),........................143-150
    circumstantial,................................145
    etiology,....................................143-145
    grudge-induced, ...148
    institutional, ...145-146
    malady of power,............................147
    power entertainment,.......................147
    power positioning,....................146-147
    premeditated,..................................145
    temptation (to),........................148, 149

R

Redemption,...........................52, 53, 78-81
    God's plan of,.............15, 92, 120, 155

Reflection
    disorder,................74, 83, 99-132, 140,
        143-150
    retroflexion,....................................148
    successful, ...60, 72, 128,

Repentance,.......................................22, 76-78
    desire for, ...59, 76-78, 80, 90, 118
    fruits of,...94
    call for, ...78

Resurrection, ...131, 157-158

S

Self-confidence
    adequate, ...42, 75, 120
    cumulative, ...69
    inadequate, ...75, 80, 90, 111, 140

Sexuality, ...137-146
    abstinence, ...17-20
    AIDS, ...101, 145, 146
    child pornography, ...143
    hetero, ...44, 140-142
    homo, ...44, 140-142
    ill-orientation (SIO), ...81, 137, 138, 140
    incest, ...143
    pedology, ...143
    pedophilia, ...143
    premarital, ...30
    prostitution, ...145, 146
    sodomitical, ...19, 25
    transmitted diseases
        (STDs), ...20, 87, 10

Spirit
    Holy, ...93
    (of) Truth, ...96

Spirituality
    definition ....xi, xii, 13

Spiritual counseling, ...13-71, 97
    aims and purposes, ...16
    (in the case of) dejection, ...124- 132
    forms, ...26-38
    goals, ...167
    group, ...39-49
    (in the case of) guilt, ...115-122
    (in the case of) jealousy, ...112-115
    main foci, ...62-69
    (in the case of) resentment, ...99-110
    resistance to, ...154
    (in the case of)
        suicide bombing, ...127-132
    techniques, ...50-62
    truth-oriented, ...59, 66-69,
    ultimate, ...91, 92

T

Techniques
    active listening and reflection
        of feelings, ...101
    (for) Assisting People with
        Life-related Issues
            (TAPLI), ...70-98
    bridging, ...52
    bringing to a high level of
        awareness, ...116
    burden transference, ...140
    clarification, ...50, 53
    clarity of purposes, ...149
    definition and contrast, ...140
    emphasizing the meaning of
        forgiveness, ...104
    disquieting the TC, ...117, 118, 135
    exercise toward total
        forgiveness, ...106
    exploring the specifics of
        forgiving, ...102
    facing resistance, ...105
    fraternizing, ...57-61
    giving feedback, ...61-62
    increasing the will of, ...132
    introducing self, ...50
    metaphor, ...130
    metaphoric questions, ...149
    minimal encouragement, ...52

(being) perseverant, 53, 102
processing conflict of
    doing God's will, ... 103
putting the counselee
    under God's care, ... 105
realistic acceptance, ... 159
retrospection, ... 103
self-disclosing, ... 54
sharing experience, ... 54-57
to spiritual counseling, ... 50-62
spiritual inversion, ... 131
validation, ... 156
working focus, ... 46

Spiritual counselor,
    ethics, ... 151-163
    ultimate, ... 79, 90, 91, 120
    experiences, models, and
        promotes the TRUTH, ... 69, 66-69
    ultimate spiritual, ... 62, 67, 79, 80,
    wonderful, ... 88-96

Suicide, ... 118-127
    bombing, ... 127-132
    impugnation, ... 126

CPSIA information can be obtained at www.ICGtesting.com
Printed in the USA
BVOW09s0639030516

446476BV00002B/3/P